Ralph Nelson Elliott

Ralph Nelson Elliott (1871-1948) led an adventurous and productive life. He enjoyed a remarkably successful accounting career, involving book authorship, magazine contributions, extensive travel and even a U.S. State Department appointment. Elliott published his first book on the stock market at the age of 67. An inspiration to anyone facing his "declining" years, Elliott's evident genius reached full flower in the last decade of his life, when he brought a great gift of knowledge to mankind.

Elliott was of that rarest of breeds, a true scholar in the practical world of finance. His revolutionary theory of stock market behavior goes way beyond the usual limitations that are characteristic of the bulk of the literature. As A. Hamilton Bolton, founder of the *Bank Credit Analyst*, said, "He developed his principle into a rational method of stock market analysis on a scale never before attempted."

In fact, the Wave Principle is far more than a useful analytical method. Over the years, it has had a profound effect on those who not only have the ability to recognize a theory of immense practical value, but who can appreciate the aesthetic beauty of the human experience in the abstract. The Wave Principle has fascinated philosophers, mathematicians, psychologists, theologians and financiers alike. Now, after being out of print for decades, the original works of R.N. Elliott have been made available in this one complete volume.

Robert R. Prechter

Robert R. Prechter, Jr. co-authored *Elliott Wave Principle -- Key to Stock Market Profits* in 1978, and in 1979 began publishing *The Elliott Wave Theorist,* a financial forecasting publication covering the stock market, interest rates, precious metals, the economy and social trends. Mr. Prechter has been named "one of the premier timers in stock market history" by *Timer Digest,* "the champion market forecaster" by *Fortune* magazine, "the world leader in Elliott Wave interpretation" by The Securities Institute, and "the nation's foremost proponent of the Elliott Wave method of forecasting" by *The New York Times.*

Today Mr. Prechter is president of Elliott Wave International, the largest market analysis firm in the world. EWI serves institutional clients in analyzing all major global stock, bond, interest rate and currency markets, as well as metals and energy markets, 24 hours a day. In that capacity, Mr. Prechter writes for EWI's *Global Market Perspective*, a monthly 100 page booklet of Elliott Wave analysis on worldwide financial trends.

Mr. Prechter attended Yale University on a full scholarship and graduated in 1971 with a degree in psychology. His studies of the Wave Principle developed from a deep fascination with the stock market and its intimate reflection of the human experience. Mr. Prechter's latest endeavor is an exposition of a new theory of historical causality based upon the patterns of human interpersonal dynamics.

R.N. ELLIOTT'S MASTERWORKS

The Definitive Collection

Edited, foreworded, and with a biography
by Robert R. Prechter

Published by New Classics Library

R.N. Elliott's Masterworks
Copyright © 1980/1994/2005/2017 Robert R. Prechter
Third Edition 2017
Second Printing 2018
1980 title: The Major Works of R.N. Elliott

Printed in the United States of America

ISBN: 978-1-61604-108-3
Library of Congress Control Number 20015934493

Publisher: New Classics Library
Gainesville, Georgia USA

Elliott Wave International
www.elliottwave.com
Address for comments: customercare@elliottwave.com

This book is dedicated to
Alfred John Frost,
a dear friend.

The Foreword and about half of the biography were initially published in *The Major Works of R.N. Elliott* (New Classics Library, 1980), which is now out of print. This volume features a greatly expanded biography, upgraded footnotes, and the Selected Essays section, making *R.N. Elliott's Masterworks* a truly comprehensive anthology of the author's important writings. Completists may wish to obtain *R.N. Elliott's Market Letters 1938-1946* (New Classics Library, 1993), which contains all of his additional publications.

ACKNOWLEDGMENTS

A number of people have been instrumental in this project. A.J. Frost provided a copy of *The Wave Principle* and copies of the Elliott Wave Supplements to the *Bank Credit Analyst,* and collaborated on the forewording comments. Alfred H. Kingon, editor-in-chief of *Financial World* magazine, generously consented to the republication of Elliott's 1939 articles. The New York Public Library yielded much information, and is the only library known to have a photocopy of the original *Nature's Law.* Claire Chartrand, an associate of the late Hamilton Bolton, helped clear up a few cloudy areas on the available reproductions. The Library of Congress provided the material for the Selected Essays section.

One of the main reasons a comprehensive republication of Elliott's works has not been attempted before was the prospect of the formidable illustrating job necessary to do justice to Elliott's concepts. His two books are rather roughly illustrated and a mere photographic reproduction would not have sufficed. Robin Machcinski successfully tackled this job, and we are proud to feature her work herein. Arthur Merrill of Merrill Analysis, Inc. provided his invaluable photographic talents toward the reduction of the illustrations to camera-ready size. The copy editing for the current edition was done by Jane Estes and Karen Latvala. The jacket design was crafted by graphics artist Pamela Kimmons.

For acknowledgments relating to Elliott's biography, see the Author's Note on page 15.

CONTENTS

FOREWORD

Hamilton Bolton said in 1953, "For every one hundred investors who have heard of the Dow Theory, there is probably not one who knows about Elliott's Wave Principle." In the service of justice, the time has come to remedy this oversight of history.

For decades a demand has existed for reprints of Ralph Nelson Elliott's major writings, but until now no one has seen fit to bring all the books and articles together in one professionally illustrated volume. I undertook this project in response to demand from readers of Frost's and my book and out of my deep concern that the form of the original discovery not be lost in the dustbin of history. It is for those who have an appreciation for the historical record and who wish an understanding of the development of the Wave Principle through its discoverer, R.N. Elliott, that this book is published.

History is replete with examples of innovators and discoverers, men years or even centuries before their time, whose ideas reached so far ahead of their contemporaries' that they were ignored by the professional establishment of their day. While Elliott was not ignored, he most certainly was not afforded the recognition he deserved.

In my experience, there are two categories of people who have stood in the way of providing Elliott's Wave Principle a wider audience. The first is made up of those who reject it, including both those who dismiss any such ideas out of hand and those who grasp the theory but choose not to believe it because they will not expend the energy required to find out if it is true.

A neutral response to unreasonable rejection of the Wave Principle would have been impossible for the discoverer of this remarkable phenomenon, who undoubtedly feared that his discovery would go entirely unnoticed if he were not able to convince at least a portion of the investment world of its validity. The eloquence of *The Wave Principle* and the intensity of *Nature's Law* partly derive from Collins' and Elliott's desire to convince the investment establishment not only that the Wave Principle was a valid theory, but also that it was the truth behind the progression of the stock market, and that in fact it reflected the law governing the form of the natural path of all human activities. My goal with this book, however, is not necessarily to convince readers that "Elliott is the way," but merely to make available knowledge of the Wave Principle to those who have enough sense and energy to use it.

As for the second category, I find that among those people who understand the theory's immense value and apply it successfully, most have done their best to keep it secret. I have been asked several times by students of the Wave Principle to refrain from publishing any material at all on Elliott's great innovative work for fear that "too many" people would start using the Wave Principle in their investment timing, thus diluting the utility of the theory.

I must say that at times I have had second thoughts. The Wave Principle frequently can call turns and project targets with such incredible accuracy that I still find myself amazed. As a tool for explaining the otherwise surprising and indecipherable ways of the market, it has no equal.

However, the reader must realize that, despite the basic simplicity of the concept itself, "Elliott" analysis is not that easy to do if your goal is to do it well. On the other hand, it is very easy to do haphazardly, and most part-time practitioners do exactly that. Even if the Wave Principle were to become popular, there would be so many opportunistic hacks floating about their ill-considered opinions that the truth probably would be lost to the investment majority in the ensuing babble. The degree of uncertainty in wave pattern recognition, moreover, ensures enough forecasting errors that the average person will dismiss it after discovering the imperfection of its application. For most people, the best approach, even by far the best approach, is not enough, as they demand the Holy Grail of perfection.

In addition, let me say that even among devotees, it is one thing to recognize that the Wave Principle governs stock prices while it is quite another to predict the next wave and still another to profit from the exercise, as anyone who ever has attempted to turn a good market forecasting approach into money knows full well. None of us can escape our human nature, a nature that involves us in the universal design whether we wish it to or not. I have met few men who invest or trade with a completely rational program based on reasonable probabilities without allowing greed, fear, extraneous opinions or irrelevant judgments to interfere. To a man of superior discipline, the Wave Principle will yield a fortune; but then so will many other methods. What no other method of reading the market *can* give you, however, which the Elliott Wave Principle makes possible for the first time, is a framework within which to observe, reflect upon and enjoy the beauty of nature in the social activity of man.

Thus, in the end, I find myself persuaded by the nobler words of both Elliott and Collins, who agreed in their letters that what is important above all else is the "search for Truth." This search is a project for all mankind, and keeping dramatic new concepts from others will only hinder progress.

If the Wave Principle is nature's way of giving us a peek at the future, we must nevertheless realize that it is only a peek, not the full panorama. Foretelling the future with exactitude all the time is not one of the blessings available to man and likely never will be. Elliott himself, despite his great achievement, was not fanatical about his ideas. He knew that the Wave Principle, for all of its value, was not the be-all and end-all. "The discovery of the Wave Principle," he said, "has only opened the door to real progress."

As you read Elliott's works, it may help to recall his words of guidance to Charles J. Collins when he said, "I hope you appreciate that application of rules requires considerable practice and a tranquil mind."

— Robert R. Prechter, Jr., 1979

A BIOGRAPHY OF
RALPH NELSON ELLIOTT

by

Robert R. Prechter

AUTHOR'S NOTE

Until now, nothing whatsoever had appeared in print pertaining to Elliott's personal life or his activities prior to discovering the Wave Principle. The facts I was able to put together were gleaned partly by studying his books and market letters, corresponding with the Library of Congress, and talking with former associates. Howard Fay and Brenda Taylor were helpful in providing biographical information. Journalist Peter Kendall followed several leads to excellent result. Like a determined private investigator, Market Technicians Association member George A. Schade, Jr. in over two years of research systematically uncovered a wealth of information on Elliott's lineage, family and geographical locations. He also discovered the *New York Times* article citing Elliott as a newly registered investment advisor as well as the review of *Nature's Law* in the journal, *Science Education.* Elliott Wave International's Michael Buettner explored the U.S. State Department's archives to come up with startling information on Elliott's role with the Coolidge Administration. Marie Eliades took the photo of Elliott's house in Los Angeles, and Paul Brodtkorb took the photo of Elliott's residential hotel in Brooklyn. My deepest gratitude, however, goes to Charles J. Collins, who sent me the entire file of early letters between Elliott and himself. Not only was that file one of the most exciting collections of material I have ever read, but the letters told more than any other source about the story of Elliott and his discovery of the nature of market behavior.

Significant information was obtained from the following sources: U.S. National Archives; U.S. Department of State; Church of Jesus Christ of Latter-Day Saints Family History Center (AZ) and Library (UT); Fairchild Sons Funeral Home, Inc., Garden City, NY; Kings Park Psychiatric Center (NY); Little, Brown & Company; Mrs. R. M. MacLaury; Ferrocarriles de Guatemala; Pottawatomie County Register of Deeds (KS); Los Angeles County Registrar-Recorder (CA); Lexington Genealogical and Historical Society, Inc. (IL); Graceland Cemetery Association (IL); Livingston County Circuit Clerk (IL); Montclair Public Library (NJ); California Department of Health Services; Inglewood Park Cemetery (CA); City of New York Department of Health; Arizona State Research Library; Arizona State University Libraries (including Hayden); Phoenix Public Library (AZ); Dominy Memorial Library (IL); Marysville Public Library

(KS); Oregon State University Library (OR); Brenau University Library (GA); Georgia State University Library; Chestatee Regional Library (GA) and Gainesville College Library (GA).

As you read the story of Ralph Nelson Elliott, you may be as intrigued as I am that a theory so remarkably unique, when compared to other methods of market analysis at that time and even those of today, could have been developed so late in life by a man not of Wall Street background. Bolton accurately described the enormity of Elliott's feat when he said that "he developed his principle into a rational method of stock market analysis on a scale never before attempted."

A BIOGRAPHY OF RALPH NELSON ELLIOTT

"A man's life, like a piece of tapestry, is made up of many strands, which interwoven make a pattern; to separate a single one and look at it alone not only destroys the whole, but gives the strand itself a false value."

— Learned Hand

Wave One: The Formative Years

Ralph Nelson Elliott's family tree contained some distinguished Americans. His maternal great grandfather, Jonathan Hamblett, fought as a private militiaman at Bunker Hill during the American Revolution. He was wounded in battle and later appointed one of General Washington's bodyguards. Elliott's grandfather, Hugh Elliott, was a veteran of the War of 1812. Hugh was residing in Iberia, Ohio, then at the nation's western frontier, when his son Franklin, Ralph Elliott's father, was born in 1835. Franklin became a merchant and married Virginia Nelson, who came from a wealthy farming family near Philadelphia, where her brothers and sisters each farmed 80 acres. On August 27, 1864, at the close of the Civil War, Franklin and Virginia Elliott had a daughter, Anna May. She was three years old when the family moved to Marysville, Kansas, a small community by the Big Blue River in the northeastern part of the state. Franklin had continued his father's practice of heading west with the nation as a whole, as at that time, Marysville was a bustling edge-of-civilization stop for the Pony Express and travelers on the Oregon Trail. The family's second (and last) child, Ralph Nelson Elliott, was born in Marysville three years later on July 28, 1871. The family then moved a few hundred miles east to Fairbury, Illinois, a small and prosperous farming community about 100 miles southwest of Chicago, apparently a better location for a merchant. The family lived on Elm Street, where Elliott spent his early childhood.

By the end of 1880, Elliott had moved with his parents and sister to San Antonio, Texas. During his teen years, he learned to speak and write Spanish fluently and developed a love for Mexico, the border of which was 150 miles to the south. He visited Mexico at times during his youth and in fact lived there when he was 15 to 16 years old. His sister later married a native Mexican, Bernard Nuñez.

Elliott began working at age fourteen, when he secured employment as a telegraph operator for Western Union. In 1891, at the age of 20, he left home permanently to work on the railroads in Mexico at the height of North America's great railroad boom. In 1892 he returned to the States for a brief stay with his mother and sister in Seattle. Shortly thereafter, his family moved to Los Angeles, California, where his parents and sister remained for the rest of their lives. Elliott stayed in Mexico throughout his early twenties, where he was employed variously as a lineman, train dispatcher, stenographer, telegraph operator and station agent.

Around 1896, Elliott entered the accounting profession,* though by what educational path is unknown. Because he had already learned the industry from the bottom up, he developed the specialty of railroad accounting. For the following twenty-five years, Elliott held executive positions with a number of corporations, primarily railroad companies, in Mexico, Central America and South America (including Argentina and probably Chile), many of which were U.S.-owned.

In his 25 years spent mostly in that region, Elliott became intimately familiar with all classes of people. "Latin America is a land of extremes," he later wrote in a manuscript. "Riches and poverty, health and sickness, enlightenment and direst ignorance, virtue and vice rub shoulders continually, presenting contrasts perhaps as striking as in any other part of the world." He colorfully described local styles of living that reflected great affluence and luxury as well as abject poverty and squalor, as reflected by the following excerpts:

> The wealthy Latin American builds himself a palace, drives expensive automobiles, plays bridge for a dollar or more a point, races his thoroughbreds, and enjoys his exclusive clubs, his well appointed home and its lavishly served table. His wife and children are exquisitely dressed, and are denied nothing that money can buy; their English and French are [nothing] short of perfect. His country house will boast a swimming bath, tennis courts and landscape gardens, and not infrequently a race-track and a golf course. Even [there,] his guests are furnished with the same choice imported wines and viands, served by perfectly trained domestics.

---

*Some researchers may discover library records of a Mr. R.N. Elliott (F.C.A.) who wrote a study for the Institute of Chartered Accountants in Australia. These records refer to a different person.

The home of the *peon* is usually a mere shack whose walls and roof are of leaves and grass. The floor is bare earth; furniture, if any, and cooking utensils are of the most primitive kind imaginable. Animals of all descriptions share the dwelling place. Dogs and pigs [provide] warmth. The filth and squalor is beyond description. They are ignorant ... and ridden with superstition, [and have] little desire for improvement. When drunk, ... a thoughtless word, a slight difference of opinion, an accidental push, or a quarrel over women is sufficient to provoke a bloody pitched battle with machetes, resulting in fearful gashes and not infrequently death.

When recounting a number of personal anecdotes in the same manuscript, Elliott revealed his experiences to be considerably more adventurous than one might assume given his profession. In one passage, he recalled the following incident:

Some idea of the innate savagery of the *peones* may be gathered from an experience of the writer some little time back, in a Central American port. Two laborers, both hopelessly intoxicated, were arrested and thrown into jail for fighting with knives on the beach. On the following day, when they were relatively sober, they were interrogated by the Port Commandant, and professed to be the best of friends, stating that they had been fighting *"por gusto"* (for fun). The quality of this grim amusement may be gauged by the fact that the less fortunate of the players had more than forty gashes on his face and body.

Elliott explained that wealthy landowners, with whom he often stayed, typically looked after their laborers as if they were an extended family. He recalled this scene illustrating the role of women in carrying out this duty:

Late at night, during a heavy thunderstorm, a little Indian boy came to the door of the farmhouse [where Elliott was staying] and informed the family that his brother was dying. Quietly calling for her horse, and packing some medicines and provisions in a basket, [the younger daughter of seventeen] set off for a three mile ride through the rain and wind. The writer, who was privileged to accompany her on this errand of mercy, can vouch for the discomforts of the journey, and also for the utter lack of gratitude displayed by the unfortunate sufferer, who proved to be merely under the influence of an overdose of alcohol.

Besides revealing his responsible nature and hinting at a subtle sense of humor that he displayed more than once in his professional writings, this passage at least informs us that Elliott was an accomplished enough horseman to ride three miles through a thunderstorm in the middle of the night. He further commented, "[The food] is of a most uninviting nature.... No beast that walks, flies or swims is despised from the standpoint [of edibility]. The writer has seen squirrels, lizards, parrots, foxes and even snakes, cooked and eaten with evident gusto." These myriad observations could not have been made by a man who spent all his time in comfortable hotels or corporate offices.

The challenge of conducting business in primitive conditions and in a different culture, particularly one that continually presented extreme personal and political risks, was particularly daunting. As Elliott explained, the "lack of means of communication, the shortage of labor, [and] almost impassable roads" made industry particularly difficult. "It may take one man all day," he said, "to haul a load of coffee [by oxcart] from the plantation to the railroad and return empty." The personality of the locals also presented obstacles that had to be understood and dealt with. In describing subordinates' method of dealing with superiors, for instance, Elliott observed, "The very antithesis of the [blunt] North American, he will answer questions in a courteous manner best calculated to please for the moment," irrespective of the truth. The region was also "constantly seething with intrigue," he noted, in prefacing this discussion of his situation in Guatemala years later when that country's president died:

> From night to morning, the whole country has been thrown into confusion. Soldiers are patrolling the streets and are stationed at all the public buildings. There is manifest reluctance to meet out of doors, and speculation is rife as to what turn events may take. On the one hand, nothing may happen. On the other, a few days may see the whole nation plunged into bloody civil war, with its attendant harrowing scenes of women and children being shot down in cold blood, of general chaos and of murder, rape and plunder. Everyone realizes, though perhaps unconsciously, that he is living on the brink of a smoldering volcano, and that in the very nature of things, the moment of greatest seeming tranquility may precede a devastating eruption.

An individual such as Ralph Elliott, who was at ease in dealing with such an environment, was certainly well suited to handle the transitions from "tranquility" to "devastating eruption" in the stock market.

Elliott prospered in his special niche not only by being rugged and adventurous, but ironically by being an accomplished "people person" as well. Elliott later explained that Latin Americans place tremendous value on "a suave and engaging personality," a "never failing urbanity," above all other character traits. Elliott's complex ability to deal with all strata of society, his relish of the extremes of Latin American life, and his insightful understanding of the character of the people, made him an invaluable asset to U.S.-based companies whose owners preferred to reside in a more stable setting stateside.

On September 3, 1902, in El Paso, Texas, Elliott married Mary Elizabeth Fitzpatrick (1867-1941), who was four years his senior. Mary was a native New Yorker but was working in Mexico, probably with a team of U.S. currency reform advisors to the Mexican government, when they met. This city-bred Irish Catholic woman exhibited a substantial pioneer spirit in traveling with her husband throughout the Latin American region in those days, although all indications are that they led a relatively comfortable middle class life, not infrequently socializing with the well-to-do. From time to time, the couple returned to the U.S., usually by ship and/or rail, to visit their respective families. On July 9, 1904, the couple hosted Mary's sister Anna's wedding in New York City. The groom, Milton T. Thompson, was an engineer for the Necaxa Project, a hydroelectric plant built 90 miles east of Mexico City. In 1908-1909, Elliott held the position of Superintendent of the Mexican Central Railway. He returned to the U.S. again in February 1909, when his mother died. She was buried in Inglewood Park Cemetery in Inglewood, California, where Elliott's father and sister were later buried.

In 1912, Elliott was serving as Special Auditor for the National Railroad of Mexico in Monterrey, while his wife was living in San Antonio. In a 1913 registration form for U.S. citizens living in Mexico, Elliott listed nine Mexican cities in which he had lived and worked over the preceding 21 years. At the time, he was an employee of the Veracruz Terminal Company. In early 1914, Elliott and his wife found time to take a cruise to England. They returned on the S.S. President Lincoln. The following year he was serving as the General Manager of the Frontera Transportation Company. His wife was summering in Great Falls, Montana, at the time, staying away no doubt due to the revolutionary unrest in Mexico, which probably also accounts for Elliott's frequent moves.

As Elliott practiced his profession, his corporate positions became more and more important. The main reason was that his expertise was proving much broader than simply accounting. As later documents reveal, his value to a company was primarily in the area of business restructuring. As he put it in a book in 1926, "Accounting, like everything else, is undergoing very radical steps in evolution; it is becoming serviceable in a vastly broader sense." Fulfilling that vision, Elliott financially reorganized numerous corporations by installing new systems of record keeping, anticipating future expenditures, and applying a principle of percentage allocation of revenues, which in a magazine article he later called "the only sane method of controlling any business successfully." Much like an independent business consultant, Elliott ultimately served many clients, although his approach was to sign on with companies one at a time, remaining with each one until the restructuring was complete. Elliott must have saved many corporations from chronic losses or increased their profitability, as over the years he earned a substantial reputation as a business organization expert.

The Elliotts might well have remained in Mexico for the rest of their lives, but circumstances ultimately forced their return to the United States. Beginning in 1911, Mexico experienced a series of violent revolutions that extended over the next several years. Relations between Mexico and the U.S. were strained by the Wilson administration's refusal to recognize the government of Victoriano Huerta, who seized power in early 1913. Tensions increased sharply in April 1914 when U.S. Marines occupied the Mexican seaport of Veracruz to retaliate for the seizure of a party of American sailors.

In July 1914, Huerta's government was overthrown, but the resulting coalition government soon split, and civil war broke out. On March 9, 1916, rebel general Francisco "Pancho" Villa, who controlled much of the northern part of the country, led an attack on Columbus, New Mexico. President Woodrow Wilson ordered General John J. Pershing to pursue the rebel army across the border and capture Villa. The expedition failed, serving only to increase anti-American sentiment in Mexico. Assaults on U.S. citizens and destruction of American-owned property in the country were widely reported. Railroads appear to have been a particular target of both the rebels, who destroyed tracks and rolling stock, and the federal government, which began to nationalize the railroads in mid-1914. The government's seizure of the National Railways of Mexico probably affected Elliott's employment situation.

When the Marines landed in Veracruz in April 1914, the Elliotts moved to Frontera, a small port town known for its Mayan archaeological sites, situated at the mouth of the Grijalva River on the Gulf of Mexico near the western edge of the Yucatán peninsula. Elliott may have come to the region with the railroad, as the main coastal line from Coatzacoalcos to Mérida runs through the area today. Because the area was home for several American-owned mahogany plantations and an American community of sorts, he may have sought employment and refuge there, away from the center of political unrest. Eventually, civil strife throughout the country reached a point of crisis, and in June 1916, in Elliott's words, "when the President ordered all Americans out" of Mexico, he complied and returned with his wife to Los Angeles, California.

Wave Two: Retrenchment and Consolidation

Having been thus dislodged from his longtime area of work and residence, Elliott appears to have undergone a period of dissatisfaction with his situation. Over the next four years, he changed jobs twice, investigated two others, and several times made plans to return to Latin America.

Numerous details of this period attest to Elliott's restlessness. In early 1917, he was living at 720 Beacon Avenue in Los Angeles and was employed by the Typewriter Inspection Company. On May 28, his father died, and on July 10, he began working as the export manager for Blake, Moffitt and Towne, a wholesale paper

manufacturer with offices in New York and Los Angeles and
production facilities in the northwestern cities of Portland, Seattle
and Tacoma. In December, by which time he was living at 801
Beacon Avenue, Elliott applied for a passport to travel to Cuba to
accept a position with the William P. Field Company of Havana.
In January 1918, he canceled his trip to Cuba, applying instead

Ralph Nelson Elliott prior to January 1918
(probably several years earlier)

for a passport to return to Mexico to promote export business for Blake, Moffitt and Towne. He later described the job as being frustratingly "difficult...under existing conditions." In his passport application dated January 25, he listed an ambitious itinerary that included visits to Sinaloa, Sonora, Colima, Jalisco and Nayarit in Mexico, as well as Guatemala, El Salvador, Honduras, Nicaragua, Costa Rica and Panama. The outcome of this journey on behalf of his employer, or even whether it took place, is unknown, as it was not mentioned in his next passport application. The revolutionary sentiment still in the air in Mexico could have affected the export business and therefore the anticipated success of the trip. Fearless of the political climate, Elliott was back in Mexico the following year, living in Tampico from July to December 1919 and working as an auditor for the U.S.-owned Pierce Oil Corporation. He also secured a job for his sister May as a bilingual stenographer at a school and office of stenography in Mexico City. During these months, his wife resided in the popular resort area of Asheville, North Carolina, staying in the U.S. undoubtedly because of the potential danger that still existed in Mexico.

It is fortunate for biographers that Elliott traveled so much and that upon the advent of World War I in 1914, passports were required of U.S. citizens for the first time. His various passport applications, held by the National Archives, contain a good deal of information. They reveal, for instance, that he was 5'8" tall, had blue eyes, brown hair, a complexion described alternatively as "ruddy" and "fair," and wore eyeglasses. Photos taken in his mid-to-late forties show a man with a sturdy frame, a hardy appearance and an air of self-assurance, all of which well served Elliott's active life.

Elliott's main goals during this time were to perform the type of work that he enjoyed and to return to the region where he had lived most of his adult life. He obviously found his employment during this time unfulfilling, possibly because he was doing business development work or simple accounting instead of the structural organizing that he enjoyed. His low opinion of standard accounting was expressed unequivocally in a 1924 magazine article:

> I believe it is safe to say that most accountants do not like their calling, and this being the case, can you expect that others, who are not familiar with the terms and objects, will relish discussions on the subject? When I introduced myself to one

young lady and opened the subject of accounting, she said that the very word "accounting" made her sick at her stomach. Now, I do *not* like accounting, but I *do* like the work I am doing.... I am not exactly an accountant, but possibly the word "efficiency" comes nearer to it; however, that sounds about as bad. We all like efficiency in others, but not in ourselves. Now I am going to sugar-coat my financial and accounting pills so that you will like them.... *What I am trying to do is help you make money.*

That last sentence certainly reveals a drive that would later make stock market forecasting an attractive vocation for R.N. Elliott. For now, however, that was the furthest thing from his mind as he searched for something that would challenge his organizational talents.

Elliott returned to Los Angeles briefly in December 1919 (perhaps to be with his sister for the Christmas holidays), then traveled to the affluent Village of Ridgewood, New Jersey, where he and his wife visited with the Thompsons for a few weeks in January, 1920. During that time, they arranged for an apartment in New York City at 142 West 82nd Street. Unemployed at the time, Elliott aggressively continued his quest to secure suitable employment in Latin America, where he preferred to reside.

In March, Elliott again applied for a passport, this time to travel to Mexico City and Tampico "to attend to some property acquired during a long residence in Mexico." This visit was to have been followed by travel to Cuba, where he had been offered the job of Standard Rules Instructor with the Cuba Railroad Company. Elliott's abilities obviously were widely known and highly regarded in Latin America, since he was offered this position despite the fact that the company just offered it to someone else. As the company's vice president and general manager wrote to Elliott, "If we thought you would come, we would notify this party that the offer to him was withdrawn." Such energetic solicitations for Elliott's services were not unusual. The position he had considered accepting in Cuba three years before had been offered to him in an urgent cable that read in part, "Your services badly needed." Apparently, he was the most talented bilingual accountant and corporate reorganizer available to these companies.

Then came an abrupt change in Elliott's life. For whatever reason, he suddenly called off his trip and ceased his efforts to find employment and residence in Latin America. Perhaps the reason was simply that in his fortuitous move to New York City he had found another place that suited his adventurous nature.

Wave Three: Productivity and Progress

Elliott, now in his early fifties and with a new base of operations in New York City, maintained a remarkably busy schedule over the next seven years. Later letters to Charles J. Collins reveal that he traveled to Canada, Germany, England and France, though for what reason (personal or business) is unknown. His largest company reorganization outside the railroad field was Amsinck & Company, an export-import house of five hundred employees.

Elliott once again decided to specialize, and in response to a newly popular industry, quickly developed a second specialty as a business consultant to restaurants, cafeterias and tea rooms, which was as well suited to New York City as his railroad specialty had been to Mexico and Central America. He displayed his usual energy in establishing this new niche, and in the process increased his professional stature yet further, this time by writing for a professional journal. In the summer of 1924, Elliott joined the editorial staff of the New York based monthly business magazine, *Tea Room and Gift Shop*.

Though the term "tea room" is now quaint, tea rooms were a booming business in the 1920s, just as coffee shops are today. Their popularity was spreading rapidly to the point that entrepreneurs from experienced restaurateurs to housewives were trying their hands at them. *Tea Room and Gift Shop* averaged 30 pages an issue, sold for 20 cents an issue ($4 in today's money), and boasted 3000 professional readers around the world. Elliott's arrival at the magazine was marked with some fanfare, with nearly a full page devoted to introducing him to its readers. Here is an excerpt:

Mr. Elliott Joins Our Staff

We are glad to be able to make good so soon some of the promises of a "bigger and better" *Tea Room and Gift Shop* made in the August number. One of the very important steps toward increased service to our readers is the addition of Mr. R.N. Elliott to the corps of experts in the various problems of our field.... Mr. Elliott will conduct a department devoted to the financial phases of tea room operation.... Mr. Elliott, in his consulting practice, has been able to locate the financial

TEA ROOM
AND
GIFT SHOP

Tea Room of Jennie C. Benedict & Co., Louisville, Ky.

Flap-Jack Alley in Constantinople
Gifts That Grow
Quality—the Shortest Road to Volume
Mr. Elliott's Column
Foods and Cookery for the Tea Room

NOVEMBER, 1924   20c. A COPY

Mr. Elliott's Column

R. N. Elliott

Our readers are invited to submit their problems to this department. Write fully and frankly to Mr. Elliott, care Tea Room and Gift Shop, and your question will be answered. Your name will not be printed.

INCORPORATION VERSUS INDIVIDUAL.

My dear Mr. Elliott: Will you please discuss the advantages and disadvantages of a corporation as related to tea rooms? I am sure others besides myself would be very grateful.

Answer: To incorporate means to give life to a new entity by means of a charter issued by the State and relieves the owners of personal responsibility beyond the investment in stock. That is to say, if one invests $1,000 in a corporation, and has fully paid for the stock subscribed for, that person cannot and cannot be called upon for further payments to make good any losses of the corporation. Tradesmen are, of course, familiar with this fact, and until they may have acquired confidence in the corporation itself, are reluctant to give credit unless secured by a responsible individual. However, if credit is not needed, this disadvantage is of no importance.

When the owner, or owners of a corporation, decide to sell an interest in the concern, it is done by the simple means of issuing stock, or one holder may sell any portion of the stock which may have been subscribed for. In other words, an interest in the corporation can be very easily purchased or sold by this means, which is not so simple in a partnership.

One person may desire to own a corporation entirely and this is possible with the sole exception that there must be three directors and each must own stock, altho the quantity is not specified by law; therefor, one person may own 998 shares of stock, and the others one share each, making 1,000 in all, which may represent the entire authorized issue.

It is, of course, desirable that one person and not two should control the policy of any business. Where there are two or more who have an equal voice, there is liable to be indecision, which is frequently more harmful than a wrong decision. Therefore, if two or more persons enter into business and incorporate, one should own, or control through friends, at least 51% of the stock.

In the event of the death of a stockholder in a corporation, the corporation does not therefore cease to exist, but the title to the stock of the deceased holder becomes the property of the heirs. If there are several heirs, the stock may be subdivided among them in accordance with the terms of the will or law, all of which can be done without affecting the operations of the corporation.

In the case of a partnership between two or more persons, if one should die, the partnership ceases immediately, and legal complications arise which may affect the continuance of the business, and thereby jeopardize the interests of the surviving partners.

In the event of the death of a partner, the question of what the interest is worth immediately arises. A purchaser has to be found for the deceased's interest and it is not always easy to agree upon the value of the interest. If the shareholder in a corporation dies, this does not complicate the continued operation of the business, and the value of the heirs' interest can be more easily arrived at by means of the percentage of dividend previously paid. That is, the stock should be worth on the basis of the percentage of revenue that it produces, taking into consideration the expected life of the business. If the corporation holds a three year lease it cannot be definitely assumed that revenues from the business will be produced after that time for the reason that permanency of location is the prime asset of this class of business.

The legal expense of incorporation is insignificant, not much, if any more, than a legally drawn partnership, but there are certain formalities which have to be attended to in incorporation. These are not frequent, however, and are easily taken care of by anyone familiar with the laws governing corporations.

If one person desires to derive all of the revenue from a corporation, it is not necessary to dissolve the corporation. The expense of incorporation has already been taken care of, and there only remains the continued annual formalities. Two other persons must hold at least one share each, the three forming a directory. It is advisable to continue this status for the reason that, conditions may change during the life of the leaks, the violations of administrative principles, which have prevented [an] adequate return.... Mr. Elliott has the accounting background, and what is exceedingly important, the business acumen, to be of great service to our subscribers.... His outlook is not confined to accounting, but includes kindred matters as related to the general problems of the operation of an eating place.... We have hesitated to apply such a label as "Accounting," "Operating Costs," or "Finance" [to the subject]. Although Mr. Elliott is thoroughly equipped in accounting knowledge and is a consultant in general tea room, restaurant and cafeteria operation, he is primarily a business man.

Elliott's monthly contribution was entitled simply, "Mr. Elliott's Column," and generally ran about two pages. Each one was announced on the front cover and accompanied by his photo, one of only two writers' photos in the publication. Elliott's first article, which appeared in the September issue, presented some basic ideas and solicited questions from the business people who read the magazine. Subsequent columns answered the questions submitted. Elliott practiced what a Department of Commerce bulletin from the time called "scientific management," and argued that accounting was "just coming into its own" and becoming far more than just bookkeeping, as he himself had demonstrated during his many years of company reorganization. His attitude toward the food service business, and to business in general, is reasonably well expressed in the following collection of comments culled (seperations omitted) from his seven articles:

> Tea rooms apparently well patronized are supposed [by the prospective entrepreneur] to be "coining money." [However,] "Survival of the Fittest" is true in tea rooms as in other classes of business. Competition is a vital factor. It is [my] object to caution prospective owners against misconceived ideas, so that failures may diminish. It is all very well and proper that recipes, decorations, etc., should receive due attention, but after all, you are in the tea room business to make money. Many tea room owners may think they are making a profit simply because they have more money in the bank at the end of each month, but this is not necessarily a fact. Expenses which do not occur every day should be anticipated. Assuming that the financial fundamentals have been properly considered, the question is whether you are making money, and if not, WHY. To be able to ascertain where the difficulty lies, it is necessary to keep

records. Aside from keeping records which the government may require for income tax purposes, one might as well not keep any books at all unless they are handled in such a way as to give reliable information as a guide for future action. The subject is a very broad one and requires verbal and graphic explanation.

His advice was not merely technical but came from experience. For instance, he urged hopeful novices first to obtain employment at a successful establishment at any wage offered, assume as many duties as possible over a period of time, and learn the business from the bottom up, a path that he himself had taken in developing his railroad accounting specialty. He further advised that people not "follow a business that does not appeal to them," regardless of the apparent financial benefits, an adage that he certainly lived by. His warnings against borrowing to start a business reflected numerous experiences with companies burdened with debt, which he considered one of four primary reasons for business failure (the other three being inexperience, insufficient capital and inadequate records).

Other comments from his columns reflected ideas that served him well in the future. For instance, his admonition that "indecision is frequently more harmful than a wrong decision" later directed his unhedged calls on the market. His idea that record keeping is primarily "a guide for future action" was directly applicable to his approach in studying the stock market, and his penchant for "graphic explanation" helped him accomplish it. His general observation that "every business that is new[ly fashionable] is liable to be overdone periodically" hinted at his experience with business cycles and knowledge of boom-and-bust fads. He even discussed the psychology of satisfied customers and explained where to find honest opinions about a business' shortcomings, directions that reflected a healthy self-esteem that later allowed him, when he was unknown among market professionals, to solicit the opinion of the nationally known investment counselor and writer, Charles J. Collins, concerning his Wave Principle discovery.

Then, as today, the restaurant business presented a strong attraction for many prospective entrepreneurs, resulting in substantial competition as well as a high failure rate. As a result of both factors, the industry was hungry for advice. Elliott's commentary was popular, and the opening letter addressed to him in the November issue began, "Your column is most interesting and I can plainly see that *Tea Room and Gift Shop* will have to be enlarged to accommodate your correspondence." The esteem with which his column was held in the restaurant accounting and management field is reflected by the fact that in late 1924, Columbia University invited him to speak on the subject. Elliott was unable to accept the invitation, as he was once again on his way out of New York on business from his then-residence at 216 West 79th Street.

Elliott's aggressive mobility and corporate service over the years occasionally brought him into contact with influential people in the academic and political world. His personal charm served him well, and his fascinating range of experience and steadfast integrity must have made him an enjoyable associate.

One of Elliott's contacts was Dr. Jeremiah Whipple Jenks, a distinguished lawyer, academician, political advisor and author of nearly two dozen books on politics, social issues, religion and business. During the mid-1920s, Jenks was Chairman and President of the Alexander Hamilton Institute in New York and Research Professor of Government and Public Administration at New York University. Elliott undoubtedly met Jenks through professional association, as Jenks had also served on the board of directors of several railroads, including the Pacific Railways of Nicaragua. The two men may have become acquainted as early as 1903, when Jenks was a professor of Political Economy and Politics at Cornell University. He had spent some time in Mexico that year serving as a consultant to its government on matters of currency reform at a time when Elliott was an accountant for the

Dr. Jeremiah Whipple Jenks

Photo: Culver Pictures

Mexican railroad. What's more, because Jenks' time in Mexico coincided with Elliott's marriage, and since both Mary Fitzpatrick and Jenks had traveled from New York, it seems reasonable to speculate that Mary may have been working for Jenks when she met Ralph Elliott. Whatever the date, at some point Jenks' and Elliott's common interests in the railroad industry, finance and Central America brought them together. The characters of the two men appear quite different, Jenks a Victorian moralist of the academic and political world and Elliott an earthy, practical professional in the corporate world. Nevertheless, their common interests led to a mutual respect and friendship.

One of Jenks' main goals was promoting a strict code of virtues as a solution to social problems, and in researching his position, he became widely read on the subject of human nature, particularly as expressed in social action. In one book (*The Political and Social Significance of the Life and Teachings of Jesus*), written in 1906, he included the following comments and quotations:

> Every society is built upon human nature, and is the product of heredity and environment. Each society will differ from every other society, but when the question is one of fundamental moving forces, human beings are much the same in all times and countries.
>
> "To understand man, however, we must look beyond the individual man and his actions or interests, and view him in combination with his fellows." — Carlyle
>
> Very frequently, men in association as groups or societies or nations act in ways quite different from those of individuals.
>
> "A large part of all the social action in which many individuals take a concerted part is impulsive rather than deliberate; and, therefore, many of the dramatic events of history have been impulsive social actions." — Giddings

Needless to say, this line of thinking is fundamental to the Wave Principle and indeed validated by it. It is possible that some of the ideas about human nature that Elliott ultimately expressed in his books on the stock market percolated from discussions with Jenks on the subject years earlier.

Elliott's longtime association with Jeremiah Jenks proved fortuitous in providing Elliott a fascinating responsibility as well as a bit of adventure. Jenks, in addition to his other activities, had served on a number of government commissions, including the High Commission of Nicaragua. In 1912, the long-standing liberal government of Nicaragua was overthrown by a coup. The U.S. Marines entered the country to effect a turnover of administrative control to the U.S. government for the stated purpose of protecting American interests in Nicaragua. After a dozen years, the U.S. State Department tired of its role and appointed the High Commission to advise it on how to help stabilize the Nicaraguan government enough to allow the U.S. Marines to withdraw. The Commission rapidly set up national elections, which were held in November 1924. The newly elected coalition government in Nicaragua then contracted with Dr. Jenks, as reported by *The New York Times*, "to revise the banking and financial laws of Nicaragua" and "to establish a new banking system in the country." U.S. banking interests apparently wanted to finance and modernize the Nicaraguan railroad system, an effort which would have interested both Jenks and Elliott. One of Jenks' first actions was to set up the National Bank of Nicaragua and serve as a director.

At Jenks' recommendation, Ralph Nelson Elliott was chosen by the U.S. Department of State to assume the post of Chief Accountant for Nicaragua. On December 18, 1924, Elliott met with Secretary of State Charles Evans Hughes in Washington, D.C. to receive his formal appointment and instructions. The following week he applied for his passport, and in January 1925 set sail for Nicaragua, accompanied by his wife.

The State Department invitation and acceptance were effected so swiftly that while Elliott was making plans to leave New York, an advertisement for his consulting services, as well as his column, ran in the January issue of what was now called *Restaurant and Tea Room Journal.* His last column, which had been submitted in December to meet the publishing deadline, ran in the February issue, at which time Elliott was on the high seas to Central America.

The ship arrived in Managua in February, and Elliott immediately began to apply his extensive experience in corporate reorganization to reorganizing the finances of an entire country. The Jenks mission arrived shortly thereafter, on March 24, 1925, and began advising the newly elected coalition government in what was probably a joint effort with the State Department's appointees.

Though originally scheduled to stay as long as two years, Elliott served in his official government position only until June

817.51

9wu w x.37. blue

NewYork Dec 15,24

Dr. Francis White,

    Latin Amn Affairs.

    Referring to Dr Francis White Chief Div Latin
American Affairs Washington DC referring
Dr J W Jenks conversations state department
Saturday Mr R N Elliott has accepted appointment
chief accountant Nicaragua stop Requests you
arrange appointment secretary Hughes December
eighteen please telegraph collect Dr Jenks office
thirteen Astor place

               Secretary to Dr Jenks.

2.00pm

TELEGRAM SENT.

Department of State

Washington, December 15, 1924.

Doctor Jeremiah W. Jenks,

    Alexander Hamilton Institute,

        Astor Place, New York City.

    The Secretary of State will receive Mr. Elliott at
10:45 Thursday, December 18.

               Francis White

Mary Elizabeth Fitzpatrick Elliott,1924

Ralph Nelson Elliott, 1924

of the same year, when the U.S. extricated itself from Nicaragua. At that time, the U.S. recalled all State Department appointees as well as the Marines under the assumption that calm and order had been sufficiently restored.*

From Nicaragua, Elliott returned to the U.S., but only for a month. Whether or not there had been any causal relationship to the termination of his column four months earlier, *Restaurant and Tea Room Journal* was folding. Upon discover ng that the magazine had just mailed its last issue, Elliott applied for an executive position with the International Railway of Central America, a U.S. company based in New York whose stock was traded on the New York and London Stock Exchanges. He was hired immediately as its General Auditor, another top executive position. The salary of $9000 a year (equivalent in today's money to $180,000 a year *after* taxes) reflected Elliott's corporate earning power at the time. Ralph and Mary Elliott promptly set out once again, on a nine-day voyage to the company's center of operations in Guatemala City, Guatemala, arriving on August 3. This was to be Elliott's last professional position.

While serving in Guatemala, Elliott wrote a comprehensive 176-page book entitled *Tea Room and Cafeteria Management*, an extension of his earlier magazine articles. The book was published in August 1926 by Little, Brown & Company. The first favorable review appeared in *The New York Herald Tribune*, and apparently its international edition as well, on August 8. As the reviewer noted, "Mr. Elliott has had years of experience as [an] organizer of many different lines of business." *The New York Times* Book Review printed a favorable critique in its August 15 edition. The reviewer commented that "Mr. Elliott writes with authority upon all these matters because of his wide and varied business experience and observation."

A practical guide to opening and managing a restaurant, *Tea Room and Cafeteria Management* deals primarily with "the economical aspects of the preparation of food as a business."

---

*The Marines left Nicaragua in August 1925 after a 13-year span of U.S. occupation. Without U.S. support, the ruling coalition immediately collapsed under rebel pressure, and within months civil war was raging. The Marines were sent back to Nicaragua after less than a year's absence and stayed until 1933, completing a 21-year span of occupation.

TEA ROOM AND CAFETERIA MANAGEMENT

By R. N. ELLIOTT

Mr. Elliott, for many years an organizer and analyst in various lines of business, has recently specialized in tea rooms and cafeterias. In this book he aims to prevent the inexperienced from losing their precious capital and to assist owners in making the greatest possible profit.

He has covered every aspect of the business, from the choice of a location to making out the income-tax report, touching on rentals, names, equipment, decoration, help and menus; on buying, on advertising; the system of accounting and other matters of vital importance which may be easily overlooked or improperly handled. This informative volume should certainly open the eyes of any one pot fully acquainted with the details of tea room and cafeteria management and will undoubtedly help many an owner to get far better returns on his investment.

Mr. Elliott is already known to many tea room and cafeteria managers through his regular contributions to the *Tea Room and Gift Shop Magazine*.

Contents: Capital; Location and Accommodations; Leases and Ventilation; Decorations; Names and Signs; Hostesses; Food and Menus; Portions; Pricing Food on Menus; Necessity for Accounting; Analysis of Expenses; Insurance; Repairs; Replacements and Taxes; Reconciliation of Bank Balances; Employees; Their Wages; Schedules; Tea Room and Cafeteria Compared; Fluctuations; Surplus Food or "Left-Overs"; Buying; A Quiet Kitchen; Advertising; Public Opinion of Your Tea Room; Lists of Equipment; Conclusion.

176 pages. 12mo. Cloth. $1.50

Boston   LITTLE, BROWN & COMPANY   Publishers

Tea Room and Cafeteria Management by R. N. Elliott

This new book offers an invaluable guide to owners and managers as well as to prospective entrants into the tea room and cafeteria business, every phase of which is here discussed.

Price $1.50

Book cover: front and back

Elliott's book concerns not only the financial end of the business but the aesthetic as well. Ads for the book referred to Elliott as "an expert organizer." Indeed, as he certainly must have done with all his positions in business, he gave great attention to detailing, arranging, analyzing and planning, abilities that were later manifest in his exposition of the Wave Principle. Several passages reveal bits and pieces of Elliott's background, interests and personality, including once again his subtle sense of humor. For instance, after discussing the absolute necessity of obtaining adequate capital for start-up purposes, a precondition that many would-be restaurateurs he knew had naively insisted upon ignoring, he commented:

> On the other hand, circumstances may arise where, there being a real demand for a restaurant in a certain neighborhood, patronage may be relied upon from the start. Such conditions, coupled with the possible fact that the owner possesses, in that particular locality, a house furnished with all necessary equipment which can be utilized for the purpose of a tea room, may be successfully taken advantage of to open a restaurant with very little initial outlay. Here the owner will pay no additional rent and will, so to speak, merely assume the responsibility of feeding a larger family. He may also, more nearly to invest himself with all the Utopian advantages, be possessed of a vegetable garden, chicken run and perhaps even a cow or two.

Elliott may have written this paragraph for the benefit of those who might otherwise have taken a course at the Lewis Hotel Training School of Washington, D.C., which Elliott noted in correspondence was "in the habit of trying to persuade people that a tea room can be started with $50."

Several paragraphs in the book reveal Elliott's interest in business cycles. His profession would have brought such cycles powerfully to his attention, and his interest in them was obviously keen. In a chapter entitled "Fluctuations," he commented:

> It is a well-known fact that prosperity and depression follow each other in cycles, and the waves of these are extremely variable, but nevertheless certain. This is not the place to discuss the causes of these cycles; suffice it to say that they are very real.

Ralph Nelson Elliott in October 1926

Elliott referred to business cycles in his conclusion poetically as "the ebb and flow of circumstance," a phrase that uses the liquid metaphor he later called "waves."

The publication of this book announced Elliott's decision to resume his career as a restaurant management specialist, and he began to make plans accordingly. Mary Elliott returned to New York in June in anticipation of being soon joined by her husband. The last of the several Spanish language letters and telegrams that Elliott wrote or received as an executive in Guatemala is dated October 15, 1926. His passport application to return to the U.S. is dated October 21, and his corporate correspondence is indexed until October 25, at which time it ceased. According to International Railways records, an "Interim" General Auditor had been appointed by mid-November 1926, by which time Elliott had returned to New York City. Though the International Railways of Central America was headquartered at 17 Battery Place, New York, Elliott had taken a sabbatical and was not on company business. He had returned to New York with a definite goal in mind: to promote the book and cement his stature as the preeminent consultant in the restaurant management field. From his temporary base at the Wolcott Hotel on Fifth Avenue, Elliott issued numerous communications to the publisher regarding their coordinated book promotion.

As important as Elliott's professional activities were to him, they were no longer his only passion. The State Department appointment in Nicaragua had focused his talent for problem-solving in an entirely new realm, and Elliott found that he had a contribution to make to politics as well as to business. During his few weeks in New York, Elliott brought another recently concluded project to the attention of a publisher, as revealed in a letter residing in State Department files that Elliott wrote on February 23, 1927, to Secretary of State Frank Billings Kellogg. The letter mentions a memorandum he had written "a year or more ago," near the start of his tenure in Nicaragua, in which he had proposed a broad economic plan for the U.S. to implement in Latin America. Elliott noted that talks were then underway between the State Department and Nicaraguan President Adolfo Díaz "on lines proposed in my memorandum." Apparently, ideas that Elliott had formulated during and after his brief tenure in Nicaragua were already substantially shaping U.S. economic policy in the region.

CONSULTANT
BUSINESS PROBLEMS
PERSONAL INVESTMENTS

RECD

INDEX BUREAU
DEPT. OF STATE

FEB 28 27

R. N. ELLIOTT
548 SOUTH SPRING STREET
LOS ANGELES, CALIF.

ROOM 337
PHONE TUCKER 1893

DEPARTMENT OF STATE

Reply 3/2

February 23, 1927.

To the Honorable Secretary of State,   March 4, 1927.
Washington, D. C.

Sir: Attention Mr. Morgan,
                              Latin American Division.

        I have noted by this morning's newspapers
that conversations are taking place between the President of Nicaragua and yourself on lines proposed in my
memorandum of a year or more ago, copy of which was left
with Mr. Morgan. Both General Diaz and Mr. Eberhardt
are familiar with the plan I developed.

        When I last had the pleasure of seeing Mr.
Morgan, I advised him that I was preparing an elaboration of my plan and contemplated publishing same. A firm
of publishers in New York expressed a willingness to
publish such a book, provided the text were approved.
I am today sending them the text, and take pleasure in
sending you a copy of the typoscript, hoping that you
will find it serviceable. I have lived in Latin-
America most of my life, and my natural inclination is
to view things from an economic standpoint. I am
quite thoroughly convinced that commercial development
and financial control will eliminate revolutions, raise
the peon to the level of a potential consumer, remove
the menace to the Monroe Doctrine, and, incidentally, assist
in the progress and prosperity of the entire world,
particularly the United States. In fact, I believe that
such a scheme would stabilize prosperity in the United
States to a remarkable degree, for two or three decades.

                    Yours respectfully,

                    R N Elliott

    The main purpose of Elliott's letter was to obtain the blessing of the State Department for publication of another volume he had begun writing immediately after the publication of his restaurant book. The 100-page typescript (a carbon copy of the original with handwritten emendations) that Elliott forwarded to the State Department constituted about half of the planned book. Its theme was a larger exposition of his previously proposed U.S. economic policy toward Latin America. Elliott explained that he had found a publisher in New York who wished to proceed, but only if the State Department approved the text, perhaps because the book dealt with current and potentially sensitive policy matters. The Department's reply was pointedly noncommittal, thanking Elliott for his courtesy in bringing it to their attention, but declining further comment. If indeed the Department had been engaged in talks with President Díaz, it may have preferred to present the ideas as those of the State Department rather than of one individual. The typescript was eventually filed in the United States National Archives. Sixty-seven years after it was sent, it was discovered during research for this biography.

The Future of Latin America is a remarkable document, not only because it is a hitherto unknown work by R.N. Elliott but also because of its content. For one thing, the volume is a treasure trove of information on Elliott the man, revealing him as an individual of wide-ranging experience, as indicated by the excerpts quoted earlier in this biography that were taken therefrom. Various passages express a deep understanding of Latin American culture and a genuine love of the region, its arts, and its people. The treatise further reveals Elliott's knowledge of the various idioms of the Spanish language, Spanish literature, "the richness and beauty of which treasure," he said regretfully, "are seldom suspected," and the region's music, whose "gayest measure," he noted, "has always an underlying and undefinable note of pathos."

Elliott identified the Latin American as "a charming and puzzling mix of inconsistencies, the best of good fellows when properly approached, [with a] perception and intuition little short of marvelous." His occasional blunt criticisms of the region's customs and character further attest to the objectivity of his observations as well as his compelling desire to deduce the meaning of things:

> [T]he Spanish American is unfortunately rather a man of words than of action. There have been, of course, many thousands of striking exceptions, but as a general rule Latin Americans seem unable to overcome that mental inertia that has led them to suffer for centuries under the oppression of political abuse, without any organized attempt at reform.
>
> A study of some of the constructions of the Spanish language is also of great interest in attempting to understand something of Latin American thought. A servant, guilty of having dropped a plate or glass will invariably say, "*se cayo*" (it fell). He will never say, "I dropped it," but prefers to endow inanimate objects with life rather than admit that he himself could possibly have had any part in the disaster. The same idea

is reflected in matters of relatively great importance. Nothing is ever *made* to happen. It just "happens," whether it be an epidemic or a revolution. There appears little desire or effort to probe the causes of discomfort or disaster. This "don't care" spirit is to be met with in all countries of Spanish America.

Elliott recognized that the chief obstacles to economic progress in Latin America were a staggering burden of debt and a somewhat cavalier attitude toward its repayment. His assessment of the situation at that time could just as well have been a description of the region's various modern day "debt crises." "The financial history of almost all of [these nations]," he said, "is one long tale of default," due to Latin America's having "not yet accepted the fact that the payment of debts is a moral obligation." He blamed this attitude on a political process that allowed unrelenting plunder and favoritism and on a citizenry that allowed it. The extent of the political corruption he revealed in this paragraph:

> The Machiavellian ingenuity displayed by dishonest administrators in enriching themselves at the expense of their compatriots almost passes belief. The writer has on several occasions made careful study of the methods of these fraudulent administrators, and has compiled figures relative to the net loss resulting to the defrauded nations by the dishonesty and maladministration of those in power. The results were staggering, and indicated in some instances a filtration of more than 50% of the national revenue. For obvious [personal safety] reasons, it is, of course impossible to give concrete examples.... This state of affairs tends to discourage thrift, industry and initiative.... There are cases on record where unduly high rates of interest [were accepted], leaving the question of payment to be dealt with by future administrations. If they continue along the downward path which they have chosen, there is no end in sight but economic suicide.

Elliott's analysis of the social and economic problems of Latin America set the stage for his comprehensive proposal for creating economic stability and lasting prosperity in the region. Before beginning, he dismissed the traditional view of the U.S.'s role in the region with respect to the Monroe Doctrine, the origin of which, he pointed out, was less noble than commonly believed. "As far as the writer can see," said Elliott, "there has never been any attempt to outline a constructive foreign policy along practical lines."

To achieve that end, Elliott outlined a plan to be implemented, not unilaterally but by mutual agreement, "whenever a Latin American country approaches the United States with a request for financial or political aid, ...[when it is] in such dire financial straits that its very national existence is threatened." The plan required the host country to allow unobtrusive yet thoroughly integrated U.S. developmental administration in exchange for a number of reforms, including assistance in the issuance of national debt payment bonds guaranteed by the U.S. government, the retirement of old debt to European creditors, full payment of internal debt, tax reform, the revision of all tariffs, civil service reform, and the chartering of an American bank to handle the finances of the region. Money raised from the U.S. guaranteed bond sales would then finance development of the country's infrastructure in the form of railroads, waterways and ports, all to the ultimate end of building a strong enough economy to pay off the bonds. The host country would gain the structural base for economic growth and stability, and the U.S. would gain "new outlets for surplus production and capital" through increased investment and trade. Neighboring countries, he presumed, would recognize the benefits reaped by the first nation to adopt the plan, and follow suit. He advocated a corresponding public information campaign in both Latin America and the United States, designed to overcome the Spanish Americans' justifiable aversion to foreign presence as well as what Elliott saw as the U.S.'s provincial attitude in not involving itself more substantially in "promoting good will [and] mutual prosperity and advancement" overseas, and in "initiating Latin America into the secrets of the prosperity of the United States," which he saw as a "moral obligation to mankind." That duty, moreover, involved "absolutely no right or justification in attempting to influence national thought [or culture] in any way whatsoever." Given the mutual benefit Elliott envisioned, he concluded, "it is simply a business proposition."

It is not unreasonable to assume that Elliott's memorandum and manuscript had a role in shaping later U.S. policy toward Latin America. In many ways his proposed program resembles later efforts such as the "Good Neighbor" policy of the Franklin D. Roosevelt Administration and the more recent pro-development policies of the World Bank. Certainly, Elliott earned the respect of the Coolidge Administration, as an internal State Department letter dated February 2, 1929, listed him as a potential appointee for another government post in Nicaragua.

Whatever political influence Elliott's ideas for Latin America may have had, it is of secondary importance to Elliott's later achievement in discovering the Wave Principle. In that regard, *The Future of Latin America* is primarily meaningful in revealing a mind that was comfortable in assimilating mountains of detail while simultaneously holding the big picture in perspective to the end of solving a major puzzle or dilemma, a prerequisite ability for discovering and codifying the Wave Principle.

One passage in particular contains a clear hint of Elliott's disposition to see pattern in the nature of things:

> The preceding chapters may have led the reader to the conclusion that the problems of the United States and of Latin America lend themselves to mutual solution. *By a seeming coincidence, but what may well be a provision of nature working in accordance with laws not yet properly understood,* all those things which the United States lacks are to be found in profusion in Latin America, and the needs of Latin America are such as the United States is best fitted to provide for. (Emphasis added.)

Here Elliott implies that nature tends toward a compensatory balance, in which scarcity of one sort is countered by abundance of another sort. This idea hints at the rhythmic, or dynamic, balance that he later found in the stock market.

In a section describing the hazards of political succession in the region, Elliott writes, "By a curious coincidence, while writing this paragraph, the author received news of the death of the president of the country where he happened to be residing." This statement indicates that Elliott was writing then in September 1926, when Lázaro Chacón succeeded to the presidency of Guatemala.

Elliott was working on *The Future of Latin America* as he brought his career in the region to a close. With one book sold and a new one in progress, Elliott had two promising reasons to return to the United States. There was a third reason, though,

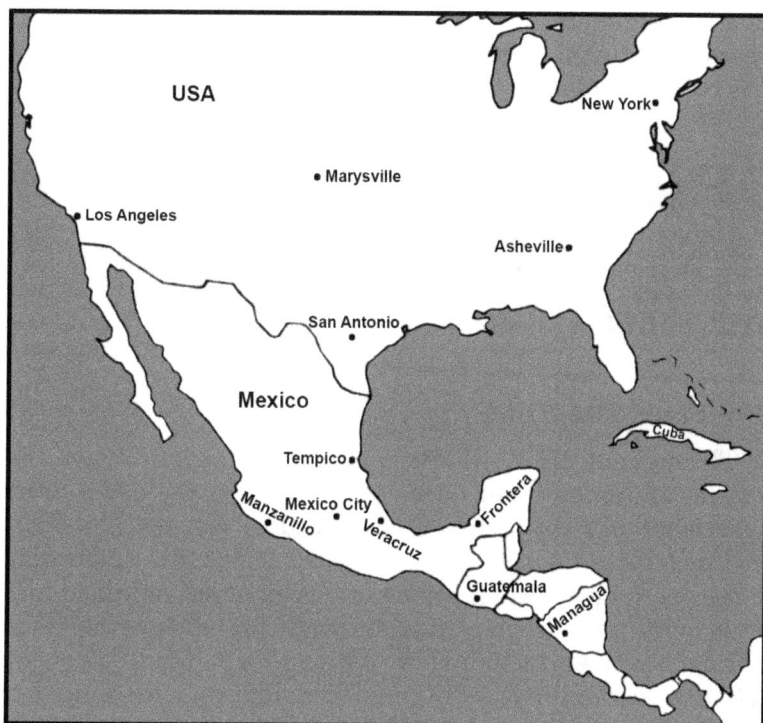

R.N. Elliott's personal and professional locations

one not nearly as happy. After decades of health and vigor, and ironically just as he was preparing to return for an unspecified time to the U.S., Elliott suddenly found himself suffering from a severe alimentary tract illness caused by the organism *amoeba histolytica*. Though Elliott's lifestyle had been rather adventurous for decades without serious repercussion, time and chance had caught up with him, and New York offered the promise of an expert medical review.

Unfortunately, the illness stubbornly persisted during the month or two that he was developing book promotion strategy in New York. By January 1927, Elliott had left New York City and taken up residence in Los Angeles, his old home base from ten years previous, in an apartment hotel suite at 548 South Spring Street. Having left behind all his old business contacts, he concentrated every effort toward relocating his consulting business while attempting to recover from the malady that had stricken him. Curiously, for a man who later connected the

Fibonacci sequence of numbers to human life, this change of careers and lifestyles occurred when Elliott was 55 years old, 21 years before his death.

Wave Four: The Crash

Throughout 1927, Elliott remained intensely active. He sent the aforementioned letter and manuscript to the State Department in February and continued to market *Tea Room and Cafeteria Management,* which sold for $1.50. Elliott sent the book to reviewers, got copies into bookstores, obtained lists for the mailing of circulars, and arranged for advertisements in several magazines, including the January and June 1927 issues of *Good Housekeeping.* Additional favorable reviews poured in from *The New York World*, the National Restaurant Association, which invited him to speak in Buffalo, New York, on September 26, 1927, and others. He advertised for clients, probably using language similar to that in his ad from the January 1925 issue of *Restaurant and Tea Room Journal,* which read:

R.N. Elliott
May be engaged to
Report on locations, capital and reserve,
Report on present status of a business,
Keep books on a basis that provides a guide for action,
Take care of income tax,
Consult on all matters pertaining to tea rooms, cafeterias, etc.

My system is adapted to out-of-town owners.
Inquiry does not involve obligation.
The cost of my service comes out of additional profits.

That last guarantee could only have been made by a man who was confident of his ability to add value to a business.

Elliott's reputation, based on a distinguished career, his new book, and a long list of references, was once again soaring. His goal of securing a sufficient number of clients in his new location was rapidly being fulfilled. Though he had prudently retained the professional option of returning to Central America, the persistence of his medical condition made such a return inadvisable, while the rapid pace of his newest success gave him every reason to remain in the United States. The two situations combined to prompt him to settle down. In December 1927, after thirty-six years of intense work, travel and hotel living, Elliott secured a more permanent residence at 833 Beacon Avenue, Los Angeles. The property's 5,150 square-foot, three-story house had been built in 1905 and converted to apartments in 1920.

Just when Elliott's future appeared its brightest, his independence and financial security seemingly assured, disaster struck. Instead of recovering from his illness, Elliott's condition worsened. By 1929, his affliction had developed into a debilitating case of pernicious anemia, involving chronic fever, dysentery

833 Beacon Avenue, Los Angeles, Elliott's home from 1927 to 1938

Photo 1990 by Marie Eliades

and weight loss, leaving him bedridden. The adventurous and productive R.N. Elliott was forced into an unwanted retirement. His book on Latin America, whether because of the State Department's noncommittal response or his accelerating debility, was never published. He could no longer travel, and had to abandon his consulting practice. Several times over the next five years, he came extremely close to death. Each time, he managed to recover. His professional photograph in *Financial World* magazine a decade later shows that the relentless affliction took its toll, leaving Elliott much thinner than in earlier years.

The Discovery

Despite being physically debilitated by his malady, Elliott needed something to occupy his acute mind while recuperating between its worst attacks. As circumstances would have it, he was living then through the most exciting period in U.S. stock market history: the peak years of the roaring bull market of the 1920s and immediately thereafter the most dramatic bear market smash on record. These events sparking his interest, he read Robert Rhea's 1932 book, *Dow Theory*, and became one of the first subscribers to Rhea's stock market service, *Dow Theory Comment* (1932-1937). It was around 1932, then, that Elliott began turning his full attention to studying the behavior of the stock market. He began pursuing a mission that he had enunciated for all responsible men in his manuscript on Latin America. "There is a reason for everything," he said then, "and it is [one's] duty to try to discover it." Elliott dedicated the rest of his life to finding out whether there was any rhyme or reason to the stock market. As it turns out, he discovered that it had both.

Not unlike the Dow Theory genius Robert Rhea, who suffered from tuberculosis and was bedridden at the time, Ralph Elliott, who spent long hours on his front porch recuperating and studying, began to make some fascinating observations concerning the movement of prices on Wall Street. His essential path of inquiry, i.e., looking for patterns in aggregate stock price movement, was undoubtedly directed initially by exposure to the tenets of Dow Theory. However, Elliott's ultimate discovery was all his own, as over a period of several years he painstakingly uncovered the Wave Principle of market behavior by studying empirical evidence. "The more desirable the goal," Elliott had said once before, "the greater the trials which have to be met and conquered for its achievement." In investigating the possibility of form in the marketplace, Elliott examined yearly, monthly, weekly, daily, hourly and even half-hourly charts of the various indexes covering seventy-five years of stock market behavior. He constructed the hourly charts from a data series that began for the Dow Jones Industrial Average on October 5, 1932, and the half-hourly charts from figures he collected off the tape in the trading room of a brokerage house.

Around May 1934, just two months after his final brush with death, Elliott's mission began to be fulfilled. His numerous observations of general stock market behavior began falling together into a general set of principles that applied to all degrees of wave movement in the stock price averages. Today's scientific term for a large part of Elliott's observation about markets is that they are "fractal," thereby coming under the umbrella of what is today called chaos science, although he went far further than most studies today in actually describing the component patterns and how they link together. The former "Expert Organizer" of businesses, through a meticulous study of detail, had uncovered the organizational principle behind the movement of markets. When he started applying this principle over the next several months to expectations for the future path of the stock market, he felt, as he later put it, "something like the inventor who is trying to become proficient as an operator of a machine of his own design." As he got more proficient in the application of his newly discerned rules and guidelines of wave formation and corrected initial errors in their formulation, they began to amaze him with their accuracy.

Though Elliott never enjoyed full recovery from his illness, his health improved after these several trying years, and his old energy began to return. However, after years of absence from his lifelong profession, his previous success and renown were no longer a ticket to further advancement in his former field.

At this point in his life, Elliott's finances were at a precarious low. His savings, which had appeared more than adequate nearly seven years earlier, were almost entirely dissipated due to the expense of his illness, the impossibility of pursuing his counseling business, a dependent wife and several seemingly safe investments that had suffered tremendously in the 1929-1932 bear market smash. His depleted financial condition, his developing fascination with the stock market, and his undeniably important discoveries combined to prompt Elliott's decision to undertake a new profession. He decided to "begin all over again," as he put it, "especially in work that I like, which is half the battle." So, at the age of 64, Elliott launched a new career and started what he later referred to as "Wave number five of my own life."

Wave Five: The Wave Principle Revealed

By November 1934, Elliott's confidence in his ideas had developed to the point that he decided to present them to at least one member of the financial community. For quite some time, Elliott had subscribed to a market service founded and edited by Charles J. Collins and published by Investment Counsel, Inc. (later Investment Letters, Inc.) of Detroit. He was particularly impressed by it. Elliott felt that he had learned enough about Charles Collins through his stock market publication to trust him with his discovery. This assumption, to Elliott's great advantage, proved correct. After an 8-year recession in fortunes, Elliott was about to embark upon a 13-year rise.

On December 2, 1934, Collins, president of Investment Counsel, received from Elliott a letter marked "PERSONAL and CONFIDENTIAL," dated November 28. Therein Elliott explained that he had discovered three novel features of market action: recognition of wave termination, classification of wave degree and time forecasting, which were "a much needed complement to the Dow Theory." He even forecasted that the market advance then unfolding would be followed not by a correction, as had been the case with the two previous legs of advance, but by "a major bear collapse." This is exactly what happened later, as the dramatic market decline of 1937-38 erased 50 percent of the market's value in twelve months.

Elliott asked Collins to finance a trip to Detroit so that he could present his observations completely to him, in hopes that Collins would decide to use the technique of the Wave Principle in his stock market letter to their mutual benefit. Elliott even commented that Collins, if he preferred to keep it secret, need not inform his readers that he was using the Wave Principle as a basis for his investment advice.

Collins was intrigued but not convinced. He filed Elliott's letter and returned a standard response to the effect that he would be happy to monitor Elliott's "calls" on the market, by telegram collect or by air mail letter, for one complete market cycle to see if they had any real merit. If they proved accurate, then he would consider further steps.

Collins had developed this method of putting off the numerous correspondents who continually offered him systems for beating the market, on the assumption that any truly worthwhile system would stand out when applied in current time. Not surprisingly, the vast majority of these systems proved to be dismal failures. Elliott's principle, however, was another story.

Although Collins assured Elliott he need not divulge his method, Elliott began sending Collins a series of letters and charts outlining the basis of what he referred to variously as "wave theory" or the "Five Wave Principle." Elliott stressed that since his financial status was difficult, he wished to acquaint Collins with the theory and prove its value without waiting two or more years for a complete market cycle.

Included with Elliott's second letter to Collins dated December 9, 1934, was a brief but thorough exposition of the Wave Principle, including an introduction, which constituted the first words Elliott ever wrote to another on his theory of the stock market:

> The market may be likened to a river. It has rather well defined borders of uniform width, occasionally becomes blocked by barriers and suddenly breaks away from them. When the channel is narrow the speed is greater and vice versa. It curves according to resistance.

As passages in his two earlier books had already suggested, Elliott's interest in mathematics, rhythm and repetition was keen. He was using fixed-time cycles in his analysis at that time, and referred specifically to a nine week cycle in stock prices, variable to twelve weeks, which is still quite regular today. This interest turned out to be only a temporary diversion, but kept him thinking in the right direction. "All life and movement consists of vibrations," he said in his second letter, "and the stock market is no exception." Except for such occasional comments, Elliott stayed focused on his empirical observations, which increasingly revealed patterns that far eclipsed the simple concept of repetitive cycles. These observations ultimately accumulated to the point of gelling with his grander notions into a practical and deeply satisfying understanding of the market's patterns, as well as their mathematical base.

Elliott's letters to Collins revealed a firm belief in the virtue of individual initiative, which virtue he certainly practiced himself, and a recognition of the harm of government regulation of business. One letter referred to the "unprecedented unconstitutional meddling in economics by politics." In another letter, he discussed the plight of the railroads, with which he was familiar from long experience:

> I see little or no hope of activity in durable goods so long as Regimentation is displacing Individualism. But for Individualism there would never have been anything to regiment. The rails have been in a secular decline since 1906 [when] politicians and labor unions combined to harass them. The Utilities are getting their dose of politics now; their treatment is reflected in the averages to the sorrow of thousands of innocent investors.

During this letter writing period, Elliott continued to discover new tenets of the Wave Principle as his studies grew more thorough. While previously attempting to count five waves in every movement, for instance, he came to conclude that all "triangles, periods of hesitation, flats, are equivalent to 'corrections' of the ruling trend." Later he found that "diagonal triangles are inevitable terminations of movements of their degree."

Since Collins was in Florida that winter as was his custom, it was not until January 4, 1935, that he began responding to Elliott's "flood of letters," as Elliott himself put it, a task that for a few weeks had been left to an associate. On January 11, Collins sent a telegram to Elliott asking him to dispatch a wire when a particular minor declining wave they were tracking had ended.

A week later the Dow Jones averages were still in a declining phase and, as Elliott put it, "the wiseacres around here are very bearish." At that time he was forecasting that the Rails would break their 1934 low but the Industrials would not, a prediction that must have struck Collins later as uncannily accurate. His first telegram in response to Collins' request for pinpointing the bottom of the correction was dated January 15, 1935, and read, "CORRECTION ENDED LAST HALF HOUR TODAY." The call was perfect, and a rally ensued immediately. On January 22, Elliott recognized the rally as a corrective style advance, and after the close he wrote to say, "the picture is bearish again." The rally peaked two trading hours later. He then forecast that the Industrials would slip below 99 to 96, and the Rails would crack 33, as larger waves 3, 4 and 5 downward unfolded.

Most of the predictions that Elliott made in his barrage of letters (even those that took years to prove) were correct, many to perfection. However, in the approach to the actual bottom, which was made at 96 as Elliott had first forecast, he changed his mind several times in an attempt to call the low exactly to the hour. Elliott's changes of mind, newly discovered tenets and occasional wave relabeling bothered Collins, who wrote Elliott a long and courteous letter on February 15 pointing out weaknesses in Elliott's methods and enclosing some of his own work on a five wave theory as applied to long-term price movements. He suggested that in order to remedy his financial situation, Elliott manage some risk capital and begin a letter service to be circulated to a select group while he developed his theories to completion. Toward that end, Collins offered to introduce Elliott to Dow Theorist Robert Rhea.

Elliott countered Collins' grounds for delay by listing the various imperfections in Collins' own market letter's investment decisions of the previous two years. He strongly reaffirmed his wish to become associated with Collins, whose letters, he stated, were so well done that there was "no comparison between your letters and those of any other service that I have ever seen."

On February 19, 1935, Elliott mailed Collins seventeen pages of a hastily organized yet meticulously detailed treatise entitled "The Wave Principle." He sent twelve more pages and five additional charts over the next two months along with his regular correspondence. The first page of the treatise contains Elliott's statement of the utility of the Wave Principle:

> A careful study of certain recurring phenomena within the price structure itself has developed certain facts which, while they are not always vocal, do nevertheless furnish a principle that determines the trend and gives clear warning of reversal.

Collins thereafter began to write Elliott more frequently and sent him several books, book recommendations and articles of interest, including *On The Relation of Phyllotaxis to Mechanical Laws* (1904), a pamphlet by Professor Arthur Henry Church of Oxford University. Phyllotaxis is the term for the arrangement of leaves on a stem, which in some plants had been found to follow the Fibonacci sequence. These mailings indicate that it was Charles Collins who introduced Elliott to the concept of Fibonacci numbers and their manifestations in natural phenomena. Thus,

he must have been the first person to notice that the number of
Elliott's waves reproduced the Fibonacci sequence when counted
at successively lower degrees. These observations ultimately
provided the spark needed for Elliott's theories to gel into their
final form five years later. One book that Collins sent was Sir
James Hopwood Jeans' *The Mysterious Universe* (1930), which
contained the following passage:

> Many would hold that, from the broad philosophical
> standpoint, the outstanding achievement of twentieth century
> physics is not the theory of relativity with its welding together
> of space and time, or the theory of quanta with its present
> apparent negation of the laws of causation, or the dissection of
> the atom with the resultant discovery that things are not what
> they seem; it is the general recognition that we are not yet in
> contact with ultimate reality.... To borrow Locke's phrase, "the
> real essence of substances" is forever unknowable. *We can only
> progress by discussing the laws which govern the changes of
> substances, and so produce the phenomena of the external world.*

In referring to the repetition of the five wave pattern in the
stock market, Elliott responded, "Possibly the reason why I have
not yet, and possibly never will know why this series occurs is
because it is a law of nature. The laws of nature, and incidentally
economics, are ruthless, which is as it should be."

Collins' traditional skepticism was abruptly dispelled with
the next occurrence. The Dow Jones averages had been declining
throughout early 1935, and Elliott had been pinpointing hourly
turns with a fair degree of accuracy. In the second week of
February, the Dow Jones Rail Average, as Elliott had predicted,
broke below its 1934 low of 33.19. Advisors were turning negative
and memories of the 1929-32 crash were immediately rekindled as
bearish pronouncements about the future course of the economy
proliferated. The Dow Industrials had fallen about eleven percent
and were approaching the 96 level while the Rails, from their
1933 peak, had fallen fifty percent to the 27 level.

On Wednesday, March 13, 1935, just after the close of
trading, with the Dow Jones averages finishing near the lows
for the day, Elliott sent his famous telegram to Collins and
flatly stated the following: "NOTWITHSTANDING BEARISH
(DOW) IMPLICATIONS ALL AVERAGES ARE MAKING FINAL
BOTTOM."

Collins read the telegram on the morning of the next day, Thursday, March 14, 1935, the day that marked the closing low for the Dow Industrials that year. The day prior to the telegram, Tuesday, March 12, marked the closing low for the Dow Jones Rails.

The precise hourly low for the Industrials occurred at 11 a.m. the following Monday, thirteen trading hours after Elliott's telegram was sent, with the Rails holding above their prior low. The opening selling pushed the Industrials just cents below Thursday's low and a hair's breadth above Elliott's target of 96. The thirteen month corrective wave was over, and the market immediately turned to the upside.

Two months later, Elliott's call had proved so precisely and dramatically correct as the market continued on its upward climb that Collins, "impressed by his dogmatism and accuracy," wrote and proposed that Investment Counsel subscribe for payment to Elliott's forecasts and commented, "we are of the opinion that the Wave Principle is by far the best forecasting approach that has come to our attention."

Elliott responded with a proposal that Collins subscribe to his market timing service for a period of two years. Then, if Investment Counsel were still satisfied with Elliott's success after the two year period, Collins, whom Elliott considered a master writer, would prepare a book on the Wave Principle suitable for public distribution. Elliott stipulated that the book should carry Collins' name as author, but Elliott was to receive full credit for the discovery and development of the Wave Principle. The copyright was to be in both their names. Elliott apparently felt that Collins' name would be useful in giving the book wider acceptance and distribution. He added that if Collins wished, he would have the option to substitute Elliott's name as author but Collins would forfeit any copyright claim as a result.

Collins accepted Elliott's terms and invited Elliott to Michigan to be his house guest for three days over a weekend in the summer of 1935. Elliott went over his theory in depth and thoroughly familiarized Collins with the working details of the Wave Principle.

For the next two years, pursuant to their agreement, Collins received and monitored Elliott's calls on the market. His accuracy remained true, and at the end of the second year, in March 1937, Collins began working on Elliott's first monograph, *The Wave Principle*, which was based on Elliott's original treatise.

Throughout this time, Elliott had maintained contact with several acquaintances from his accounting days, notably George P. Robinson. Robinson had a financial consulting firm in New York City that served corporate clients. While communicating with Collins, Elliott had also presented the theory of the Wave Principle to Robinson, who had become increasingly interested in the stock market as a tool for corporate financial investment. Aside from Collins and Elliott, Robinson is the only person known to have used the Wave Principle prior to the publication of Elliott's book. Robinson and his associate Todd H. Becker (later an investment manager for a group of ore exploration companies in Toronto) took Elliott's work seriously and spent time studying it. In March 1937, as Collins began work on *The Wave Principle*, Robinson and Becker, probably while corresponding with Elliott, precisely called the 1937 top using Elliott's new discovery. As Becker recalled in a telephone conversation, "It was so clearly the fifth of the fifth wave up."

THE ROAD TO WALL STREET

By 1938, Elliott was so involved with the Wave Principle that he insisted that if he were to be taken into Collins' organization, Investment Counsel's stock market service would have to use his approach exclusively, a proposal that Collins could not accept. However, in appreciation of Elliott's decision to confide to him the details of his discovery, and in fulfillment of their agreement, Collins completed *The Wave Principle*, which was published on August 31, 1938. The 8 1/2" x 11" monograph was copyrighted by Elliott and printed in dark blue softcover with no cover markings. An estimated five hundred copies were printed.

The first chapter of *The Wave Principle* makes the following statements:

> No truth meets more general acceptance than that the universe is ruled by law. Without law, it is self-evident there would be chaos, and where chaos is, nothing is.... Man is no less a natural object than the sun or the moon, and his actions, too, in their metrical occurrence, are subject to analysis.... Very extensive research in connection with ... human activities indicates that practically all developments which result from our social-economic processes follow a law that causes them to repeat themselves in similar and constantly recurring serials of waves or impulses of definite number and pattern.... The

stock market illustrates the wave impulse common to social-economic activity.... It has its law, just as is true of other things throughout the universe.

Within weeks after publication of this ground-breaking book, Elliott packed up his belongings and moved with his wife to the Standish Arms Hotel, 169 Columbia Heights, Brooklyn, which afforded a spectacular view of the Brooklyn Bridge and lower Manhattan across the East River, as well as Staten Island, Governor's Island and the Statue of Liberty. His new residence was ideally situated for launching his new career, being a short subway stop from Manhattan's financial district. Ironically, it was an area with which he was already familiar, having prepared accounting reports for Wall Street area restaurants in his former life. By April 1940, Elliott and his wife had moved to an apartment at 202 Pierpont Street in Brooklyn Heights, across the street from Columbus Park. It is interesting that while both of Elliott's personal corrective waves (two and four) took place in Los Angeles, his sharpest advancing waves (three and five) took place in New York City.

The Standish Arms Hotel (note bust of Miles Standish on facade)
169 Columbia Heights, Brooklyn, New York
Elliott's home in 1938
Photo 1990 by Paul Brodtkorb

The good fortune that Elliott had provided to George Robinson and his clients the year before returned to Elliott's favor, since Robinson made his offices available to Elliott any time he wished to utilize their resources. For his part, Charles Collins graciously provided Elliott some financial assistance, referred to him a number of discretionary accounts, and helped him set up his office at 25 Broad Street, where Elliott began managing some speculative funds for several well-to-do clients. Then on November 10, three months after *The Wave Principle* was released, Elliott published the first in a long series of Interpretive Letters, which outlined and forecast the path of the market in terms of the Wave Principle. He issued the one to four page letters irregularly ("as the occasion requires"), ranging from three to seven issues annually between November 10, 1938, and August 6, 1945. Elliott initially priced his Interpretive Letters at $60 per year and continued to make available his monograph, which he called "the Treatise," for $15. R.N. Elliott was finally back in the saddle, and as independently in business as he had planned eleven years before.

For a number of years, Investment Counsel's advertisements in *Barron's* had described Collins' market letter as "A weekly service based on The Dow Theory." Immediately following publication of *The Wave Principle*, new ads appeared referring more generally to "analyses of significant economic and technical trends." Clearly, Collins no longer depended only upon Dow Theory but used the Wave Principle as well. Yet Collins never mentioned the Wave Principle in his market publication or advertising. His reasons were later stated in a 1957 letter to A. Hamilton Bolton, where he commented, "I did not give the 'Elliott' reason for my target, as I think the less his principles are discussed, the better working tool they will prove." In fact—reflecting a common view of the day—Collins several times counseled Elliott against overly publicizing his findings, a sentiment that he voiced again in a 1963 letter to Bolton with respect to Elliott's *Financial World* articles. (That letter also revealed the sad story of what happened to the bulk of the correspondence between himself and Elliott.)

Despite Collins' sentiments, Elliott considered exposition of his discovery a necessary step and insisted on it. His views on revealing knowledge had already been articulated in *The Future of Latin America* when he wrote that, "Gone are the days when happily revealed secrets were jealously guarded for the personal advancement of their possessors. It has been proved time and time again that true and lasting success lies in the dissemination of knowledge rather than in its concealment."

800 BUHL BUILDING
DETROIT 26, MICHIGAN
December 23, 1963

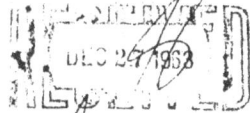

Dear Hamilton:

Re the Elliott series in the Financial World — he wanted wide publicity for his system. I tried to argue him out of it as I thought he had something unique and should build up a following without broad-scale disclosure of how he did it. He said no, he thought he would profit by the publicity. As a then existing or previous regular contributor to the Financial World (I forget which now), I had an entree with the management and induced them - after some demur on their part - to give publicity to Elliott. Since you have republished the series I thought the above would be of interest. I threw away a cartload of Elliott's correspondence some years back, but if I run into any more do you want it — otherwise I'll clean it out.

Don't bother to acknowledge, unless you want any of Elliott's papers.

Regards,

C J Collins
ag

Hamilton Bolton, Esq.
Bolton, Tremblay & Company
1245 Sherbrooke Street W.
Montreal 25, Canada

Collins had been writing regular feature articles for *Financial World* magazine and in early 1939, at Elliott's urging, he contacted the editors and introduced them to Elliott and his work. As a result, Elliott was commissioned by *Financial World* to write twelve articles on the Wave Principle. After their initial "announcement" on March 29, the magazine opened the series with the following statement:

> During the past seven or eight years, publishers of financial magazines and organizations in the investment advisory field have been virtually flooded with "systems" for which their proponents have claimed great accuracy in forecasting stock market movements. Some of them appeared to work for a while. It was immediately obvious that others had no value whatever. All have been looked upon by *The Financial World* with great scepticism. But after investigation of Mr. R.N. Elliott's Wave Principle, *The Financial World* became convinced that a series of articles on this subject would be interesting and instructive to its readers.

The first of Elliott's articles appeared in the April 5 issue, and their publication continued regularly into July. These definitive articles established Elliott's reputation with the investment community. They had great staying power and survived in various forms over the years, while the monographs were never reprinted.

Broadening the Principle

In late 1939, after the publication of the *Financial World* articles, Elliott began writing in-depth follow-up essays on various technical aspects as well as broader implications of the Wave Principle. These quickly evolved into a formal Educational Service, which he published from 1940 to 1944 and for which he charged $60 per year. One of Elliott's earliest "Educational Bulletins" was a ground-breaking work that lifted the Wave Principle from a comprehensive catalog of the market's behavioral patterns to a broad theory of collective human behavior unparalleled in the fields of economics and sociology.

Since 1935, Collins had been sending books to Elliott on the role of the Fibonacci sequence in nature. By 1940, Elliott had read Baldassare Boncompagni's publication of Leonardo Fibonacci's original works and two books by Jay Hambidge on the subject

R. N. ELLIOTT, 1939
Photo: *The Financial World*

of "dynamic symmetry," a term used by Euclid to describe the designs that result from nature's purposeful employment of what are now called Fibonacci mathematics. Hambidge was an American artist who until his death in 1924 applied the principles of geometry to art and architecture in several books. Elliott also read *Nature's Harmonic Unity: A Treatise On Its Relation to Proportional Form* (1912) and *Proportional Form* (1920), both by Samuel Colman and C. Arthur Coan, and *The Curves of Life* (1914) by Sir Theodore Andrea Cook, all of which discussed the role of the Fibonacci ratio in nature's patterns. Elliott's additional important observation from his 1938 book that the Wave Principle applied to data series outside the stock market was another impetus to his investigation into the broader meaning of his discovery.

By the early 1940s, Elliott had developed to completion his concept that the ebb and flow of human emotions and activities follow a natural progression governed by laws of nature. The culmination of this train of thought was a treatise of a transcendent importance equal to that of his original book. On October 1, 1940, Elliott published his first discussion of Leonardo Fibonacci's "Summation Series of Dynamic Symmetry" in an Educational Bulletin entitled "The Basis of the Wave Principle" under the subheading "How the Wave Principle Works, and its Correlation with Mathematical Laws." In it, he tied the patterns of collective human behavior to the Fibonacci, or "golden" ratio, a mathematical phenomenon known for millennia by mathematicians, scientists, artists, architects and philosophers as one of nature's ubiquitous laws of form and progress.

This ground-breaking presentation led to what appears to have been an incident of intellectual piracy. On May 19, 1941, less than eight months after Elliott's treatise was disseminated to his small list of subscribers, *Barron's* published an article authored by "Edson Beers." Edson Beers was a pseudonym of Edson Gould, Jr., whose middle name was Beers. The article, "A New Idea for Speculators: Applying the Principles of 'Dynamic Symmetry' to the Stock Market," purported to introduce this unquestionably novel idea yet neglected to mention Elliott, its original and foremost proponent. Gould confirmed in a telephone conversation that the editor of *Barron's* told him he had received a call from Elliott, who was (justifiably) angry about the article. The 1941 edition of Garfield Drew's book, *New Methods for Profit in the Stock Market*, referenced this controversy when he said, "The same elements of dynamic symmetry which Beers believes apply to the patterns of stock price movements are likewise the basis of Elliott's 'Wave Principle,' although Elliott says he made this discovery after empirically working out the Principle." Drew then showed Beers' list of Fibonacci numbers of months between various turning points in the Dow, which echoed Elliott's similar list in "Table B" from his October 1940 treatise. In a telephone conversation with me, Gould inaccurately recollected that his article on the subject had appeared in March 1935 (the date of one of his forecasts in *Barron's* based on fixed-time cycles), thus predating Elliott's work, when in fact it was published six years later. Despite gentle probing, he declined further comment on the subject. History was kind, however, and in ensuing decades afforded Elliott full credit for his remarkable intellectual achievement.

BRANCHING OUT

Elliott's subsequent Educational Bulletins expanded further upon his thesis as he came across new observations and ideas. Titles included "Technical Features," "Alternation," "The Basis of the Wave Principle," "Duration or Time Element," "Inflation," "Dynamic Symmetry," "Two Cycles of American History," "The Law of Motion" and "Nature's Law" (a precursor to his second monograph).

Elliott's other services included:

– Forecast Letters marked "Confidential," which were sold at "conventional fees." These one page bulletins provided investment timing recommendations "for those who desire prompt advice when important reversals are due in averages and individual stocks."

– Special reports for "business executives" designed to assist in detecting "peaks and nadirs of production."

– A service called "Information" whereby nonsubscribers were allowed to send a stamped self-addressed envelope and ask Elliott any question about the Wave Principle. Elliott responded with a quotation of the fee he required for his response and, upon payment, the answer. "This novel service," said Elliott, "fills a long felt need."

– A 61.8% ruler, which Elliott probably created using a drafting instrument called a "proportional divider," the fulcrum of which can be moved to obtain different ratios of measurement. Elliott's ruler enabled the user to ascertain without the bother of calculation when the ratio between two lengths was 61.8%. Elliott offered it for sale at 25 cents.

Elliott wrote in 1935, "waves do not make errors, but my version may be defective. The nearer one approaches the primary law, the less errors will occur." By virtue of all his painstaking study, Elliott rightly considered himself the sole authority on his discovery. Toward the establishment of that position, he delivered the following warning on the front page of *The Wave Principle*:

When a newly discovered phenomenon is disclosed, self-appointed "experts" immediately appear. Considerable

63 Wall Street, New York
Elliott's office location from 1942 to 1947
Photo 1990 by Robert R. Prechter, Jr.

25 Broad Street, New York
Elliott's office location from 1938 to 1942
Photo 1990 by Robert R. Prechter, Jr.

experience is required to interpret correctly waves which are in process of formation.... No interpretation of the Wave Principle should be accepted as valid unless made by me or by a student directly licensed by me.

In fact, Elliott did have a class of students whom he taught at irregular intervals from his small office at 25 Broad Street. Carroll Gianni, a member of the New York Stock Exchange, was an occasional student of Elliott's from 1939 to 1941. He described the one hour sessions as informal but Socratic, with Elliott firmly in the position of professor.

On November 2, 1940, *The New York Times* published an article on page 25 of its "Business & Finance" section headlined, "SEC Lists Advisers in Investing Field." It names 605 individuals from New York, New Jersey and Connecticut who had registered with the Securities and Exchange Commission under the Investment Advisers Act of 1940, which became law that year on August 22. The list includes W.D. Gann & Son, H.M. Gartley, Inc., Henry Wheeler Chase, Putnam & Co., Bernstein MacAulay, Delafield & Delafield, Fenner & Beane, Smith Barney, Shearson Hamill, Spencer Trask, Lehman Brothers, Lowry & Mills, Mansfield & Staff, J. & W. Seligman & Co. and Elliott's colleague George P. Robinson. The number and quality of names on this list and the article's temporal proximity to the passage of the Act indicate that this is most or all of the SEC's inaugural class of registered investment advisers. Among them was the entry, "Ralph Nelson Elliott, Fahnestock & Co.," a listing that finally tells us with which brokerage firm Elliott was affiliated.

On August 31, 1941, Elliott received major publicity. *The New York Times*, in a section titled "Financial Books," reviewed *New Methods for Profit in the Stock Market* by Garfield A. Drew (see excerpt on pp. 307-8) and commented,

> This book, by the director of accounts of United Investment Counsel, Inc., is a study of the chartists. It goes thoroughly into the Dow theory and its various offshoots, studying each and giving charts to show their results. The "natural rhythm" methods for determining market action, says, the author, "have been far more correct in recent years than mere chance seems to account for, and R.N. Elliott's record is carefully documented with unimpeachable outside sources."

On December 30, 1941, Elliott's wife Mary Elizabeth, who had remained with him throughout his travels, career changes and medical misfortune, died at age 74. They had been married thirty-nine years. A few months later, in the spring of 1942, Elliott moved his office to 63 Wall Street through an interesting chain of events. Philip K. Sweet, then president of Fundamental Investors, Inc., had worked for Edgar Lawrence Smith in the late 1920s with Anthony Gaubis, who in 1934 became associated as a junior partner with Charles J. Collins at Investment Counsel. Gaubis had met Elliott in 1938 at Investment Counsel and later introduced him to Sweet in New York. Sweet, who admired Elliott's work, offered him an office at 63 Wall Street where Fundamental Investors was located. Elliott accepted, and moved his business from 25 Broad Street to its new location.

Around this time, Elliott licensed at least one student of whom there is some record, a man named Richard Martin, who published four market letters entitled "The Wave Principle" from March to August 1942. Elliott made certain to protect his discovery even from his proteges and had the letters copyrighted in his own name. Mr. Martin's career with Elliott was brief, however, possibly because he found himself in disagreement with Elliott on the outlook for the market. While the position of the market under the Wave Principle often allows several possible outcomes, rarely is their order of probability a proper point of contention. While Elliott was willing to discuss different points of view, he rightly considered his interpretations expert and refused to sanction deviations. Martin dropped from view but reappeared in 1943 as author of a booklet called *Trend Action, A New Method of Forecasting*. The booklet proposed an analysis of the market in a fashion similar to Elliott's, but now purported to be refined from a system developed by Frank H. Tubbs and published in 1929 as part of a course titled "Tubbs Analytics." It was once suggested that Tubbs was annoyed that Elliott had exploited "his" discovery. However, Tubbs' surviving literature dismally fails to indicate anything but a superficial similarity to Elliott's Wave Principle, thus negating any claim of plagiarism.

Throughout the first half of the 1940s, Elliott investigated further in the fields of philosophy, art, dynamic symmetry, mathematics, physics, botany, and even Egyptology and pyramidology. One of the articles he read was "Do You Know Your Emotional Cycle?", which appeared in the November 1945 issue of

Redbook magazine. The article discussed the work of Dr. Rexford B. Hersey, a scientist who discovered the cyclicality of human emotions (today called biorhythms). He also read *Prophecies of Melchi-Zedik in the Great Pyramid* by Brown Landone, *Life's Riddle Solved* (1945) by Dr. John H. Manas, president of the Pythagorean Society, and other volumes, some of which are listed in the References section at the end of *Nature's Law*. More and more, his concept took on a wholeness that fit into what he eventually came to call "Nature's Law" and "The Secret of the Universe."

Some time prior to 1944, Elliott corresponded with Manly P. Hall, founder of The Philosophical Research Society, Inc., a private research and educational organization in Los Angeles, California. Elliott requested permission to reprint the picture of Pythagoras that Hall had contributed to John Manas' book. Permission was granted, and Elliott reproduced the picture in *Nature's Law*. Hall, who chronicled man's search for the secret of "universal wisdom" and who maintained that "all the universe is eternal growth," may have influenced Elliott's thinking by the time he wrote *Nature's Law*.

During these years, Elliott visited his old friend, investment counselor George P. Robinson, almost daily in his offices at 14 Wall Street. Robinson employee Howard Fay became friends with Elliott and visited him several times at his home in Brooklyn Heights. Fay describes Elliott as "intelligent and sharp," but "ornery at times," and less than patient with those who disagreed with him.

By 1945, Elliott was established to the point that he was advertising for Graphics Stocks, a monthly range chart service published and updated every two months. Obviously his students needed charts, and F.W. Stephens, the distributor, felt that Elliott could supply him some business by recommending them as ideal for illustrating the principles of wave movement. Annual subscriptions sold for $50.

How ironic it seems that the owner of a challenging market analysis business and a man of increasingly expansive philosophical thoughts would take the time to write a dry practical booklet, based on his earlier career as an accountant, entitled "Farm Tax Accounting As You Go," published in January 1945. It is as if, with only a few years left to live, Elliott was not only branching out in several avenues of investigation and thought but also finishing projects long planned yet previously left undone.

The Wave Principle offers Three Services:

1. "Interpretive Letters", issued as occasion requires, are intended for those
   who wish to learn The "Secret of the Universe".
   Business Managers may learn to detect peaks and
   nadirs of production.

2. "Forecast Letters" are intended for those who desire prompt advice when
   important reversals are due in Averages and
   individual stocks.

3. "Information" for non-subscribers: Ask any question you wish and enclose
   a stamped, self-addressed envelop. I will advise
   the fee for the answer. This novel service fills
   a long-felt need.

63 Wall Street, New York 5 N. Y.   R. N. Elliott.

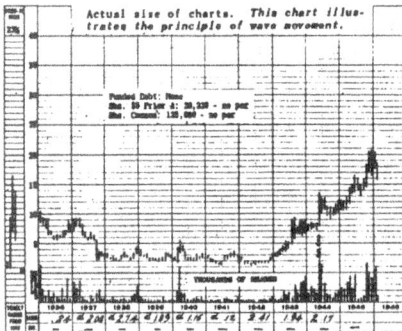

The Final Years

During the last three years of his life, Elliott's clients continued to call him, mostly for advice on the very short term moves in the market. However, he ceased to solicit new business. Elliott wrote the last of his Interpretive Letters in August 1945 and spent the rest of the year and the first five months of 1946 putting together what he obviously considered his definitive work, *Nature's Law—The Secret of the Universe. Nature's Law* incorporates part of *The Wave Principle* and includes the additional discoveries and observations that in the intervening years had been detailed in his Educational and Interpretive Letters. This final monograph includes almost every thought Elliott ever had concerning the theory of the Wave Principle.

The reader of that volume should keep in mind that Elliott was a pioneer. Much of his discovery was recorded as it was formulated, and little time was available to spend on cosmetic editing. At 75 years of age and still suffering from anemia, Elliott undoubtedly felt a sense of urgency about getting his final thoughts on the Wave Principle into print, an urgency that took precedence over a well organized text. In an effort to get the book out before age and ill health finally caught up with him, Elliott opted for speed and inclusiveness over the meticulous organization evident in his previous articles and books. Indeed, many of the pages were inserted directly from his Educational Letters. Despite the lack of cohesion that more time for planning would have allowed, the book is nevertheless a major contribution to market literature.

The publication date of the book was June 10, 1946. It was printed in an 8½" x 11" buff colored softcover ring binder, and the reported 1000 copies sold out quickly to various members of the New York financial community. While copies of *The Wave Principle* and each market letter Elliott wrote had been meticulously sent to the Library of Congress, Elliott apparently neglected to send a copy of *Nature's Law*. But his book did get reviewed. The February 1947 issue (Vol. 31, No.1) of *Science Education*, a journal based in New York, included the following appraisal by "A.W.H.":

Elliott, R.N. *Nature's Law—The Secret of the Universe*, New York: 63 Wall St., R.N. Elliott, 1946, 64 p.

This is a loose-leaf booklet stating some theories of the author relating to what he calls nature's law which is based upon his concepts of rhythm, periodicity, and mathematical relationships in life activities—apparently operating in both individual and social life. Discussions refer, in the main, to the stock market, but with references to Egyptian pyramids, Pythagoras, and Hersey—the last concerned with emotional cycles in people. Many diagrams and mathematical calculations abound in the 64 pages. The last page of the book advertises three services which the author will undertake to supply on application; and services in stock graphing furnished at stated prices by a distributor in New York.

For nearly five years, Elliott had been living alone. By this time, the only immediate relative of Elliott's still living was his widowed sister, May. Relatives through marriage included only his wife's niece and nephews, Mrs. Marcella Thompson Makinson of Upper Montclair, New Jersey, and her brothers, Milton, Jr. and Ralph Thompson, both of whom lived in California. Howard Fay described Elliott as becoming quite lonely in his apartment at the Standish Arms Hotel during this time. Nevertheless, he was visited occasionally by a few Wall Street friends, one of whom was Robert M. MacLaury, a broker with Lord Abbott and later a vice president of Kidder Peabody. MacLaury often brought him his business correspondence when he was too ill to come to the city to collect it. Garfield Drew's 1948 edition of *New Methods for Profit in the Stock Market* mentions another friend, Mr. John C. Sinclair of the Francis I. duPont & Co. brokerage firm. He refers to him as Elliott's "collaborator," which probably means that Elliott had authorized him as an interpreter of the Wave Principle.

Elliott managed to issue at least two additional periodical pages, in July and December of 1946, but his chronic anemia was catching up with him, severely affecting his health once again. By 1947, Elliott's Wall Street friends persuaded him to admit himself to Methodist Hospital in Brooklyn for a health review. These same friends probably helped Elliott move on June 14 to Kings Park State Hospital, one of New York's leading psychiatric hospitals, a type of facility that in those days also served as a home for the elderly. There Elliott's basic needs were satisfied as he lived out the last months of his life. Elliott and Collins continued their occasional meetings and remained friends and correspondents. According to accounts, Elliott remained mentally as sharp as ever through most of his final year. His death certificate notes that he slipped into a typical senile deterioration shortly before his death.

Elliott died at 8:50 a.m. on January 15, 1948. The cause of death was listed as chronic myocarditis, a persistent inflammation of the heart muscle that had led to arteriosclerosis. As with the amoebic infection that led to the forced retirement from his earlier career, Elliott almost certainly contracted this illness during his time in Central America. In that region, chronic myocarditis is often caused by a type of parasitic infection called Chagas' disease, which can cause death many years after the initial exposure.

One former trader claimed that Elliott's friends took up a collection (a common practice when a deceased left no immediate relatives) for his cremation, which took place two days later at the Fresh Pond Crematory in Middle Village, New York. Records of Fairchild Sons Funeral Home indicate that arrangements for the cremation were made by the Elliotts' niece (the daughter of his wife's sister, Anna), Marcella Makinson, a long-time resident of Montclair, New Jersey. She received Elliott's ashes, as she had Mrs. Elliott's six years earlier. In reviewing the records on file at the funeral home, a representative remarked that in all her years at the facility, she had hardly seen a sketchier record. The few details were provided by Mrs. Makinson, who stated his occupation as "investment counselor." *The New York Times* published the following obituary on January 17, 1948:

> ELLIOTT — Ralph Nelson, Jan. 15, 1948, the husband of the late Mary F. Elliott. Funeral services at the Fairchild Funeral Home, Brooklyn, 1 P.M. Saturday, Jan. 17. Interment private.

On December 18, 1953, Elliott's sister May, who had lived sixty years in Los Angeles, died at the age of 88. She was buried alongside her parents at the Inglewood Park Cemetary in Los Angeles. May left no children, and as Elliott was childless himself, he thus had no direct or indirect descendants.

The Wave Principle After Elliott

After Elliott's death, none of his students attempted to continue his publication where he left off. Yet his legacy was so powerful that his method aided the success of a major market educator, C. Ralph Dystant, and three of the greatest forecasters in the history of market analysis: Edson B. Gould, E. George Schaefer and A. Hamilton Bolton.

C. Ralph Dystant (1902-1978) founded Investment Educators in 1946 for the purpose of teaching technical analysis methods. One of his occasional speakers was Ham Bolton. Dystant was the first independent person to include instruction on the Wave Principle in a course. By 1966, he was charging $2100 for it. Dystant eventually wrote a 300-page book on the subject titled *The Fifth Wave—Stocks: A Critique of Elliott Wave.*

Edson Gould (1901-1987), who developed the "Three Steps and a Stumble" rule (based on the Fed's interest-rate moves) and the "Sentimeter" and used cycles and seasonal patterns in his work, was famous for making precise market predictions. He claimed that his methods of forecasting were all his own except for the Decennial Pattern, which was developed by Edgar Lawrence Smith. When asked about the basis for his highly specific forecasts, he often replied by citing his "Three Step" rule, i.e., "expect three steps but be prepared for a fourth," which is either a slight expansion on Dow Theory's "three phases" or a generalization of Elliott's basic principle. Gould's price charts were typically notated with numbers and letters, and he continually expected and forecasted "three phases" (or sometimes "three stages") on the upside, separated by two corrections. Moreover, correspondence between Bolton and Collins that mentioned Gould always referred to his analysis as "implying that wave III may not yet have ended," or concluding that "the rise from June 1962 inaugurates his Wave Five," and the like, implying that they knew he was using the Wave Principle.

Gould started with the Elliott wave idea that bull markets have a similarity of form and then observed the time and price ratios between them to make some of the most accurate long term forecasts in stock market history. For instance, in 1963 he forecasted a major high for the Dow Industrials of "1066 in July 1966." The orthodox top of the bull market was registered at 996 in February 1966, while the price peak was registered seven years later at 1061 (the "theoretical intraday" high was 1067). In

October 1972, he predicted a low in the 640-650 range for August 1974, which he adjusted in March 1974 to "550-650 in October or November." The double bottom of October/December of that year registered an intraday low at 570. In November 1979, with the Dow depressed in the three-digit range, Gould forecasted a Dow peak of 3475 for January 11, 1990, successfully indicating the scope of the upside potential that lay ahead. No approach other than Elliott's Wave Principle has ever allowed such bold forecasting. According to market technician Tim Burton, in February 1980 at an Investment Seminars, Inc. conference, Gould "mentioned that he really invented the Elliott wave before Elliott did but didn't get credit for it." All the evidence — from Elliott's original letter in 1934 to Gould's use of a pseudonym in his *Barron's* article to the timing of his and Elliott's respective articles to the testimony of Charles Collins to the utter lack of any Gould-produced literature on the Wave Principle whatsoever — utterly negates this claim. It is perhaps instructive to note, moreover, that all three of Gould's most famous forecasts had been essentially made previously (and more accurately, as they ultimately turned out) by acknowledged Elliott wave analysts. In 1960, Bolton forecasted "Dow 999" (having forecasted "Dow 1000" as early as 1953); in 1970, A.J. Frost forecasted "Dow 572" (Collins and Bolton having called for 535 as early as 1966); and in 1978, Frost and Prechter forecasted a Dow near 3000 in *Elliott Wave Principle* (which Prechter revised in 1982 to Dow 3885, with the Dow then in the 900s). Though Gould never credited the Wave Principle or its practitioners for his forecasts, they appear at least to have merited a mention.

Dow Theory expert E. George Schaefer (1908-1974) knew Elliott and began publishing the *Dow Theory Trader* (1948-1974) the year Elliott died. There is some evidence, but no proof, that Schaefer kept a close eye on the market's message from the standpoint of the Wave Principle. For instance, author and technical analysis innovator James Dines, one of Schaefer's early subscribers, recalls that Schaefer mentioned the "three phases" of the 1920s bull market. Thus, just as one Dow Theorist (Robert Rhea) had inspired Elliott, who began publishing the year after Rhea died, so Elliott may have provided inspiration to Schaefer, in effect returning the favor. In a nearly perfect long-term performance, Schaefer turned bullish on stocks in 1949, catching the entire postwar bull market right up to the orthodox top in 1966. He turned bearish and stayed that way throughout the Cycle wave IV bear market until he died in the summer of 1974. His two long-term signals were thus identical to Bolton's (see discussion below). The influence of the Wave Principle upon Dow Theorists carried through more explicitly to Richard Russell, who while conferring with A.J. Frost published a number of remarkable Elliott Wave forecasts in his *Dow Theory Letters* during the bear market years of Cycle wave IV.

Though Elliott's concepts powerfully shaped the work of several of this century's most successful market forecasters, it was A. Hamilton Bolton, the brilliant analyst of Bolton-Tremblay, Ltd. of Montreal, who truly kept Elliott's name and the Wave Principle alive. Bolton, who was a stock broker at the time, read Elliott's *Financial World* articles in the spring and summer months of 1939. He made a point of contacting Elliott on one or two occasions on his trips to New York and corresponded continually with him until Elliott's death. In 1946, the year *Nature's Law* was published, Hamilton Bolton and Maurice Tremblay formed a money management firm and began publishing *The Bank Credit Analyst,* a monthly market analysis based upon Bolton's pioneering research on the relationship between bank credit statistics and trends in the stock market. As a result of his consistent success in forecasting with this method of "fundamental" analysis, Bolton commanded great and ever-increasing respect within the investment community, particularly among institutional investors.

While bank credit statistics were Bolton's bread and butter, the piles of correspondence to Collins, Frost and others show that he was captivated by the Wave Principle. Five years after starting his monthly publication, Bolton decided to assume the task of publicly analyzing the market in terms of what was by then referred to as the "Elliott" Wave Principle. His first exposition on the subject appeared in a 1953 "supplement" to *The Bank Credit Analyst.* The long-term bullish forecast it presented, at a time when to most analysts the market appeared "high," was not only daring, but accurate. Bolton's analysis proved so popular that the Elliott Wave Supplement became an annual feature published each April. His thoughtful commentary and dramatic success with the Wave Principle kept Wall Street interested in the concept for thirteen years.

Elliott's Wave Principle got another small boost with the inclusion of a concise summary in Garfield A. Drew's 1955 edition of *New Methods for Profit in the Stock Market.* In it,

Drew, who may have solicited the commentary from Bolton, wrote as follows:

> After a brave start in 1949-1951, the past two years, at least, have detracted from long term 1948 forecasts of most basic cycles. If these projections had been correct, stocks should have reached a bear market low in 1951, building activity should have been on the downgrade until 1953, and 1951-1952 should have been the trough of a depression. There is one exception, however. Elliott's Wave Principle seems to have stood up better than anything else in the field of long range forecast. There was more hesitation of stock prices in 1947-1949 than originally anticipated, but the basic theory was quite correct that the next important move would not only be up, but would also exceed the 1946 top. At the same time, it was also forecast that, eventually, a fifth "wave" would exceed even the 1928-29 top for stock prices. That seemed utterly fantastic in 1948 when the 200 level would have looked "high," but with the Average having already hit 360 in 1954, it no longer appears quite so impossible of ultimate accomplishment.

In 1960, while he was president of the Financial Analysts' Federation, Bolton published *The Elliott Wave Principle — A Critical Appraisal,* the first book on the Wave Principle since Elliott's *Nature's Law.* In that volume, he made his famous forecast of a major Dow peak at 999, reached six years later almost to the dollar. He also documented (without referring to him by name) Collins' concept of a 1932 orthodox Supercycle low for stocks, Elliott's concept of a 1942 orthodox low based on a 13-year triangle, and Bolton's own interpretation of a 1949 orthodox low based on a 21-year triangle. These differences of opinion constituted a point of good-natured disagreement among students of the Wave Principle that lasted a decade. A.J. Frost recounts that Bolton, just months before his death, changed his mind on the 21-year triangle, agreeing with Collins that 1932 marked the orthodox low. Subsequent market action confirmed this wave labeling to be correct.

On February 11, 1966, two days after that decade's high and the peak of Cycle Wave III, Bolton wrote to Collins, whom he had met twice before, and asked him to contribute to *The Bank Credit Analyst's* 1966 Supplement, which was published in April. Therein Collins gave his thoughts on the market and explained the story of his relationship with R.N. Elliott. He then outlined the Intermediate, Primary, Cycle, Supercycle and Grand Supercycle wave counts for the stock market and correctly identified the top of the Cycle wave advance from 1942. At the same time, he called for an ensuing fourth wave to be made up of a large A-B-C formation carrying ultimately to about the 525 level on the Dow Industrials. Considering that the Dow at that time was close to 1000 and bears were scarce, Collins' prediction was truly remarkable, not only because it forecast the unthinkable, but because it came true. The end of the 1966-1974 correction envisaged by Collins came at 570 (intraday reading) on the Dow, just 45 points from the projection made eight years earlier. [*The Complete Elliott Wave Writings of A. Hamilton Bolton* (1993) presents both his and Collins' entire published commentary.]

A.J. Frost, as vice president in charge of administration at Bolton-Tremblay, was a business associate of Bolton's from 1960 to 1962. He became and remained one of Bolton's closest friends. They corresponded frequently and discussed in detail the market and the Wave Principle on many occasions. After Bolton's death on April 5, 1967, Frost was chosen to assume the task of writing the Elliott Wave Supplements. Frost wrote the 1967 Supplement and collaborated with Russell L. Hall on the 1968 Supplement. The last Elliott Wave publication issued by *The Bank Credit Analyst*, which had been purchased by Storey, Boeckh & Associates following Bolton's death, was Frost's 1970 Supplement, which included his famous calculation using hourly figures that the bear market then in progress would bottom at 572. The hourly low four years later was 572.20. [*The Elliott Wave Writings of A.J. Frost and Richard Russell* (1996) presents Frost's entire published commentary.]

The Wave Principle receded from public view in the 1970s. Aside from brief summaries of the theory in a few book chapters and articles, the aforementioned discussions by Richard Russell and Robert C. Beckman's *The Elliott Wave Principle as Applied to the London Stock Market* (1976) were the most ambitious writings on the subject during this period.

The Wave Principle Renewed

The recession of Elliott Wave commentary ended with the release of Frost and Prechter's 1978 book, *Elliott Wave Principle — Key to Stock Market Profits*, the first book to arrange all known aspects of the Wave Principle in logical sequence and add points of substance to the literature.

In late 1976, while I was a technical analyst with Merrill Lynch in New York, I began corresponding with A.J. Frost. I had been publishing reports since April on the status of the market in terms of the Wave Principle and was beginning research for a new book on Elliott. The Market Technicians Association contacted me in early 1977 and asked if I would arrange for Frost to speak at its annual conference in Pennsylvania that May.

When Frost and I met at the conference, we enjoyed each other's company immensely and became fast friends. Frost explained that he also was in the process of writing a book on Elliott, which was to be a collaborative effort with Ian M.T. McAvity of *Deliberations* (for artwork) and Richard Russell. Frost added that he would like to include some of my recent analytical work as a chapter. I agreed and began work on the chapter while continuing research on my own book.

Frost spent most of 1977 writing a draft summary of the Wave Principle for his book. Then late in that year, McAvity and Russell contacted Frost and explained that their busy schedules precluded their involvement with the book. Frost wrote and suggested we collaborate on the volume and in December invited me for a weekend to his home in Manotick, Ontario, to go over our plans. I spent the next seven months substantially expanding on A.J.'s draft, interrupted only by a delightful weekend visit with Frost and Collins at Collins' retreat in Florida. By July the book was completed. The next several weeks were devoted to production details such as drawing the illustrations, photographing them and developing the photos in the basement darkroom at the house of statistical market analysis pioneer Arthur A. Merrill. By August the manuscript was at the printer, and in November it was released.

In April 1979, I left my position as Market Specialist with Merrill Lynch and began publishing *The Elliott Wave Theorist*, which I hope will track the fifth wave in the current Supercycle as well as Elliott tracked the first and second, Bolton and Collins tracked the third and Frost the fourth.

In 1979, I began assembling Elliott's original writings for publication. The result is this volume, which I hope has left no stone unturned in helping make available to R.N. Elliott the wide audience his pioneering ideas so richly deserve.

— Robert R. Prechter, 1980/2005/2017

If a reader possesses Elliott memorabilia, or has any additional knowledge, no matter how trivial, about the life of R.N. Elliott, please contact the publisher.

PUBLISHER'S NOTES AND REFERENCES

The first letter from Elliott to Collins, sent in November 1934, is reproduced in *Elliott Wave Principle* (New Classics Library, 1978-2005).

"The Basis of the Wave Principle" and "How the Wave Principle Works, and its Correlation with Mathematical Laws" are reprinted in the *Selected Essays* section of this book.

All available copies of Elliott's Interpretive Letters and educational essays have been republished, along with a Foreword providing a more complete discussion of Elliott's services, in *R.N. Elliott's Market Letters, 1938-1946* (New Classics Library, 1993).

All of Bolton's annual Elliott Wave Supplements to *The Bank Credit Analyst*, as well as his book, *The Elliott Wave Principle — A Critical Appraisal*, have been republished in *The Complete Elliott Wave Writings of A. Hamilton Bolton* (New Classics Library, 1994).

A.J. Frost's 1967 and 1970 Supplements to *The Bank Credit Analyst*, Russ Hall's 1968 Supplement, and all of Richard Russell's Elliott work are included in *The Elliott Wave Writings of A.J. Frost and Richard Russell* (New Classics Library, 1996).

In Elliott's original printing of *The Wave Principle*, most of the charts and diagrams were placed in the back of the book. For easier reference, we have rearranged their placement in the foregoing material to appear within the text where they are discussed.

Minor editing, including comma placement, letter cases, spelling of some numerals and an occasionally added article, was performed throughout Elliott's material. No substantive changes were made. Where a substantive edit is required, the original text has been left intact and a change suggested in a footnote.

May 24, 1999
To Robert R. Prechter, Jr., CMT, Gainesville GA
From George A. Schade, Jr., Scottsdale, AZ
RE: Biographical Research on Ralph Nelson Elliott

I attended the MTA Annual Seminar in Manhattan Beach, California. As Elliott's mother, father and sister are buried in Inglewood Park Cemetery, a stone's throw from the L.A. Airport, I decided I would visit their grave sites and continue the research.

I rented a car and headed to the cemetery. Inglewood Park is one of the oldest cemeteries in Los Angeles and quite large. I would not be surprised to learn that movies have been filmed there, as some of the landscape looked familiar to me. The park is large, quiet and bucolic. It now has the nation's largest mausoleum.

I thought this would be easy. I told my wife, "just twenty minutes." I headed out to Sequoia 182 with a gardener. Before long, it became clear we couldn't find the headstones. We enlisted the help of a second gardener. The first gardener went looking for a better map. I was reading headstones. My wife was walking around looking for headstones. No Elliotts.

The gardeners then started digging for burial section markers. Sequoia is one of the oldest areas of the park. "It's real old," said the gate guard, and he was right. Sequoia also stands out because it is one of the areas with above ground headstones and markers. Apparently, these are no longer allowed in the park.

No Elliotts. Finally we all agreed that we were standing in Sequoia 282 (after nearly forty minutes). We looked around and noticed something unusual – a grassy area with no markers. The gardener said, "We will have to dig." I thought, "Now, this research is really going far. We are going to dig for headstones." I told the gardener to go ahead and start.

He sunk his shovel in one spot and started digging a perfect rectangle. Lo and behold! He struck a gravestone six inches underneath the lawn. Lifting the cut rectangle of grass, Virginia H. Elliott's gravestone was exposed. He then moved over two feet and again cut a perfect lawn rectangle. Franklin Elliott's gravestone was exposed. We swept them, and after a short while, the marble glistened in the sun.

As for May Elliott, she is buried on the other side of Franklin, but she was buried without a gravestone. This accords with her life. She was 88 years old when she died. She was the sole survivor of the family and realistically did not have the monies to purchase a gravestone. She was buried without a headstone, according to the park's records. I checked the burial records which show no marker.

THE WAVE PRINCIPLE

by

R.N. Elliott

R. N. Elliott

25 Broad St.

New York City.

HAnover 2 7887 Oct. 1, 1938

A remarkable phenomenon and a secret heretofore carefully guarded, is now disclosed. It lends itself to both long and short term trading and is unique because it;

    (a) Really forecasts (makes known beforehand),

    (b) Has no resemblance whatsoever to any device heretofore offered,

    (c) Requires no confirmation, mathematical calculations or costly statistical research.

One reading of the treatise will give a general idea of

THE WAVE PRINCIPLE

but, like a text book, it requires application to learn. Price $15.00

In due course Interpretative Letters, applied to the current market, will be available.

R. N. Elliott,

Discoverer.

THE WAVE PRINCIPLE

by

R. N. ELLIOTT,

Discoverer.

Permission has been granted the author
to reproduce charts prepared by:

E. W. Axe & Co.,
Standard Statistics Co. Inc.,
New York Stock Exchange,
Barrons, The National Financial Weekly.
Dow-Jones & Co., Inc.
Numbering and lettering of waves was done
by the author and is protected by copyright.

Warning: When a newly discovered phenomenon is disclosed,
self-appointed "experts" immediately appear.

Considerable experience is required to interpret
correctly waves which are in process of formation.

Long distance forecasting requires thorough
familiarity with historical precedent.   During[*]
the next few years the market will not follow
the pattern observed between 1932 and 1937.

No interpretation of the Wave Principle should be
accepted as valid unless made by me or by a student
directly licensed by me.

                                        R. N. Elliott.

New York.

* What Elliott meant was that no rallies in the few years following publication in 1938 would develop into five-wave bull markets, since a bear market of Cycle degree was still in progress from 1937. He was absolutely correct. No "bull market" occurred until 1942-1946.

I

RHYTHM IN NATURE

No truth meets more general acceptance than that the universe is ruled by law. Without law it is self-evident there would be chaos, and where chaos is, nothing is. Navigation, chemistry, aeronautics, architecture, radio transmission, surgery, music — the gamut, indeed, of art and science — all work, in dealing with things animate and things inanimate, under law because nature herself works in this way. Since the very character of law is order, or constancy, it follows that all that happens will repeat and can be predicted if we know the law.

Columbus, maintaining that the world was round, predicted that a westward course from Europe must eventually bring his ships to land and despite scoffers, even among his own crew, saw his prediction realized. Halley, calculating the orbit of the 1682 comet, predicted its return which was strikingly verified in 1759. Marconi, after his studies in electrical transmission, predicted that sound could be conveyed without wires, and today we can sit in our homes and listen to musical and other programs from across the ocean. These men, as have countless more in other fields, learned the law. After becoming thus posted, prediction was easy because it became mathematical.

Even though we may not understand the cause underlying a particular phenomenon, we can, by observation, predict that phenomenon's recurrence. The sun was expected to recurrently rise at a fixed time thousands of years before the cause operating to produce this result was known. Indians fix their month by each new moon, but even today cannot tell why regular intervals characterize this heavenly sign. Spring plantings are witnessed the world over because summer is expected as next in order; yet how many planters understand why they are afforded this constancy of the seasons? In each instance the rhythm of the particular phenomenon was mastered.

Man is no less a natural object than the sun or the moon, and his actions, too, in their metrical occurrence, are subject to analysis. Human activities, while amazing in character, if approached from the rhythmical bias, contain a precise and natural answer to some of our most perplexing problems. Furthermore, because man is subject to rhythmical procedure, calculations having to do with his activities can be projected far into the future with a justification and certainty heretofore unattainable.

Very extensive research in connection with what may be termed human activities indicates that practically all developments which result from our social-economic processes follow a law that causes them to repeat themselves in similar and constantly recurring serials of waves or impulses of definite number and pattern. It is likewise indicated that in their intensity, these waves or impulses bear a consistent relation to one another and to the passage of time. In order to best illustrate and expound this phenomenon it is necessary to take, in the field of man's activities, some example which furnishes an abundance of reliable data and for such purpose there is nothing better than the stock exchange.

Particular attention has been given to the stock market for two reasons. In the first place, there is no other field in which prediction has been essayed with such great intensity and with so little result. Economists, statisticians, technicians, business leaders, and bankers, all have had a try at foretelling the future of prices over the New York Stock Exchange. Indeed, there has developed a definite profession with market forecasting as its objective. Yet 1929 came and went, and the turn from the greatest bull market on record to the greatest bear market on record caught almost every investor off guard. Leading investment institutions, spending hundreds of thousands of dollars yearly on market research, were caught by surprise and suffered millions of dollars loss because of price shrinkage in stock holdings that were carried too long.

A second reason for choosing the stock market as an illustration of the wave impulse common to social-economic activity is the great reward attendant on successful stock market prediction. Even accidental success in some single market forecast has yielded riches little short of the fabulous. In the market advance from July 1932 to March 1937, for illustration, an average of thirty leading and representative stocks advanced by 373%. During the course of this five-year movement, however, there were individual stocks whose per cent advance was much larger. Lastly, the broad advance cited above was not in a straight upward line, but rather by a series of upward and downward steps, or zig-zag movements of a number of months' duration. These lesser swings afforded even greater opportunity for profit.

Despite the attention given the stock market, success, both in the accuracy of prediction and the bounties attendant thereto, has necessarily been haphazard because those who have attempted to deal with the market's movements have failed to recognize the extent to which the market is a psychological phenomenon. They have not grasped the fact that there is regularity underlying the fluctuations of the market, or, stated otherwise, that price movements in stocks are subject to rhythms, or an ordered sequence. Thus market predictions, as those who have had any experience in the subject well know, have lacked certainty or value of any but an accidental kind.

But the market has its law, just as is true of other things throughout the universe. Were there no law, there could be no center about which prices could revolve and, therefore, no market. Instead, there would be a daily series of disorganized, confused price fluctuations without reason or order anywhere apparent. A close study of the market, however, as will be subsequently disclosed, proves that this is not the case. Rhythm, or regular, measured, and harmonious movement, is to be discerned. This law behind the market can be discovered only when the market is viewed in its proper light, and then is analyzed from this approach. Simply put, the stock market is a creation of man and therefore reflects human idiosyncrasy. In the pages which follow, the law, or rhythm, to which man responds will be disclosed as registered by market movements that fluctuate in accordance with a definite wave principle.

The Wave Principle is a phenomenon that has always functioned in every human activity. Waves of different degrees occur whether or not recording machinery is present. When the machinery described below is present, the patterns of waves are perfected and become visible to the experienced eye.

A. Extensive commercial activity represented by corporations whose ownership is widely distributed.
B. A general market-place where buyer and seller may contact quickly through representatives.
C. Reliable record and publications of transactions.
D. Adequate statistics available on all matters relating to corporations.
E. Daily high and low range charted in such a manner as will disclose the waves of all degrees as they occur.

The daily range of stock transactions was inaugurated in 1928 and the hourly record in 1932. These are necessary in order to observe the minor and minute waves, especially in fast markets.

The Wave Principle does not require confirmation by two averages. Each average, group, stock or any human activity is interpreted by its own waves. Behavior of waves has been fairly well explored, but application is in its infancy.[1]

ENDNOTES

[1] Here Elliott suggests, correctly I think, that once one knows the Principle it is easy to recognize and follow, but it takes practice to be able to forecast the market from it. On the other hand, it is not necessary to forecast in order to trade successfully. As Elliott said in a letter to Collins, "I consider that it is far more important to *know* when the terminals are actually reached than to forecast a 'guess'."

II

STOCK MARKET WAVES

Human emotions, as mentioned in the preceding discussion, are rhythmical. They move in waves of a definite number and direction. The phenomenon occurs in all human activities, whether it is business, politics, or the pursuit of pleasure. It is particularly evident in those free markets where public participation in price movements is extensive. Bond, stock and commodity price trends are therefore especially subject to examination and demonstration of the wave movement. This treatise has made use of price movements in stocks to illustrate the phenomenon, but all the principles laid down herein are equally applicable to the wave movement in every field where human endeavor is registered.

A completed movement consists of five waves. Why this should be five rather than some other number is one of the secrets of the universe. No attempt will be made to explain it, although, in passing, it might be observed that the figure five is prominent in other basic patterns of nature. Taking the human body, for example, there are five extensions from the torso — head, two legs, two arms; five extensions from head — two ears, two eyes, the nose; five extensions in the form of fingers, from each arm, and in the form of toes, from each leg; five physical senses — taste, smell, sight, touch, hearing; and so the story might be repeated elsewhere. In any event, *five waves are basic to a completed social movement* and can be accepted without necessity of reasoning the matter out.

Three of the five waves that form any completed movement will be in the direction of the movement; two of the waves will be in a contrary direction. The first, third and fifth waves represent the forward impulse; the second and fourth waves, the contrary, or corrective. Stated otherwise, the odd numbered waves are in the main direction; the even numbered waves, against the main direction. This is illustrated in Figure 1.

Five waves of one dimension become the first wave of the next greater dimension or degree. As an example of this, the five waves in Figure 1 progressed from point M to point N. In Figure 2, however, representing a next higher degree of movement than the one just illustrated, it will be seen that the movement from M to N is but one wave of the five-wave movement M to R. The movement M to R, in turn, becomes but the first wave of a movement of still higher degree.

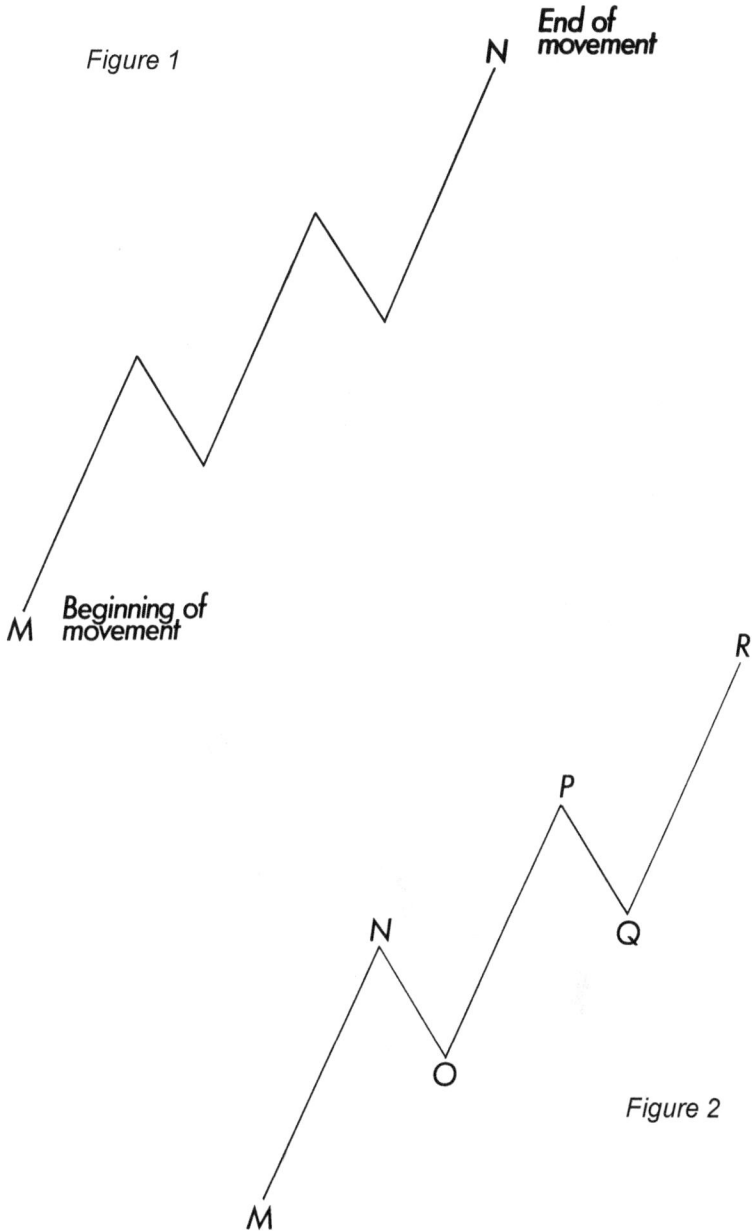

Figure 1

Figure 2

III

IDENTIFYING THE WAVES

In the preceding discussion the wave movement in stock prices was rather generally treated, the main point established being that a movement consists of five waves, and that the five waves of one movement equal the first wave of a next higher movement. At this point a second basic fact with respect to the wave movement should be introduced. This concerns a difference between the odd numbered and the even numbered waves.

Waves one, three and five, it will be recalled, are impulses in the main direction, whereas waves two and four are reverse movements. Wave two serves to correct wave one, and wave four serves to correct wave three. The difference between waves in the main direction and waves against the main direction is that the former are divisible into five waves of lesser degree, whereas the latter are divisible into but three waves of the lesser degree. In the preceding discussion, the movement M to N was shown as in Figure 3.

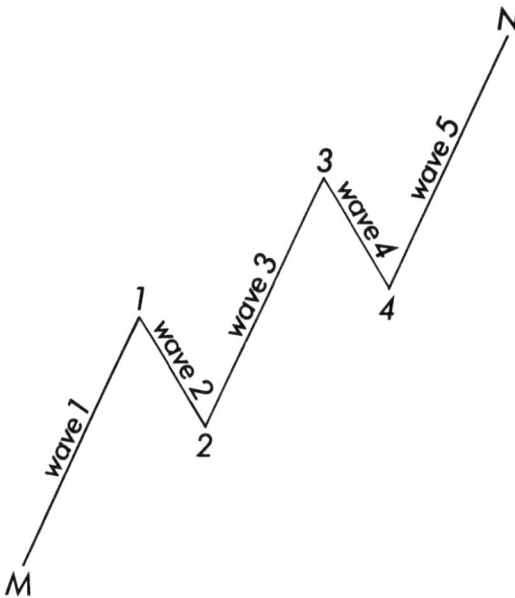

Figure 3

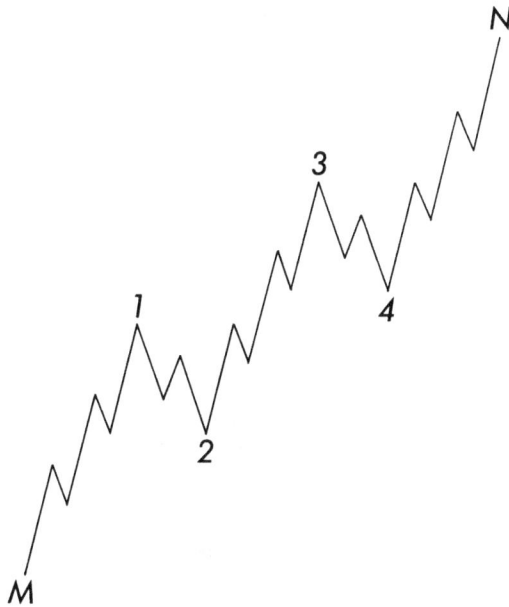

Figure 4

Were this movement also broken into waves of one lower degree, it would appear as in Figure 4.

Note, in Figure 4, that the second wave (wave 1 to 2) and the fourth wave (wave 3 to 4) are each made up of three smaller waves, whereas waves one, three, and five each have five smaller waves. The rules to be derived from this illustration — and these rules are fundamental to the whole wave subject — are:

1) Waves in the direction of the main movement, or the odd numbered waves, are made up of five lesser waves.

2) Corrective waves, or waves against the main movement (even numbered waves) are made up of three lesser waves.

To further illustrate the above rules, let us take the movement 1 to 2 in Figure 4. This was wave number two of the five-wave or complete movement from M to N, and was made up, as all corrective movements should be, of three waves. The three waves of the movement 1 to 2, however, formed, when isolated, a distinct corrective movement, and, under the above rules, the odd numbered waves (or waves a and c), since they are in the direction of the entire corrective movement 1 to 2, should each be made

up of five lesser waves, whereas
the even numbered wave (or wave
b), which is against the direction
of the movement 1 to 2 and thus
is a correction in such movement,
should be made up of three waves.
If we now present the movement 1
to 2 in terms of its lower waves, it
will appear as in Figure 5.

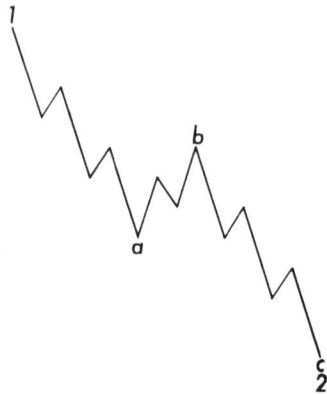

For purposes of convenience,
let us designate the odd numbered
waves of a movement as cardinal[1]
waves and the even numbered
waves as corrective waves. Let us

Figure 5

also remember that the cardinal waves will contain five waves of
a lower degree, whereas the corrective waves will contain three
waves of a lower degree. Other rules and points of interest with
respect to waves follow.

The wave movement applies to stock averages, such as the
Dow-Jones, Standard Statistics, New York Times; to groups of
stocks, such as the steels, the coppers, the textiles; and individual
stocks.[2] When individual stocks are studied, it will be found that
some are advancing while others are declining or undergoing a
corrective movement. The great majority of individual issues
will, at any given time, be following the same pattern, however,
with the result that the averages, or general market, will break
down into the wave phenomenon. It follows that the greater the
number of stocks in a market average, the more perfect will be
the wave pattern.[3]

Waves are not of uniform length or duration.[4] An entire
movement, consisting of five waves, is always due to some one or
more controlling influences, but the three upward waves (waves
one, three, and five) which, with their two corrective waves
(waves two and four), go to make up the entire movement, may
accommodate themselves somewhat to current developments.[5]
The fundamental cause behind such movement is generally not
recognized until after the effect has played out in the form of the
complete movement, whereas, during the course of the movement,
current news is available to every one and thus modifies, both
as to extent and duration, each of the five waves going to make
up the completed move.

As a general rule, it may be assumed that wave three will reach a higher level than wave one, and that wave five will go higher than wave three. Likewise, wave four should not carry to as low a level as is attained by wave two.[6] Wave two rarely cancels all of the ground gained by wave one, and wave four rarely cancels all of the ground gained by wave three.[7] The completed five-wave movement, in other words, is normally diagonal in character, as illustrated in Figure 6.

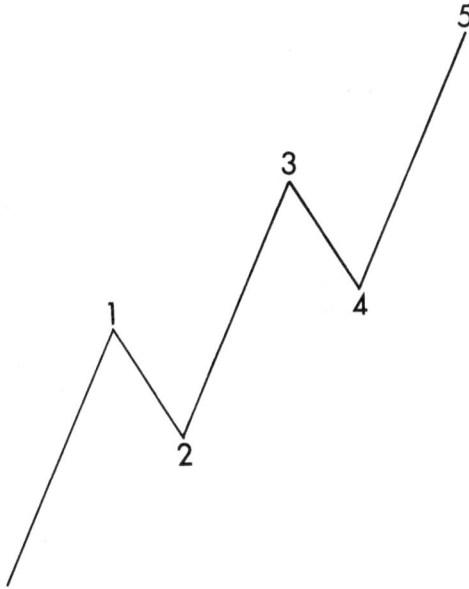

Figure 6

To properly observe a market movement, and hence to segregate the individual waves of such a movement, it is necessary that the movement, as it progresses, be channelled between parallel lines. Most stationers' shops carry in stock parallel rulers and the use of such a device greatly facilitates the channelling.

A channel cannot be started until waves numbers one and two have been completed. In Figure 7, waves one and two have ended, leaving three exposed contacts, or points which stand out alone. The first exposed contact is the starting point of wave number one; the second exposed contact is the termination point of wave number one as well as the starting point of wave number two; the third exposed contact is the termination point of wave

number two. These points, for purposes
of illustration, have been designated M,
N, and O. In preparing the channel, a
base line should first be drawn between
exposed contacts M and O. Across
exposed contact N may then be drawn a
line parallel to the base line, designated
as the "upper channel line." This upper
channel line should be extended some
distance to the right of N. When this
operation has been completed, the
channel will appear as in Figures 8 and 9.

Figure 7

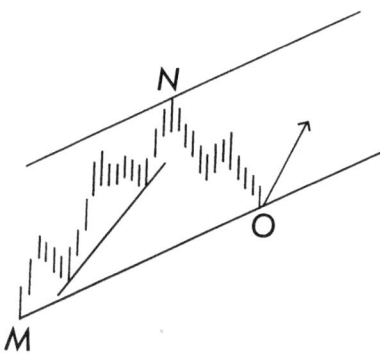

Figure 8

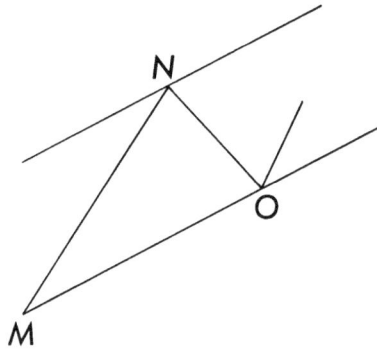

Figure 9

Wave number three should normally terminate at around
the upper channel line. If wave number three exceeds the
upper channel line, the upmovement has taken on temporary
strength, whereas if wave number three terminates below the
upper channel line, the upmovement has developed temporary
weakness. In any event, when wave three has terminated, the old
channel can be abandoned in favor of a new one. The new channel
is established by drawing an upper channel line to connect points
N and P, or termination points of waves one and three. A line, still
designated as the base line, parallel to the new upper channel line
is drawn across exposed contact O and extended to the right. It is
about this line that wave four should terminate. Figure 10 shows
both the old, or discarded, and the new channels. Of course, if
the third wave terminates at exactly the original upper channel

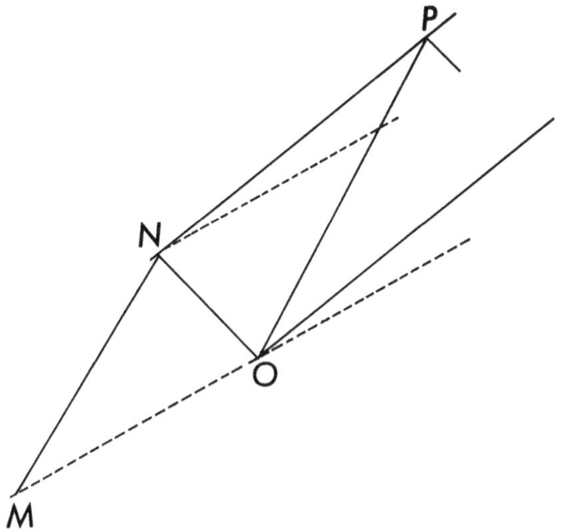

Figure 10

line first drawn from point N, the discarded channel and the new channel will be one and the same.

When wave four has terminated, either on, above, or below the new base line, the final channel can be drawn. This channel is quite important since it helps to locate the end of the fifth, or last, wave. It is on the termination of a long movement that investors and speculators must chiefly concentrate if their operations are to prove successful. The final channel is located by drawing a connecting line between the extreme terminal or exposed contact of wave number two (O) and the terminal or exposed contact of wave number four (Q). Parallel to this base line, and touching the terminal of wave number three (P) is drawn another or upper channel line. This is shown in Figure 11, the discarded first and second channels of the diagram above having been erased for clarity of illustrations. Wave five should normally terminate at around the upper channel line, although this subject, because of its importance, will be treated in detail in the succeeding discussion outlining wave characteristics.

When the fifth wave has terminated, there will be a downward movement or correction of greater proportions than those previously recorded during the progress of the channel discussed above. This wave becomes number two of the next higher degree of movement, just as the first five waves previously

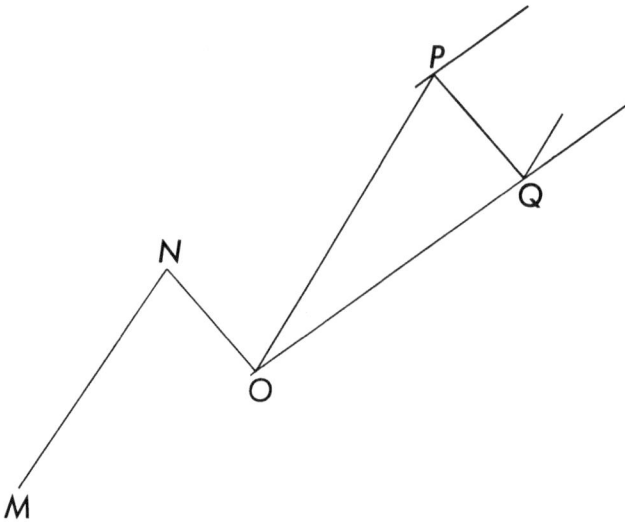

Figure 11

channeled are now renumbered as wave number one of the next higher order. Channeling on a higher scale can be started at the termination of wave number two under the same principles as laid down in Figure 11.

ENDNOTES

[1] "Cardinal" is the original term. In the *Financial World* articles, he uses the term "progressive" waves, and later in *Nature's Law*, "impulse" waves. *Elliott Wave Principle* gives these terms different, specific meanings.

[2] Use of the Wave Principle with individual stocks is less reliable than with averages since the phenomenon reflects mass psychology or, as Elliott put it, "extensive public participation in price movements."

[3] Strictly speaking, this statement is not true. An average made up of IBM and General Motors alone might better reflect the Wave Principle than an average of ten thinly traded two-dollar stocks. Moreover, I am convinced that the public visibility of a market index may enhance its utility with regard to the Wave Principle. Thus the Dow, which is made up of only thirty stocks, may be a more sensitive recorder of the Wave Principle than say, the Value Line Composite index since investors have a psychological interaction with the Dow Industrial Average that they do not experience with other indexes.

[4] He means *necessarily* of uniform length or duration. They certainly can be, and at times are.

[5] This assertion cannot be true, since any "entire movement" is merely one of the waves of a movement of larger degree. What Elliott means is simply that news appears to affect the shape of waves of Sub-Minor degree.

[6] Later Elliott contended that wave 4 should not drop below the peak of wave 1, a rule that experience verifies.

[7] If the Wave Principle is to have any consistency or value, the word "rarely" should read "never."

IV

TERMINOLOGY

In classifying the wave movement as applied to the stock market (or as discerned in any other field of human activity, for that matter), it is necessary to devise some nomenclature by which the waves of any one degree will be distinguished from the waves of a greater or lower degree. For all practical purposes the following degrees of movement will cover such studies of the stock market as are herein presented, or as the student of market trends will need in his own research work in the phenomenon. The following order is from the lower to higher degrees, five waves of one degree going to make up the first wave of the next higher degree. Five Sub-Minuette waves, for example, compose wave number one of a Minuette movement, five Minuette waves equal wave number one of a Minute movement, and so on. The order follows:

Sub-Minuette
Minuette
Minute
Minor
Intermediate
Primary
Cycle
Super Cycle
Grand Super Cycle

To avoid confusion in the lettering of waves on charts presented herein, so that the movements of any one degree can be readily differentiated, at a glance, from the movements of another degree, the following number designations have been devised for the nine movements classified above.[1]

Degree	Number	Description
Sub-Minuette	a to e	Small letters
Minuette	A to E	Capitalized
Minute	1 to 5	Arabic Numerals
Minor	I to V	Roman Numerals
Intermediate	Ⓘ to Ⓥ	Romans circled

Primary	① to ⑤	Double circled
Cycle	c I to c V	Preceded by "c"
Super Cycle	sc I to sc V	Preceded by "sc"
Grand Super Cycle	gsc I to gsc V	Preceded by "gsc"

The reader need not pay too much attention, at the moment, to the above nomenclature and its numerical designation, but will find it of increasing usefulness as his studies into stock price movements progress.

A Grand Super Cycle in stock prices got under way in the United States in 1857. The first wave of this degree of movement ran from 1857 to 1928. The second wave — representing a correction of the first wave — ran from November 1928 to 1932. The third wave in the Grand Super Cycle started in 1932 and has many years to run.

The Grand Super Cycle wave from 1857 to 1928 is referred to as "No. 1", but it may have been No. 3 or No. 5.[2] A severe depression occurred from 1854 to 1857 similar in duration to that of 1929-1932.

Wave number one[3] of the Grand Super Cycle, the upward wave that ran from 1857 to 1928, was made up of five waves which, together, may be designated as one complete Super Cycle. This Super Cycle may be subdivided as follows (see Figure 12):

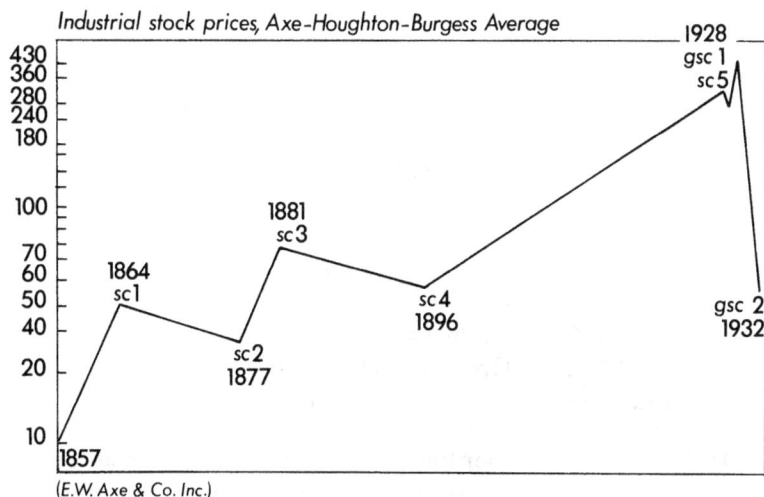

Figure 12

1857-1864 — Super Cycle wave number one
1864-1877 — Super Cycle correction (wave two)
1877-1881 — Super Cycle wave number three
1881-1896 — Super Cycle correction (wave four)
1896-1928 — Super Cycle wave number five.

The only record of stock prices available as far back as the beginning of the present Grand Super Cycle is the Axe-Houghton Index of representative issues (published in the *New York Times Annalist*) which records movements from 1854 to date.

Let us, in further illustration, now take Super Cycle wave number five and break it down into its next smaller degree. This wave, running from 1896 to 1928, under the previously stated nomenclature, would be designated as a Cycle, and this Cycle would be made up of five waves. These waves were as follows (see Figure 13):[4]

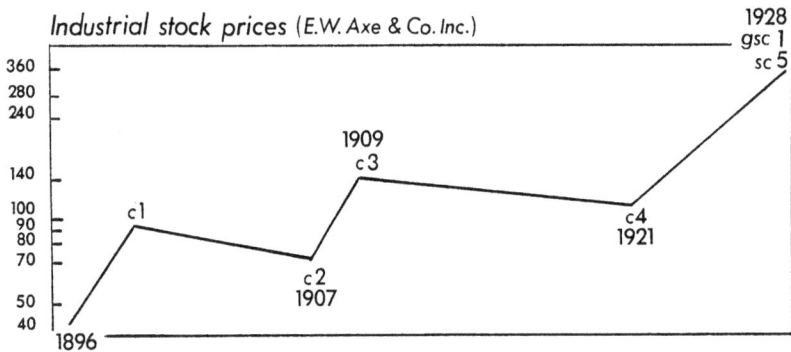

Figure 13

1896-1899 — Cycle wave number one
1899-1907 — Cycle correction (wave two)
1907-1909 — Cycle wave number three
1909-1921 — Cycle correction (wave four)
1921-1928 — Cycle wave number five.

If Cycle wave number five — the wave running from 1921 to 1928 — is now reduced to its lesser degree, it will be found to have been composed of five Primary waves, as follows (see Figure 14):

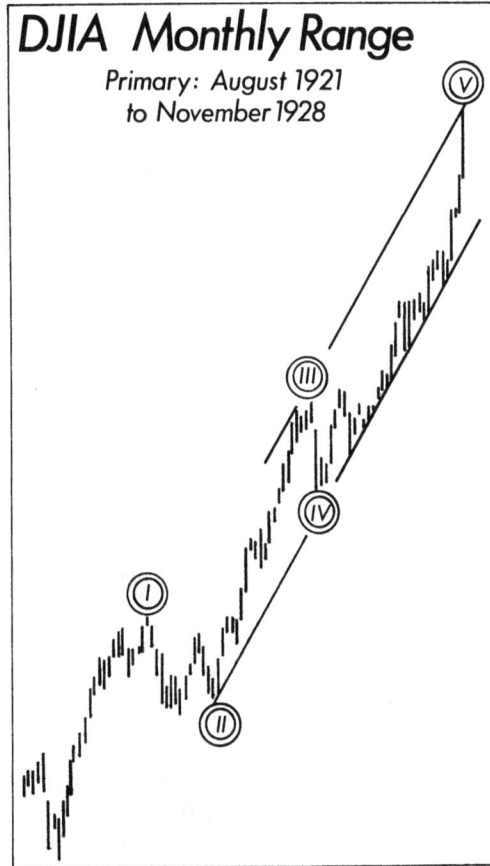

Figure 14

June 1921 to March 1923 — Primary wave number one
March 1923 to May 1924 — Primary correction (wave two)
May 1924 to November 1925 — Primary wave number three
November 1925 to March 1926 — Primary correction (wave four)
March 1926 to November 1928 — Primary wave number five.

In like manner, the Primary waves of the Cyclical wave running from June 1921 to November 1928 can each be broken down into Intermediate waves; the Intermediate waves can each be broken down into Minor waves; and so on through lesser and lesser degree until the most minute movement of record is properly analyzed and classified.

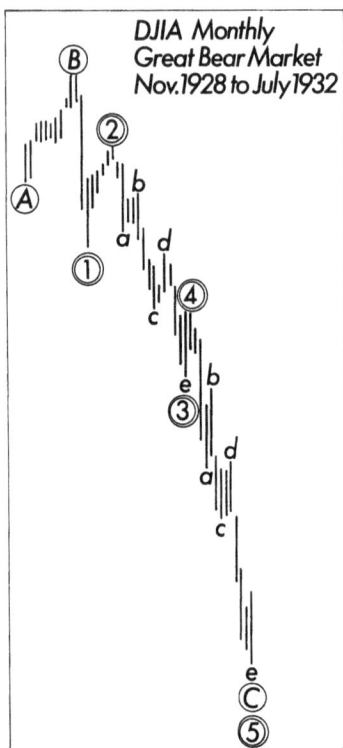

DJIA Monthly
Great Bear Market
Nov.1928 to July1932

Figure 15

November 28, 1928, with the Dow-Jones Average of thirty industrial stocks standing at 295.62, came at the end of the fifth Minuette wave of the fifth Primary wave of the fifth Cycle wave of the fifth Super Cycle wave of the first Grand Super Cycle wave. Stated otherwise, one who was tracing the stock market's pattern in terms of its decade by decade, year by year, month by month, week by week, day by day, and hour by hour fluctuations, was not confused as to its trend during any part of the past decade but was able, even, to fix not only the year and month when the great bull market terminated, but could even determine the day and hour of the end — and even the minute. From the Super Cycle down through every lesser degree to the most infinitesimal movement recorded, the market, before reaching its final peak, had to complete a fifth wave of each lesser degree. The first reversal downward in December 1928 was signalled by the extended minor fifth wave up to November 1928.

It will have been noted that the top of the fifth wave of the Super Cycle is shown as having ended November 1928 (the orthodox top) and not September 1929, the extreme high.[5] Between these points are registered (see Figure 15).

— wave A from November to December 1928 (down) and
— wave B from December 1928 to September 1929 (up in three minor waves), in an irregular reversal.

Wave C runs from September 1929 to July 1932. Wave C was subdivided into five waves down, and the irregular top signalled a fast, straight down movement.

The same irregular pattern occurred at the top of August 1937.[6] This irregular pattern is described in detail under the caption "Corrections."

ENDNOTES

[1] Frost and I have standardized a labeling system in which letters are reserved only for corrective waves while numbers are used for motive waves.

[2] Elliott's use of 1857 as a Supercycle wave low is absolutely correct, but at this time he lacked the data to be sure which number it was. He came firmly to the correct conclusion that 1857 was the low of a *second* wave of Supercycle degree in the Interpretive Letter dated August 25, 1941 (see Figure 98 in *Nature's Law*).

[3] Three, actually.

[4] Frost and I prefer the count as presented in *Elliott Wave Principle*, although we use a different data series to arrive at our conclusions.

[5] I prefer the interpretation that 1929 marked the orthodox top, a labeling that Elliott in fact uses once, in "The Future Pattern of the Market" from 1942, which is reprinted in the Selected Essays section of this book.

[6] Questionable. See Endnote 3 in Chapter XX of *Nature's Law*.

WAVE CHARACTERISTICS

In the preceding discussions an attempt has been made to state, as simply as possible, the five-wave phenomenon. In the present discussion attention will be devoted more to detail, in order that the student of the wave movement can fully master the subject, and thus be prepared to develop his own studies of price and other movements of human origin and influence.

Investors and speculators in stocks are particularly concerned with the termination point of a fifth wave, as this event marks the point at which an entire movement is to be corrected by a reverse movement of similar degree. Stock market movements of important dimensions, such as Intermediate swings running over a number of months, and Primary swings running over a number of years, will witness, at termination, a considerable price correction, and such terminal points call for disposition of stock holdings. It is likewise important that terminal corrections be identified, as these points represent price areas where long positions in stocks are to be established. In the following paragraphs the fifth wave, as well as the corrective wave, are dwelt upon rather fully. Other factors bearing on terminal points are also discussed.

The Fifth Wave

In fixing the end of a movement in stock prices, it should be borne in mind that before the movement has terminated there must be five waves of the next lesser degree of movement, that the fifth wave of such next lesser degree will also require five waves of a still next lesser degree, and so on. For illustration, an Intermediate movement will end on the fifth Sub-Minuette wave of the fifth Minuette wave of the fifth Minute wave of the fifth Minor wave of such Intermediate movement. In Figure 16, the fifth Minor wave has been broken down into its five Minuette waves, and the fifth Minuette wave has been broken down into its five Sub-Minuette waves to illustrate the foregoing principle.[1]

The fifth wave of a movement, particularly the larger such as the Intermediate and above, generally penetrates or "throws over" the upper parallel line formed by channelling the termination

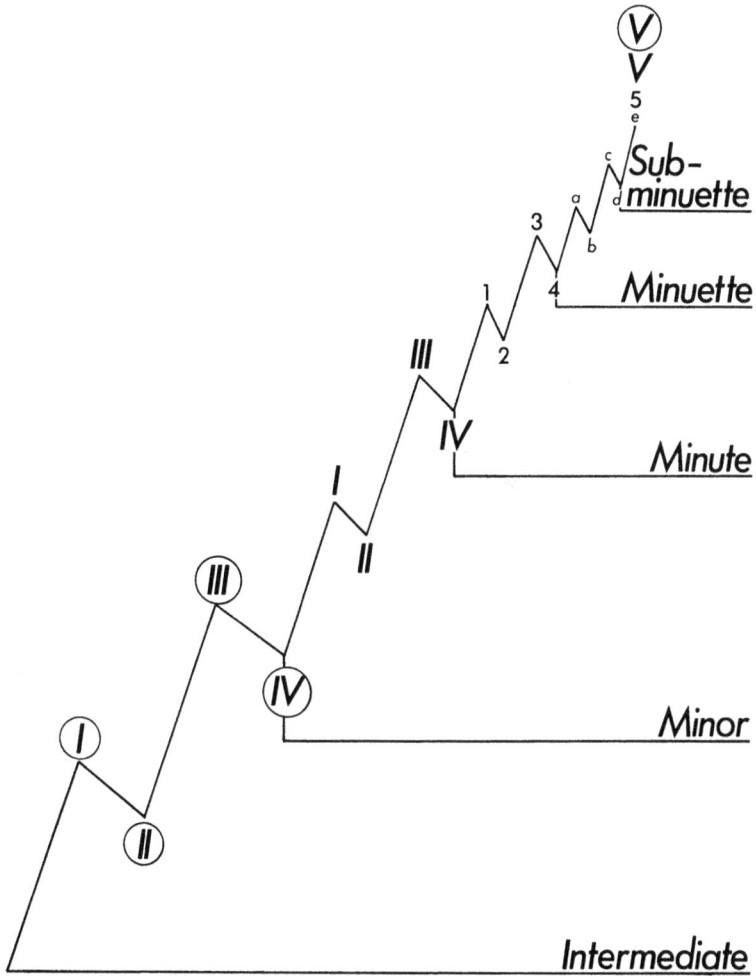

Figure 16

points of the second, third and fourth waves as described in the preceding discussion, and as illustrated in Figure 17.

Volume tends to climb on a throw-over, and when this throw-over is by the fifth Intermediate wave of a Primary movement, volume should be very heavy. When the fifth wave of any degree fails to penetrate or throw-over its upper channel line and decline occurs, this is a warning of weakness. The extent of the weakness indicated is according to the degree of the wave.

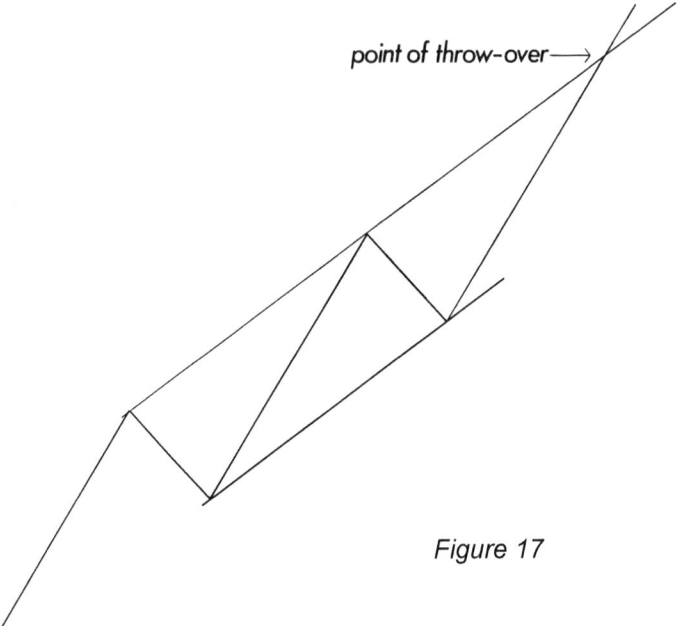

point of throw-over⟶

Figure 17

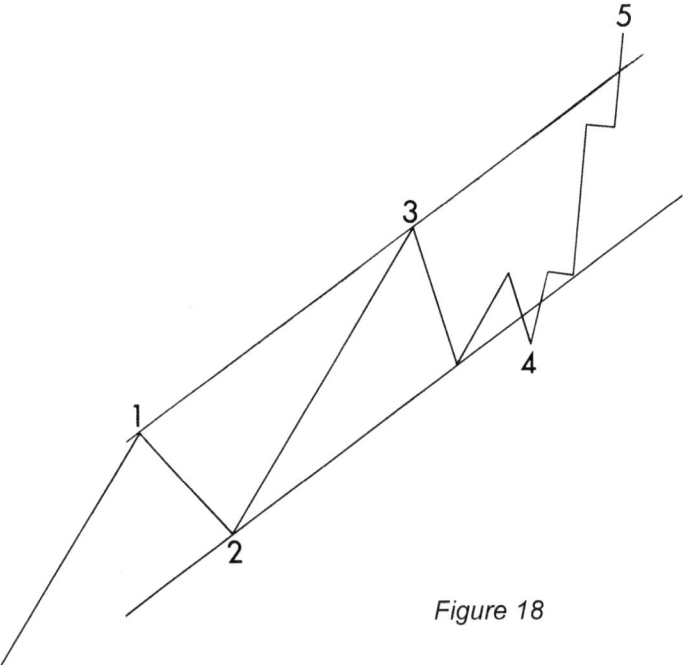

Figure 18

Sometimes, near a point of throw-over, a fifth wave will fail to immediately complete, and the fourth wave flattens out before number five starts (see Figure 18).

In locating "throw-overs," a logarithmic scale is highly recommended for those charts on which the market, or individual stocks, may be followed by means of the weekly price range, whereas an arithmetic scale should be used for daily range and hourly charts. At the tops of primary and higher degree movements the arithmetic scale is much more likely to produce throw-overs, whereas at the bottom of such movements the reverse is true; that is, the logarithmic scale is more apt to develop throw-overs. In both cases the arithmetic scale would be deceptive, in waves of say 30 points or more. To clearly illustrate one of the foregoing statements, a monthly range chart of the 1929-1932 movement of the Dow-Jones Industrial Average on both the logarithmic and the arithmetic scales is shown in Figure 19.

Fifth waves will sometimes deploy or spread out. This has been designated as one type of "stretching." In such an event the fifth wave, rather than the terminating movement of which it was a part, is followed by four other waves of lower degree. That is, the fifth wave has simply subdivided into five waves. Stretching is a characteristic of markets that are unusually strong (or weak, where the stretching occurs in a down movement). Examples of upside stretching were witnessed in the 1921-1928 upswing, the culmination of a seventy-two year advance.

Figure 19

Corrections

While the wave principle is very simple and exceedingly useful in forecasting, nevertheless there are refinements within the principle that may baffle the student, especially when wave movements are in process of formation. The best way to explain what is meant by refinements is to chart them as shown below. The examples are theoretically perfect specimens; the student will find the actual development of these patterns not so simple, in all cases.[2]

Corrections always have three waves[3] which fall into four general types, but while in formation it is sometimes difficult to forecast the exact pattern and extent.[4] Once completed the pattern indicates the strength of the ensuing move. The types shown in Figures 20 through 23 are those of very small corrections. The general outlines of patterns are the same in all degrees.

Zig-zag

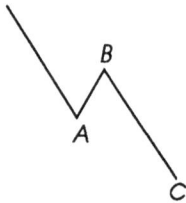

Figure 20

Flat

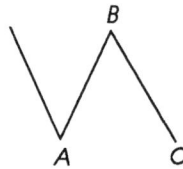

Figure 21

Irregular Types

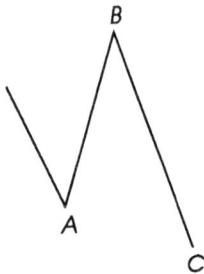

Figure 22

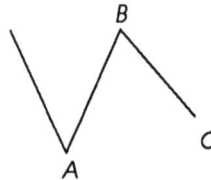

Figure 23

The same types as above, but for larger degrees, are shown in Figures 24 through 26.

Zig-zag

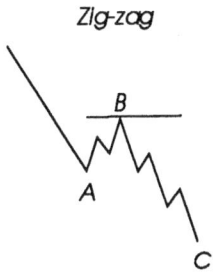

Figure 24

Flat

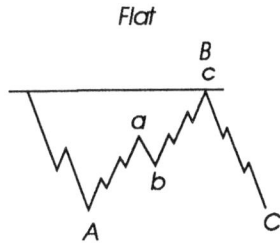

Figure 25

Irregular

Figure 26

Still larger types of corrections, although of the same general patterns, are those seen in Intermediate and Primary degrees (see Figures 27 through 29).

Zig-zag   Flat

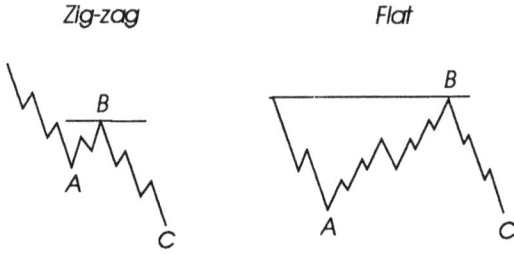

Figure 27   Figure 28

Irregular

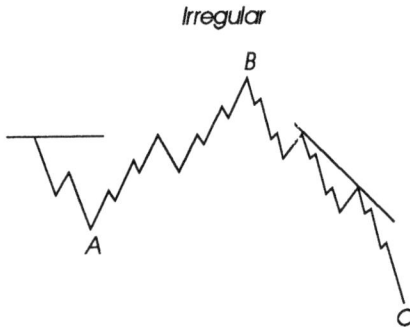

Figure 29

Extensions

Extensions may appear in any one of the three impulses, waves 1, 3 or 5, but rarely in more than one. Usually they occur in wave 5.[5] Examples are shown in Figure 30.

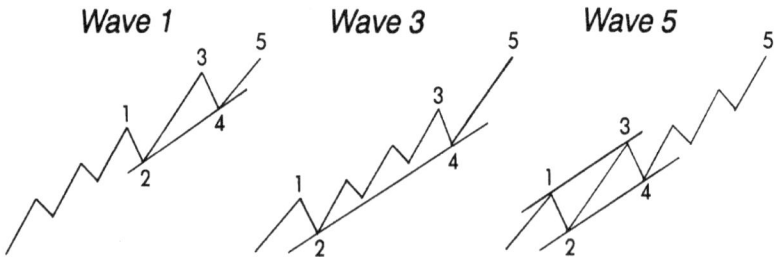

Figure 30

Extensions of Extensions

The same rules govern both extensions and extensions of extensions. In Figure 31 will be found three types of extensions of extensions and the standard type.

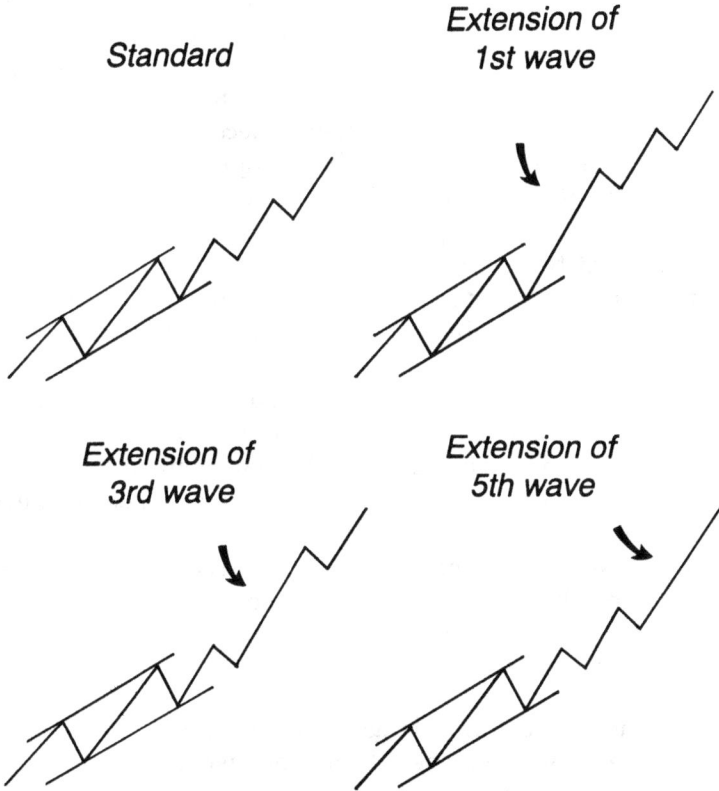

Figure 31

Behavior of Market Following Extensions

A thorough understanding of extensions is very important. Warnings of this phenomenon have been sought without success, and for certain reasons it is probable none exist.[6] However, losses can be avoided and profits obtained by learning the behavior of the market subsequent to their occurrence. The rules are:

1) Extensions occur in new territory of the current cycle.

2) Extensions are retraced twice.[7]

3) The first retracement will occur immediately in three waves to approximately the beginning of the extension (wave 2 of the extension).

4) The second retracement will occur in the usual progress of the market and travel beyond the extension.

5) However, when an extension occurs, for example, at the end of a fifth primary (where a major reversal is due) the first and second retracements become waves A and B of an irregular correction. This complies with the double retracement rules. Wave C will be composed of five waves downward, fast and probably to the beginning of the fifth primary of the preceding bull market.[8] The only example[9] of this particular kind is downward from November 1928, upward to September 1929, and downward to 1932. (See Figure 15.)

6) Occasionally extensions occur in bear markets under the same rules, such as, for example, during October 1937.

7) An extension is never the end of a movement.[10] This does not infer that higher or lower levels may not be seen even without an extension.

8) Retracement means that the travel of a described movement between two specified points is covered again. For example, a correction and resumption of the trend is a double retracement.

If a trader is holding "longs" when a downward extension appears, he should not sell then because the market will immediately retrace the extension in three waves, before seeking lower levels.

Important extensions have occurred as follows:

Industrials Upward	*Industrials Downward*
July-November 1925	November 1929
October-November 1928	October 1937
July 1933	
March 1936	

Rails Upward
February 1936

While the first retracement will occur immediately and in three waves, the second might not develop for a considerable time, but it will eventually end in the current cycle. The pattern of an extension[11] and double retracement is illustrated in Figure 32.

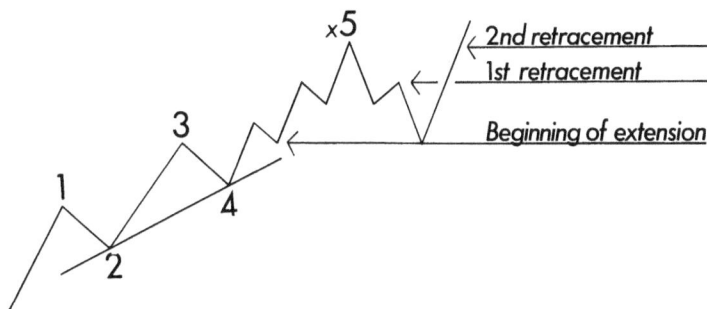

Figure 32

Irregular Corrections

Examples of corrections have already been shown but not as a part of the waves of the previous movement being corrected. Such examples are shown in Figures 33 and 34. The letters "A," "B" and "C" indicate waves one, two and three of the corrective movement, irregular pattern. Note that the second wave "B" exceeds the orthodox top (5) of the previous movement.

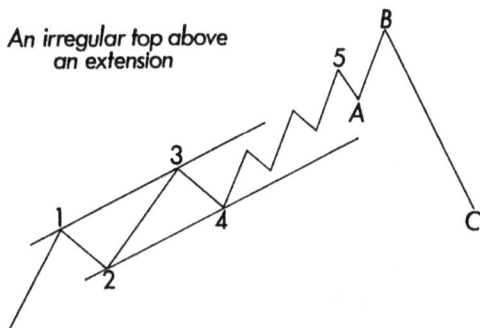

Figure 33

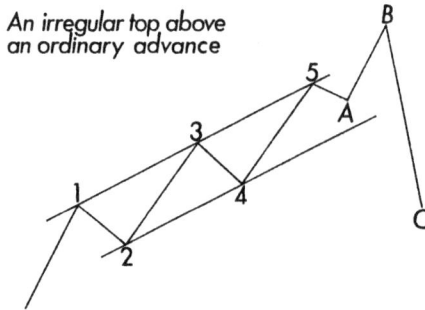

An irregular top above an ordinary advance

Figure 34

Strong Corrections

Corrections can prove useful as warnings of strong movements. Figure 35 is a regular zig-zag pattern, which indicates ordinary strength of subsequent movement. Figure 36 is a flat, indicating strong subsequent movement (see wave 4 Primary, July1933 to July 1934).

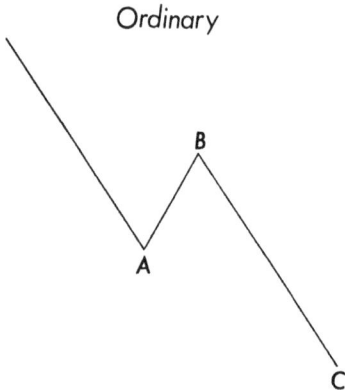

Ordinary

Figure 35

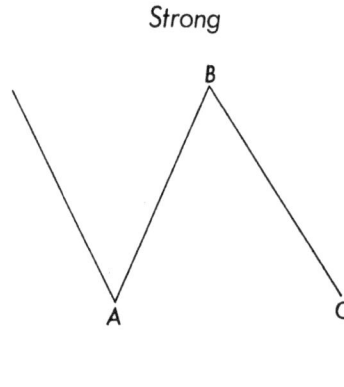

Strong

Figure 36

Figure 37 shows a pattern where the end of the correction at "2" is higher than the end of wave "A" of the correction, indicating unusual strength of the subsequent movement. (The second correction shown in Figure 37 is weaker.)

Corrections of bear trends, that is, corrections following downward movements, have the same characteristics as those of advancing movements, but in reverse (see Figures 38 through 40).

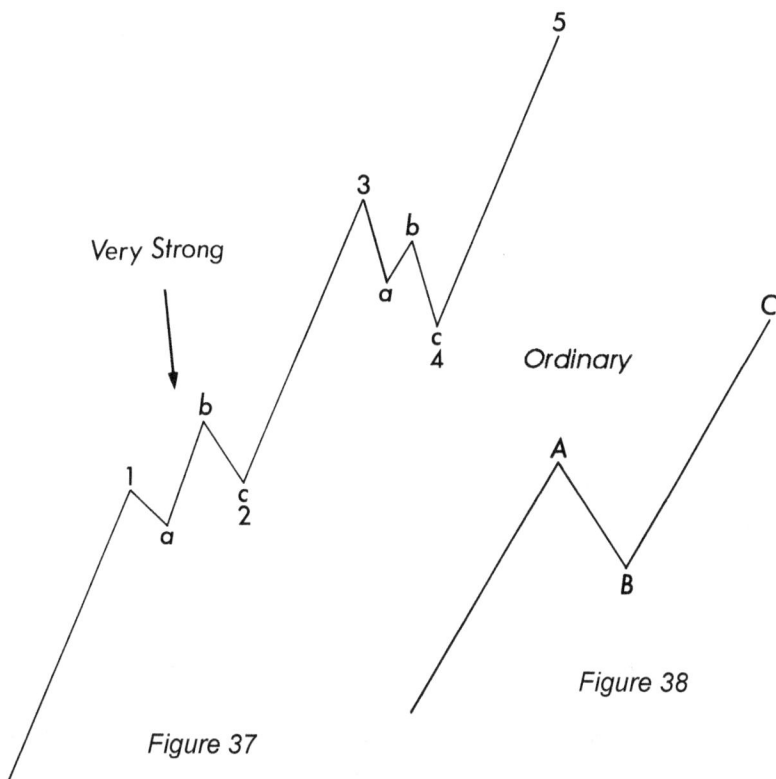

Very Strong

Ordinary

Figure 37

Figure 38

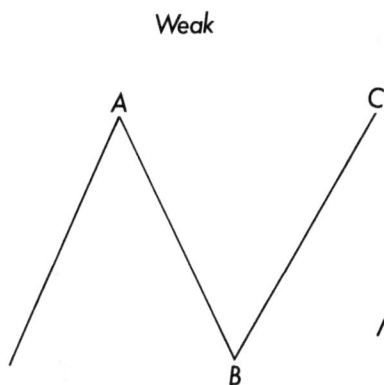

Weak

Figure 39

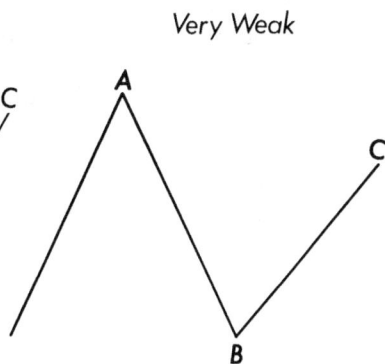

Very Weak

Figure 40

Irregular corrections in bear trends are also seen, but very rarely. Note that after a five-wave down trend, an irregular correction would appear as in Figure 41.

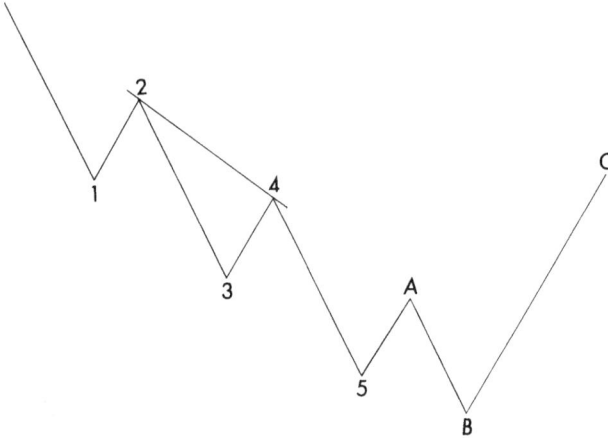

Figure 41

Failures

In the pattern shown in Figure 42, the fifth wave failed to materialize, and stock should be sold at "B." Note that there are five waves down from the top at "3," whereas a correction should be composed of three waves. The answer is that "B" is the real top from which only three waves downward were registered. That is, the decline stole two waves from the advance. Put in another way, the regular number upward is five plus the regular number down is three, total eight. In this case there were three upward and five downward, same total eight. Such patterns are rare but are a serious warning and should be acted upon immediately.

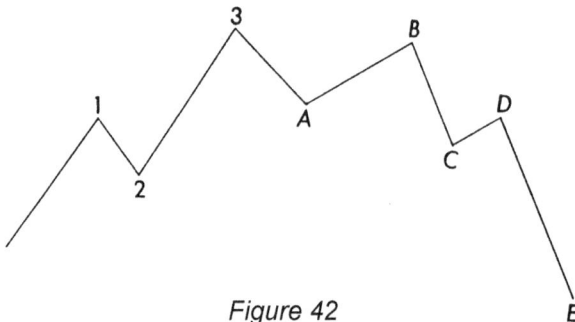

Figure 42

When the Student Is In Doubt

In the position shown in Figure 43, the trader may not know which of the following patterns will develop, i.e., an extension or an irregular correction. Volume may furnish the answer. Elsewhere it is stated that volume diminishes during the various waves of correction (zig-zags, flats, triangles), therefore if volume is extremely light in the last wave shown, then it is wave B of an irregular correction. If relatively heavy, an extension is generating.[12]

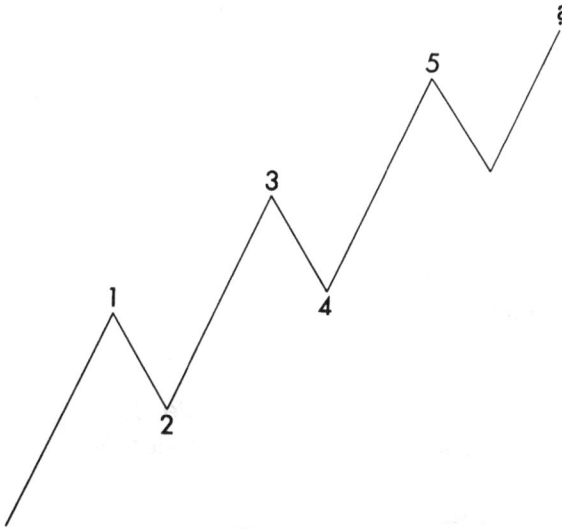

Figure 43

Triangles

Wave movements occasionally taper off to a point or broaden out from a point in the form of a triangle. These triangular formations are important since they indicate the direction the market will take at the conclusion or approximate apex of the triangle.

Triangles are of two classes — horizontal and diagonal. Horizontal triangles represent hesitation on the part of prices. At the conclusion of a horizontal triangle the market will resume the same trend — upward or downward — which it was pursuing previous to triangular hesitation. Horizontal triangles are simply hesitations and have the same significance as flats. If a zig-zag appears as wave 2, a flat or triangle will appear as wave 4 (see Figure 44).[13] If a flat or triangle occurs as wave 2, a zig-zag will appear as wave 4 (see Figure 45).[14]

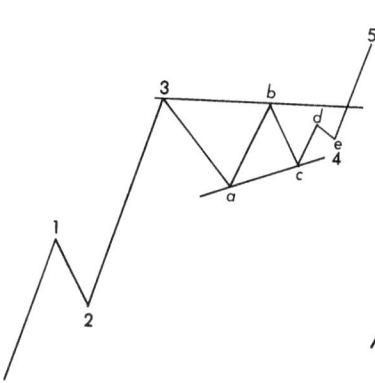

Figure 44

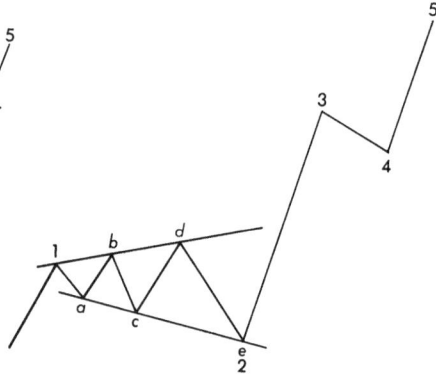

Figure 45

Examples of horizontal triangles are shown in Figure 46. They are of four types.

Ascending:
top flat, bottom ascending

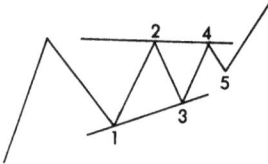

Descending:
bottom flat, top descending

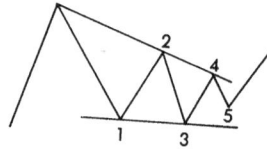

Symmetrical:
bottom ascending, top descending

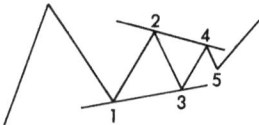

Reverse Symmetrical:
widens from start to finish

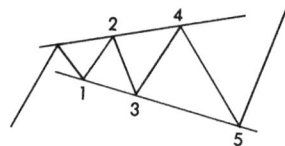

Figure 46

Examples of diagonal triangles are shown in Figure 47. They are of two types.

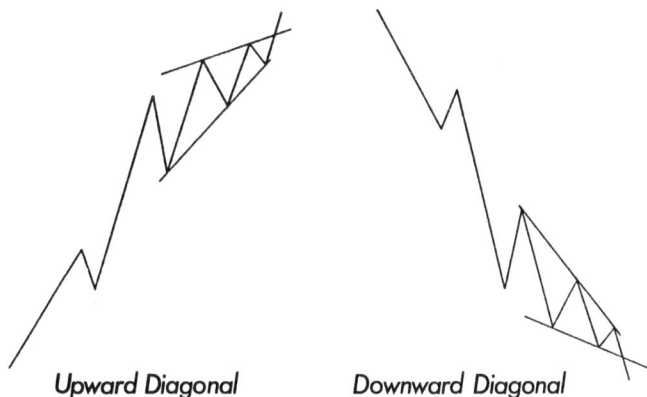

Upward Diagonal   **Downward Diagonal**

Figure 47

Triangles, whether horizontal or diagonal, as will be noted from the above illustration, contain five waves. Where there are less than five waves, the triangle falls outside the wave phenomenon, as herein discussed, and should be ignored.

The most important thing to be noted with respect to a horizontal triangle is where it begins. This is because wave number two of the triangle must be definitely fixed, and to fix wave number two it becomes necessary to identify wave number one. Wave number two is important, because when the triangle has ended the market will move from the triangle in the same direction as wave two travelled.[15] In Figure 48, the direction of wave two of the horizontal triangle is downward. At the conclusion of the fifth triangular wave, the market, which has been hesitating during the course of its downward travel M-N, will resume the decline.

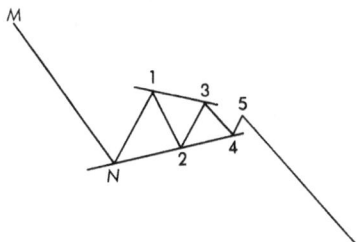

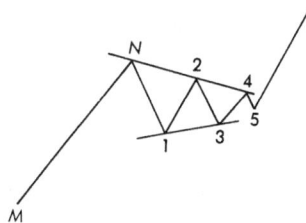

Figure 48   *Figure 49*

In Figure 49, the record of the five triangular waves is upward. The market bottomed at M and is hesitating after the upward movement M-N, prior to resuming the advance.

In Figure 50, wave two of the upward diagonal triangle is downward. The market will reverse its direction at the end of this diagonal (that is, when the fifth triangular wave has terminated) and will return to about the base of the triangle, as illustrated.

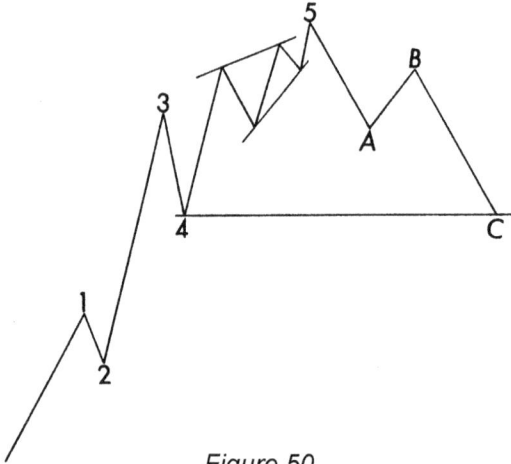

Figure 50

The fifth wave of all but reverse triangles frequently falls short of its channel or triangle line. Occasionally, however, as shown in the illustration above, the fifth wave will penetrate its triangle line.

If the last wave (the fifth Intermediate) of a Primary movement develops a triangle,[16] be prepared for a rapid reversal.

All waves in a triangle must be part of a movement in one direction. Otherwise no triangle is present, only a coincidence.

A diagonal triangle occurs only as a fifth wave; that is, it should have four waves back of it of the same degree as it will be.

When the range (weekly or daily) in a triangle embraces the entire width of the triangle, the end has about arrived. Confirmation should be required in wave number five. A throwover is not essential.

Usually triangles are quite small, and all waves are not developed in detail. For the first time, between October 1937 and February 1938, one occurred of sufficiently large proportions to demonstrate that all five waves should be composed of three Minors. Each of these five waves formed a different pattern.[17]

The Dow-Jones Industrial Average does not show this period as a triangle, but the Standard Statistics, 348 stocks, weekly range, makes a perfect picture as shown in Figure 51, a perfect triangle and the largest on record. Being a weekly range, the chart does not show the composition of each of the five waves, but another average daily range displays them as shown in Figure 66, Chapter IX.

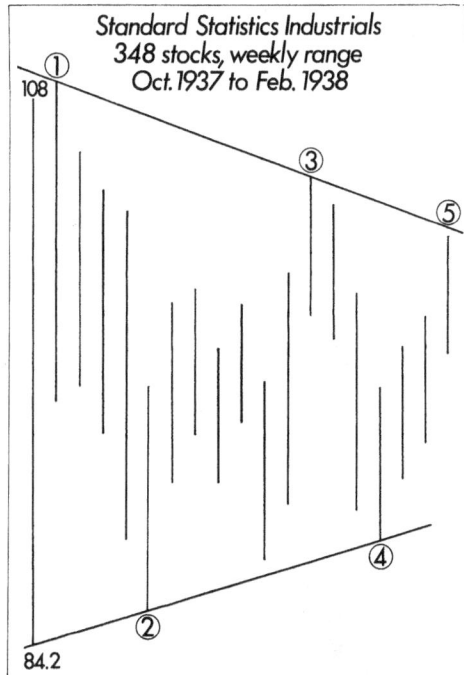

Standard Statistics Industrials
348 stocks, weekly range
Oct. 1937 to Feb. 1938

Figure 51

ENDNOTES

[1] Elliott adopted a loose form of illustration in order to make more economical use of vertical space in his books. I have changed proportions occasionally to adhere more closely to normal wave characteristics. Exceptions are the figures in the *Financial World* articles, which I left intact as Elliott had them.

[2] This type of comment helps moderate charges of Elliott's dogmatism.

[3] Unless they are triangles. Later Elliott discovered double threes and triple threes. These latter variations, along with double zigzags, were later added in *Nature's Law*.

[4] See Endnote 2 above.

[5] Despite Elliott's contention, experience shows that wave three is most often the extended wave. Elliott's experience with the 1921-1929 and 1932-1937 bull markets, both of which contained extended fifth waves, surely influenced his thinking on this point.

[6] True, as far as I can tell. There are some guidelines, as Frost and I point out in our book, but no rules. See Endnote 5 in Chapter IX of the *Financial World Articles* and the corresponding text.

[7] Extensions are retraced twice only if the extension occurs in the fifth impulse wave. Elliott clarifies this point in Chapter VI of *Nature's Law*.

[8] Usually, although not necessarily. An irregular correction will sometimes hold above the beginning of the fifth wave of the preceding bull market. See *Elliott Wave Principle*.

[9] This example is not a particularly good one. The extension in the fifth wave of the 1921-1928 rise was not retraced the first time (that is, to the "beginning of the extension") by wave A as Elliott counts it, since wave A was extremely short. Wave C as Elliott counts it *did* retrace much of the fifth wave twice, once in the October 1929 crash and again in the 1930 rally. A more straightforward count labeling the bottom of the October 1929 crash as "A" (an irregular a-b-c from the orthodox top) and the 1930 rally as "B" (an inverted zigzag) would better satisfy the double retracement rule.

[10] The orthodox end of a "movement" in the direction of the main trend is the terminal point of the fifth wave of a five-wave sequence. What Elliott appears to be saying here is that when an extension occurs in the fifth wave up, an irregular top will carry the market into new high ground, thereby extending the "movement" beyond the orthodox top of the fifth wave.

[11] Elliott's use of "x5" to notate an extended wave is useful. Few students have employed it.   ı

[12] This statement is true for small degrees but not true for waves of higher than Intermediate degree. The 1961-62 rally occurred on extremely high volume and was a "B" wave. The 1930 rally, a corrective wave advance, occurred on volume higher than that at the peak in 1929.

[13] This rule is part of what was later dubbed the rule of alternation (which is in fact a guideline, as it holds in the vast majority of impulses but not all of them).

[14] Elliott later modified his rules to indicate that a triangle always precedes the final impulse wave in a sequence. Thus, a triangle can never occur as wave two in a five-wave sequence, only as wave four (or as wave B in an A-B-C correction).

[15] This discussion is superfluous if one understands the wave position of the formation.

[16] That is, a diagonal triangle.

[17] A very important point. This is another facet of the rule of alternation.

VI

SPEED, VOLUME AND CHARTING[1]

High speed by the market in one direction almost invariably produces a corresponding high speed in the reversal, as for example, the midsummer 1932 advance covered forty points (Dow-Jones Industrial Average) or 100% in nine weeks. This was equal to 4 1/2 points per week. Note the decreasing speed of advances from 1932 to 1937 in Figure 52.

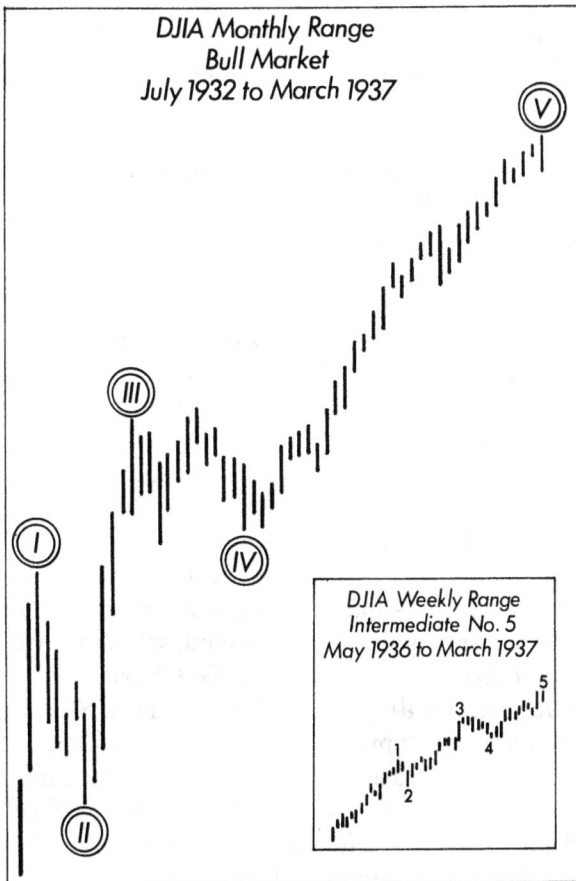

Figure 52

In fast markets like the advance of 1932 and 1933, it is essential to observe the daily as well as the weekly ranges, otherwise characteristics of importance may be hidden, such as for example, triangles and extensions.

In a subsequent heading entitled "Charting," a reference is made to "lines." In the average market, slow speed and the exclusive use of daily range may conceal important patterns. Take, for example, the period from the last week of January to the first week in June 1904, five months, during which the maximum range of daily closings (Dow-Jones Industrial Average) was only 4.09 points (50.50 - 46.41). On the daily chart, the appearance is an uninteresting line, but when condensed into a weekly range chart a perfect triangle is disclosed, with the second wave pointing upward, thus assuring the trader that the market would move upward following the end of the triangle.

Volume

Volume decreases gradually from the beginning to the end of horizontal triangles, flats and other types of corrections. Volume often helps to clarify the character of a movement. However, when markets are abnormally "thin," the usual volume signals are sometimes deceptive.

Characteristics of volume are very impressive when considered in conjunction with the five wave cycle. For example, during an advance or a decline of some importance, volume will increase during wave number one, diminish during number two, increase during number three, decrease during number four, and increase during number five. Immediately following number five, volume should be fairly well maintained, with little, if any, further progress in price, indicating reversal.

Herein reference is made to volume and ratio. "Volume" is the actual number of shares transferred, whereas "ratio" is the ratio of volume to listed shares on the New York Stock Exchange.

In its bulletin for July 1938, the New York Stock Exchange noted in chart form some interesting comparisons of volume and ratio. An upward ratio Cycle started in 1914, completed five Primaries, ending in 1929. Then began a downward Cycle, ending June 18, 1938 (see Figure 53). Precisely the same phenomenon occurred in the price of seats on the New York Stock Exchange (see Figures 54 and 55).

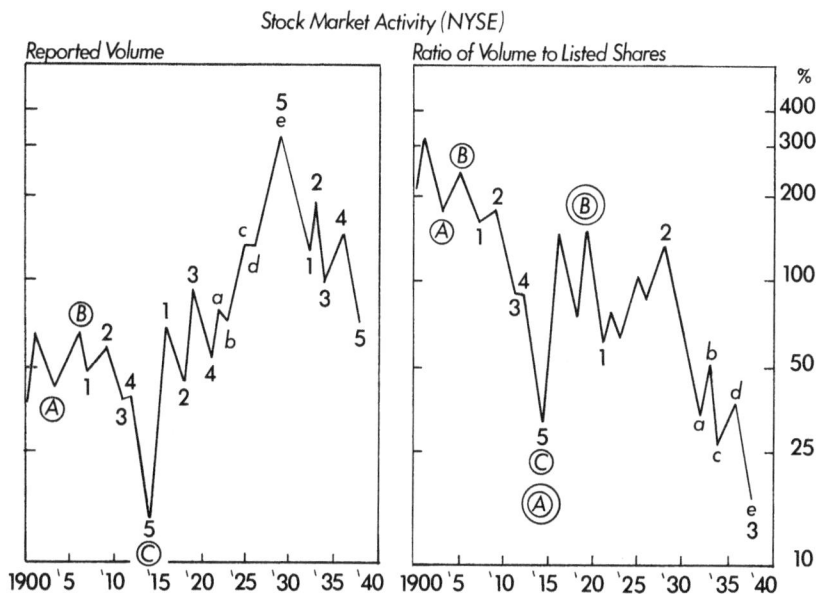

Stock Market Activity (NYSE)

Figure 53

The ratio waves are not easy to follow in minor detail for the reason that volume varies according to the momentary direction of the market. However, as fluctuations in stock exchange seats are not affected by the momentary direction of the market, these become a useful guide to the ratio scale. See Chapter X, "The Wave Principle in Other Fields."

According to the bulletins of the New York Stock Exchange, page 11, the ratio for May 1928 was 12.48%, and the ratio for May 1938 was 0.98%. I calculate that the ratio for the first 18 days of June 1938 was 0.65%. On Saturday, June 18, 1938, actual volume was 104,000 shares, equivalent to say 200,000 shares for a five-hour session. For several weeks previous to June 18th, volume was so low that long intervals frequently occurred between sales of important stocks in the averages, with the result that occasionally Sub-Minuette waves failed to appear in the hourly waves, or registered when they should not. Hourly volume was occasionally deceptive for the same reason. Fortunately such low volume should not recur for some twenty years.

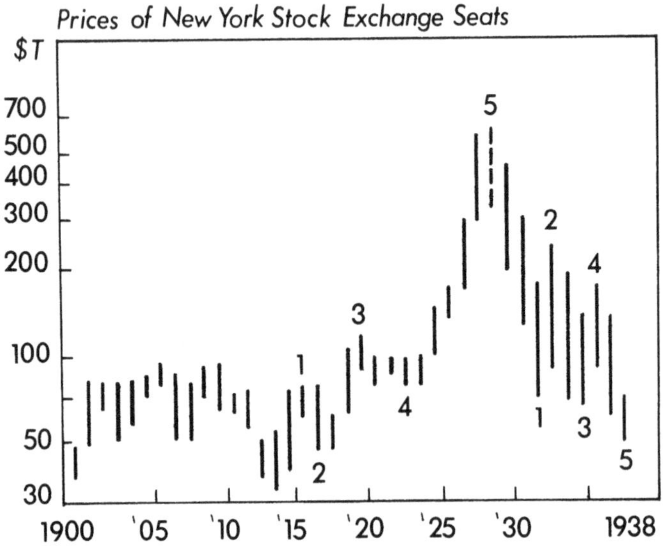

Prices of New York Stock Exchange Seats

Figure 54

On the first page of its monthly bulletin for November 1937, the New York Stock Exchange noted volume ratio to price change of the period between August 14th and October 1937, and seven other periods of equal duration. I have reduced the comparison to percentage and find that the 1937 period was, by far, the most remarkable of all.

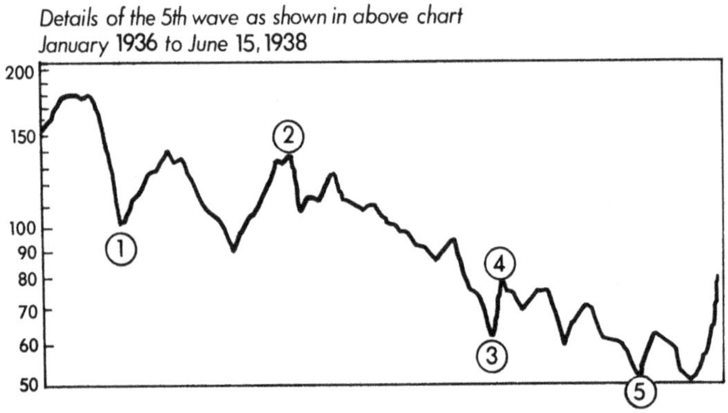

Details of the 5th wave as shown in above chart
January 1936 to June 15, 1938

Figure 55

Data obtained from the Public Relations Department relative to money value of transactions are shown in Figure 56.

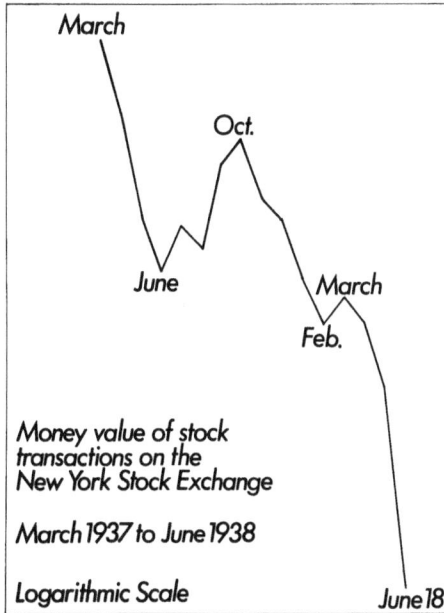

Figure 56

The following outline of comparisons is interesting:

Recent bear market

Top, March 10, 1937:	195.59
Bottom, March 31, 1938:	97.46
Decline:	98.13 points, or 50.1%.
Time:	1 year, 3 weeks.

Money value of stock transactions on the N.Y.S.E.

March 1937:	$2,612,000,000
May 1938:	499,000,000
June 1938 (est.):	187,000,000
Decline:	92.9%.
Time:	1 year, 4 months.

Price-Volume Ratio for 64-Day Periods (which was the duration of decline from August 14th to October 19, 1937. Comparisons of this with other periods is as follows:)

August 14 - October 19, 1937:   *22.2%.*
March-May 1937:   *10.9%.*
Late 1929:   *11.1%.*
February-April 1934:   *6.5%.*
Other periods: *2.1%* to *1.0%.*

New York Stock Exchange Seats
Top, 1929: $625,000
Bottom, June 15, 1938:   51,000
Decline: 92%.
Time: 9 years.

Volume decline from March 1937 to June 1938 was 87.5%.

ENDNOTES

[1] Based on the abrupt changes in organizational style (and other small points, such as spelling), I conclude that Elliott wrote and inserted Chapters VI, VII and IX after Collins' manuscript was completed.

VII

MISCELLANEOUS NOTES: CHARTING

1) Tops of big moves scatter or fan out in different groups and stocks, whereas bottoms of big moves consolidate; that is, different groups and stocks tend to establish lows simultaneously. During July 1932, for instance, bonds, stocks, production, insurance sales, and many other major spheres of human activity bottomed together (see Figures 69 through 79, Chapter X). That, of course, was a bottom to wave two[1] of the Grand Supercycle, and therefore the phenomenon was naturally drastically emphasized.

2) When, in the course of a move, the numbering becomes confused, the relative size of waves may help to distinguish one degree of movement from another. The use of the exposed contacts (that is, channeling them) should help to clarify the movement.

3) Always connect or channel two exposed contacts.

4) Always await development of point number four and the drawing of the final channel before determining culmination of the move (that is, the approximate point where wave five should end).

5) Width of channels must be preserved in all movements of the same category, or, stated in other words, the width of a channel of the same movement must be preserved,[2] except that number five may not reach the top of the channel.

6) The larger the category, the more probability of a throwover.

7) In channeling: on an advance, the base line is below; on a decline, above.

8) Strength for the main move is indicated when the base line is hugged. See the movement from January 1927 to June 1928 in Figure 14 as one illustration.

9) In order to properly visualize the wave phenomenon in its larger aspects, certain methods of charting are essential, as follows:

— Weekly range of the daily extreme high and low, on logarithmic scale, preferably exaggerated two or three times the usual practice.

— One sheet for each complete advance of five primaries, and its correction.

10) These recommendations apply to the three principal averages (Industrial, Rail, Utility), to small groups and individual stocks. The daily range of the three averages, of groups and of individual stocks in which the investor may be interested, should also be maintained, and ordinary arithmetic scale is satisfactory.

11) There are three important reasons why weekly range charts are necessary:

— Only by this method is it possible to observe the movement over a sufficient historical background in order to judge the nature of the several degrees of waves, especially the larger.

— So-called "lines" are converted into patterns of flats or triangles, composed of three or five waves, respectively, useful in determining or confirming future movements.

— Any deceptions of the small daily range are obviated.

12) Always place the particular movement under supervision, whether it be a Minute, Minor, Intermediate, Primary, or even greater degree, on one chart. Otherwise the numbering of waves, their relative magnitude, and the channeling of movements become distorted and confused.

13) The best time measures for Primary and lesser movements are weekly, daily and hourly charts. Never be guided entirely by any one of these three important time measures, but keep them all in mind in analyzing wave numbers. In fast markets the hourly and daily movements are the best guides; in slow markets, the daily and weekly.

14) For the first time since 1928, stocks, bonds and volume ratio got into gear June 18, 1938. Only with a knowledge of the Wave Principle may these phenomena be observed and followed.

15) Some items appear to have declined in five waves. In such cases, an "irregular" top occurred and wave "C" thereof was composed of five waves, as explained under the title "Corrections."

16) In some cases it is impossible to obtain figures for charting, such as real estate, for the reason that there is no central market; the items are not standardized, and prices specified in transfers are often "nominal." The solution is found in "foreclosed mortgages." Reliable figures of these are available. When foreclosures are at a bottom, real estate is at a top, and vice versa.

17) In other cases, while reliable figures are available, it is difficult to define the minor degrees. An example is volume, which fluctuates in minor degree with the momentary direction of the market. The solution is found in prices of New York Stock Exchange seats.[3]

18) Seasonal fluctuations present difficulties which may be overcome by charting a ten year average of weeks, months or quarters, using same as a ratio basis. For example, weekly statistics of car loadings are available, and the ratio of the current week to the ten year average may be charted, thus disclosing the facts needed on which to base an interpretation under the Wave Principle.

19) When two items, which do not always travel in harmony, unite occasionally, unusual disturbance may take place, such as that described under the title "Volume."

20) Not all stocks perform harmoniously. While the principal averages topped on March 10, 1937, the several Standard Statistics groups commenced to top in November 1936, increased to the maximum number in March, then gradually decreased until May. On the other hand, stocks tend to bottom simultaneously.

ENDNOTES

[1] Four, actually.

[2] I.e., "Keep the channel lines parallel."

[3] This rather cryptic assertion is better stated in Chapter VI. Even so, since seat prices are not actively traded enough to register in "minor degree," it is difficult to see how their waves could help clarify the short term trend.

VIII

APPLYING THE WAVE PRINCIPLE

As stated in a previous chapter, the investor and speculator are greatly concerned with the termination of a fifth wave, for this marks the point at which an entire movement is to be corrected by a reversal. Stock market moves of high degree, particularly intermediate movements running over a number of months and primary movements running over a number of years, will witness, at termination, considerable price correction, and the terminal points thus call for disposition of long positions. It is likewise important that terminal points of corrections be identified, as there are price areas where long positions can most profitably be re-established.

A first consideration of an operator in stocks is to determine over what type of movement he wishes to carry a long position in stocks. Many investors prefer to operate through a Primary movement, and it is this type of movement which will be discussed here, although the same principles that apply to this movement will likewise apply to a movement of lesser degree or greater degree.

Let us assume that the investor has correctly established a long position in June 1921. From his study of the Grand Super Cycle (see Figure 12) he sees that the market started as a Super Cycle movement in 1857 and that Cycle movements one, two, three and four of the entire Super Cycle movement have been completed. The fifth Cycle movement started in 1896 and is nearly completed, in that four Primary waves have elapsed from 1896 to 1921. Primary movement number five is just commencing. It will be made up of five Intermediate movements. Intermediate movement number five will not only terminate the full Primary movement, but it will also terminate a full Cycle and a full Super Cycle. The period ahead, in other words, promises to be quite interesting.

Based upon his study of Primary movements one and three preceding the fifth one now getting under way, the investor has some gauge as to the extent and length of the movement, although, as previously mentioned, these are but rough guides due to modifying events which serve to differentiate one wave of a certain degree from another wave of the same degree. A more certain guide, however, can be derived from channelling. The Super Cycle running from 1857 has completed four waves of lesser degree (Cycle movements), and thus by connecting exposed contacts of wave terminals two and four of the Super Cycle and drawing a parallel line across the terminal point of wave three, an upper parallel is established, about which line the fifth Cycle, or that running from 1896, should end, thus completing wave five of the Super Cycle movement. Similarly, the Cycle movement from 1896 has completed four waves (Primary movements) so that, as for the Super Cycle, it can be given its final upper channel line about which the fifth Primary movement now under way should terminate.

At this point the investor, whose set purpose is to hold stocks purchased in June 1921 until the Primary movement then starting has terminated, observes those rules which will help him in selling out. Some of these rules have been previously stated; others are first presented at this time.

1) The Primary movement will be made up of five Intermediate waves. Selling is not to be considered until four Intermediate waves have been witnessed, and the fifth is under way.

2) When the fourth Intermediate wave has terminated, and the fifth gets under way, it will be composed of five lesser degree or Minor waves, and selling is not to be considered until the fifth Minor wave is under way.

3) When the fourth Minor wave of the fifth Intermediate wave has terminated, and the fifth Minor wave gets under way, it will not terminate until five Minute waves have been witnessed, and selling is not to be considered ahead of the fifth Minute wave.

4) It is probable that the fifth Minute wave of the fifth Minor wave of the fifth Intermediate wave will also be made up, based upon hourly averages, of five Minuette waves, the fifth of which waves will likewise be composed of five Sub-Minuette waves. To reach the extreme top of the Primary wave starting in June 1921, therefore, it will not be necessary to liquidate holdings until the fifth Sub-Minuette wave of the fifth Minuette wave, of the fifth Minute wave, of the fifth Minor wave, of the fifth Intermediate wave has terminated.

5) The fifth waves of a Super Cycle movement, of a Cycle movement and of a Primary movement generally penetrate or "throw-over" the upper channel line established for the

termination limit of each such movement. Upper channel lines (see earlier paragraphs) have been established for the termination limit of the fifth Super Cycle wave and the fifth Cycle wave. Since the Primary movement starting in June 1921 will end a Cycle as well as a Super Cycle movement (see Figure 14), it may be anticipated that such Primary movement will not have ended until it has carried prices (on a logarithmic scale) above the upper channel lines of the Super Cycle and the Cycle. Likewise, the fifth Intermediate movement of the existing Primary — an Intermediate movement that is yet ahead — should penetrate or throw-over the upper channel line established for it.

6) Terminal points of the fifth wave of Super Cycle, Cycle, and Primary movements are usually accompanied by heavy volume of trading relative to prior waves of each such movement. Intense volume should therefore be witnessed during and near the peak of the fifth Intermediate wave of the Primary movement now getting under way.

With the above general rules in mind, the investor lets the market unfold, plotting its weekly and monthly movement in order to keep abreast of each Intermediate move as it occurs. The weekly movement is given in Figures 57 through 61. Intermediate wave one terminates in March 1923. It is made up of five Minor swings, as a glance at Figure 57 will indicate. There follows Intermediate wave two made up, as should be the case for even numbered or corrective movements, of three waves. Intermediate wave three runs to November 1925. It is succeeded by the usual three wave correction.[1]

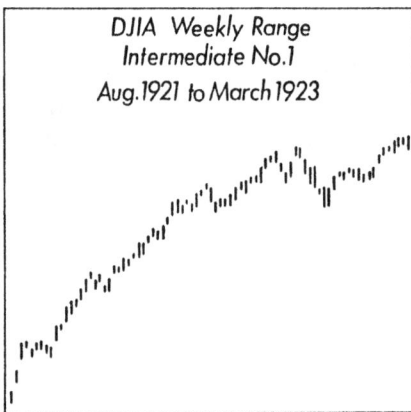

Figure 57

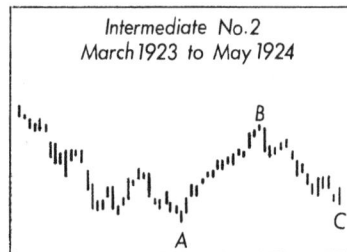

Figure 58

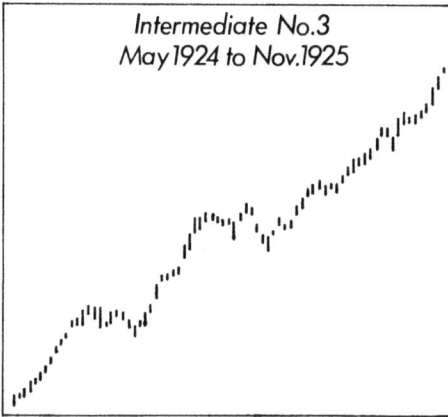

Figure 59

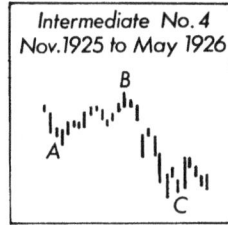

Figure 60

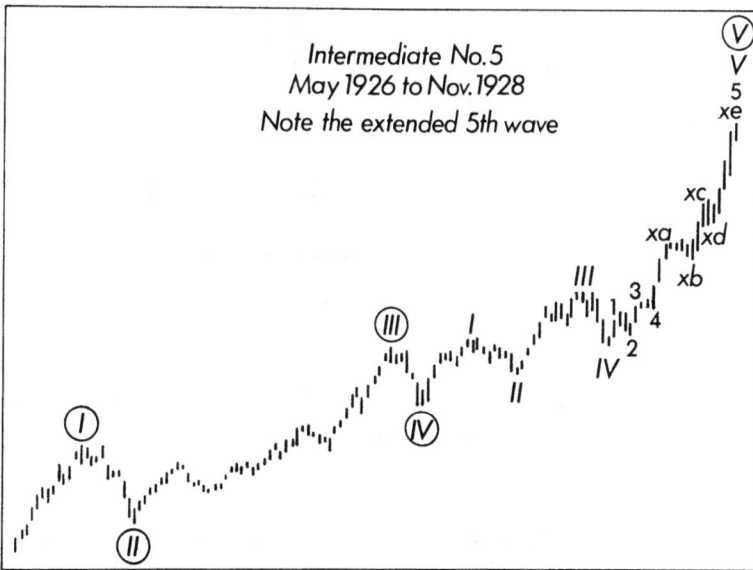

Figure 61

ENDNOTES

[1] I.e., Intermediate wave four. The abrupt termination of this discussion leads me to believe that a page was omitted from the monograph as published. In any case, the last two pages of Chapter IV can serve to complete the discussion.

IX

RARITIES IN THE 1937-1938 BEAR MARKET

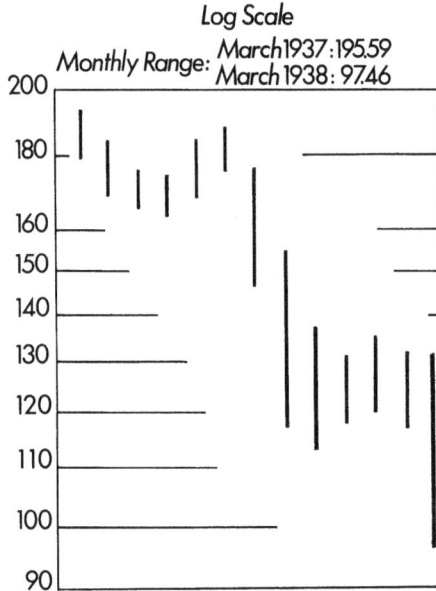

Figure 62

The 1937-1938 Bear Market (see Figures 62 and 63) provided a number of novelties, for example:

Parallelogram

August 4, 1937, at 187.31, was the "orthodox" top of a rally.1 Then followed a dip of three waves and an advance of three waves to 190.38, August 14th. Between these two dates waves A and B of an irregular correction were formed (see Figure 64). Wave C was very rapid and long, down to 115.8[2] on October 18th, and formed a perfect parallelogram. It has no particular significance for that reason. The speed and extent were spectacular, and indicated by the "irregular" top, the same as that of 1928/1929/1932 (see Figure 65).

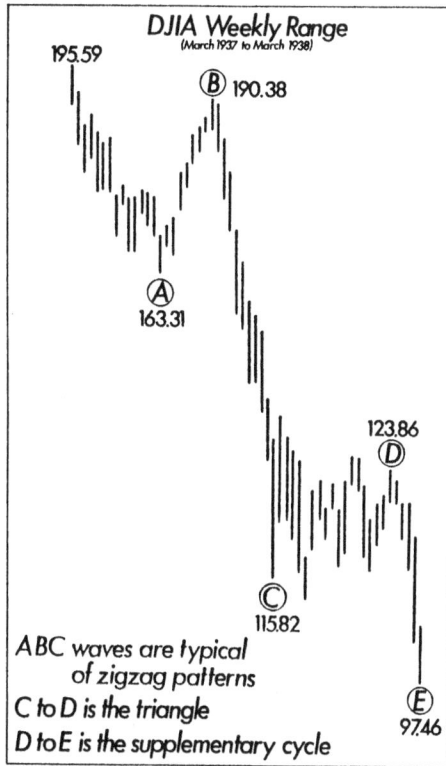

DJIA Weekly Range
(March 1937 to March 1938)

195.59

Ⓑ 190.38

Ⓐ
163.31

123.86
Ⓓ

Ⓒ
115.82

ABC waves are typical
of zigzag patterns
C to D is the triangle
D to E is the supplementary cycle

Ⓔ
97.46

Figure 63

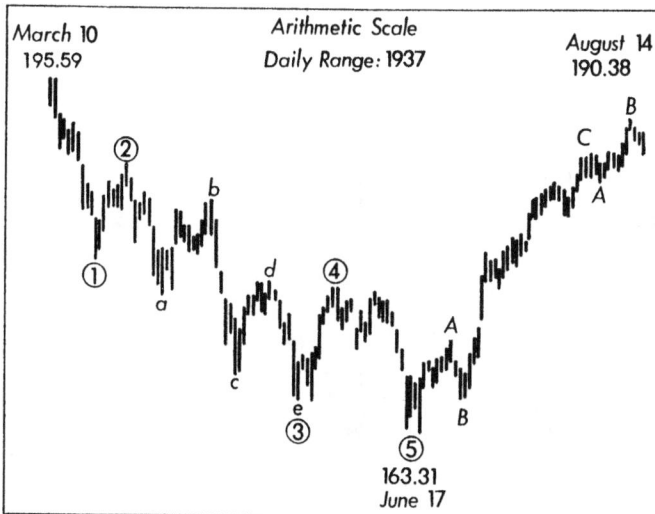

March 10
195.59

Arithmetic Scale
Daily Range: 1937

August 14
190.38

②

①

b

a

d

c

e

③

④

⑤
163.31
June 17

A

B

A

B

C

Figure 64

Figure 65 embodies the greatest number of interesting features known to the author. Note the parallelogram pattern. The "irregular" top, OT to B, forecasts a severe decline. The extension xa to xe forecasts an immediate retracement in three waves to xb and eventually lower prices than xe. The first retracement was composed of three waves as shown in Figure 66, which confirms lower levels. The zig-zag A-B-C in Figure 64 indicates that the correction subsequent to C in Figure 65 will be a flat or triangle. The triangle shown in Figure 51 reconfirms lower levels as per Figure 66, February to March 1938.

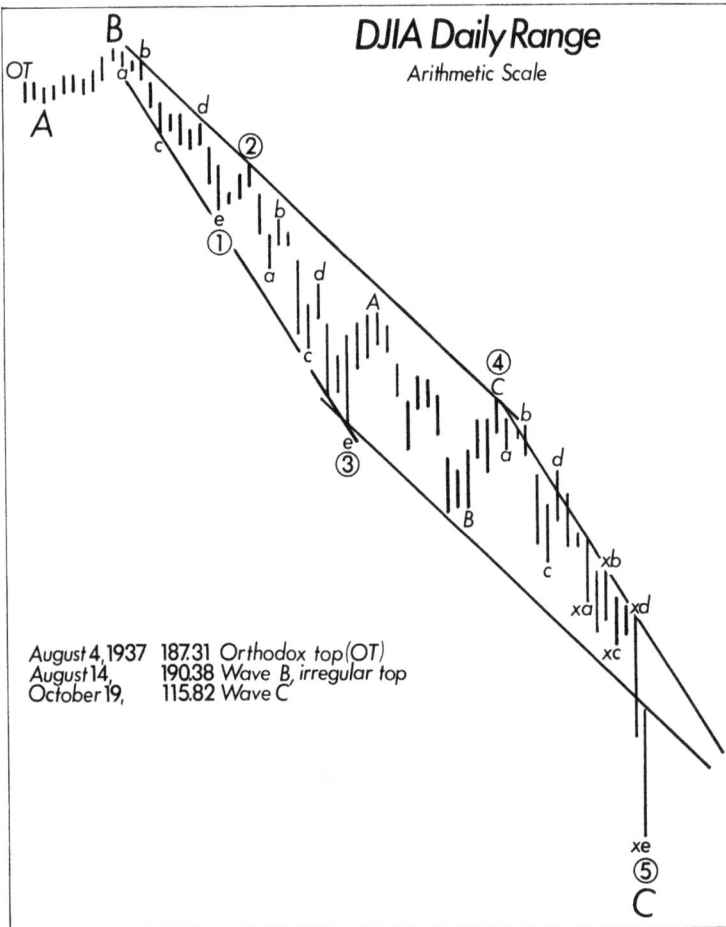

Figure 65

Half Moon[2]

This is a name given to the pattern which developed between February 23 and March 31, 1938, 132 to 97. It curved downward and at bottom was almost perpendicular (see Figures 66 and 67).

The extension down to 115.82 (refer to Figure 65) forecast this lower level. The first advance, from 115.82, being composed of three waves, confirmed. The triangle reconfirmed.

The same pattern occurred in April 1936, 163 to 141. Both were retracements of extensions. On account of the high speed it is necessary to refer to the hourly record, especially during the latter half.

From September to November 1929, wave 1 from 381 to 195 was extended and immediately retraced in 1930. No extensions appeared in waves 3 or 5 because one occurred in wave 1 as just described (see Figure 19, arithmetic scale). If the extension had

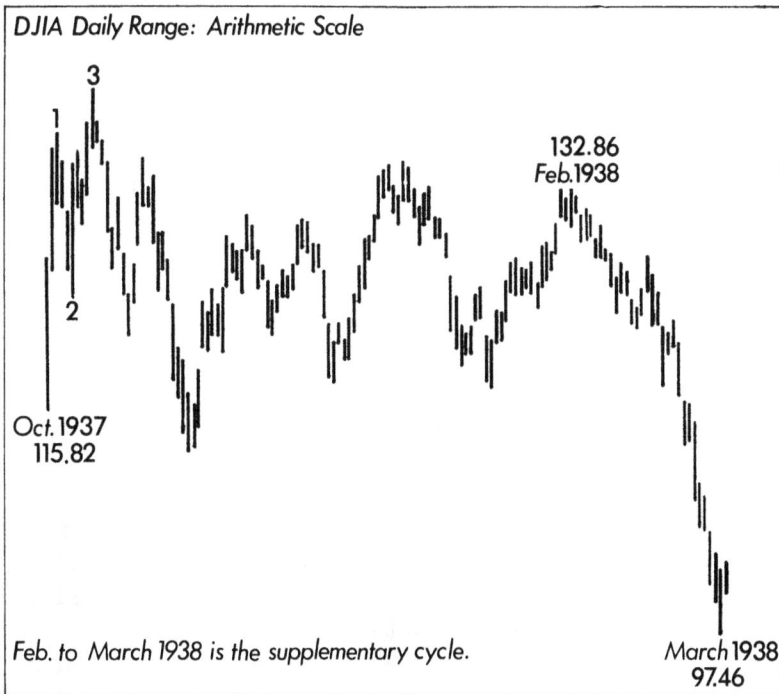

DJIA Daily Range: Arithmetic Scale

3

1

132.86
Feb.1938

2

Oct. 1937
115.82

Feb. to March 1938 is the supplementary cycle.   March 1938
97.46

Figure 66

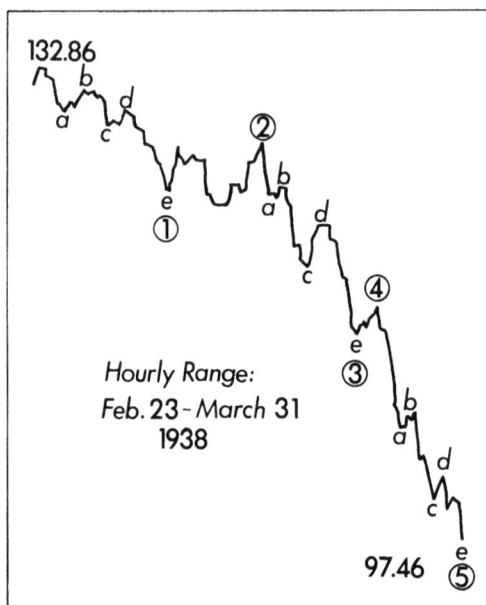

Figure 67

occurred in wave 5 instead of wave 1 during 1932, the appearance of the decline from September 1929 to July 1932 would have been the same as the "half moon" of February-March 1938.

Supplementary Cycles[3]

Insofar as records disclose, 1938 witnessed the first Industrial Supplementary Cycle (see Figures 66 and 67), February 23 to March 31, 1938, 132 to 98. Heretofore termination of wave "C" with five waves has been the end of major corrections, as in 1932.[4] This same phenomenon occurred in the Rails and Utilities between December 1934 and March 1935.

The movement from 97.46 to 121.54 (see Figure 68) is composed of five waves and is the first upward five wave pattern of this degree since March 1937 and confirms that 97.46 of March 31 was the bottom of wave A of the bear market.[5]

The 106.44 level of May 27 is the end of a typical flat correction from 121.54.

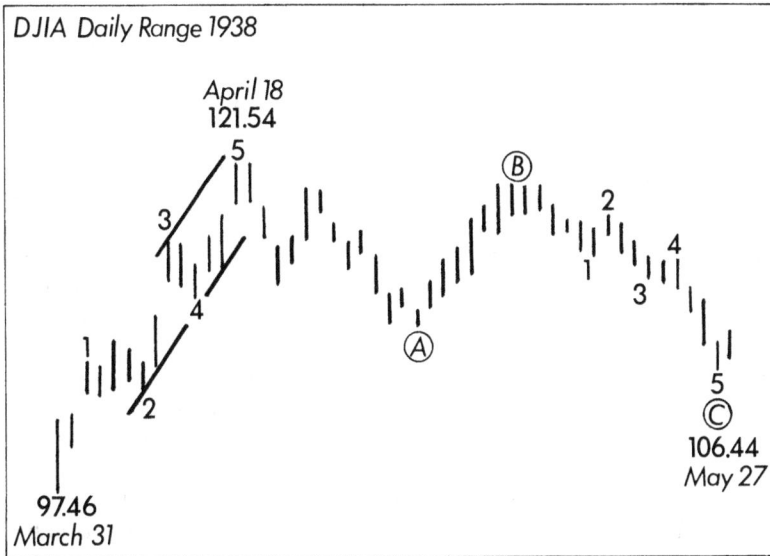

DJIA Daily Range 1938

April 18
121.54

97.46
March 31

106.44
May 27

Figure 68

ENDNOTES

¹ Elliott should have interpreted this entire picture differently.
The supposed waves A and B at the upper right of Figure 64 are way
out of proportion to the huge C that follows. Wave C as he labels it
is actually wave three of the five-wave decline that he labels wave Ⓒ
in Figure 63. The orthodox top of wave two is on August 14 at 190.38
and is followed by five waves down for wave three, as it should be. A
correct count for Figure 64 would be as follows: Where Elliott has a 1,
put 1; where he has b, put 2, completing an irregular correction that
subdivides perfectly; where he has c, put 3; where he has d, put 4;
where he has ③, put 5. Then an irregular correction upward follows:
where he has ④, put A; where he has ⑤, put B; then a C can be placed
at the August 14 high on the top of a clear nine-wave advance (five
waves with extension).

² These comments are important in predicting the speed of
corrections. Unfortunately Elliott never expanded on these thoughts
in later writings.

³ Elliott's use of this term is confusing initially. He doesn't define
it and fails to illustrate his thoughts completely. What he is saying
is that where he expected an A-B-C bear market, he got five waves
down instead. His "supplementary cycle" is merely the fifth wave of

a five-wave count, whereas at the time of writing he felt that it was somehow an additional decline following an A-B-C correction.

⁴ The 1937-1938 decline forms a clear five-wave pattern (see Figure 63), which completes only wave Ⓐ of the Ⓐ-Ⓑ-Ⓒ bear market of 1937-1942. While this fact seems to elude Elliott in these paragraphs, other sentences clearly indicate otherwise. In two instances (the first page of the book, and the final sentences in this chapter, which were originally placed with Figure 68), he makes it clear that he recognizes the correct interpretation. It appears that he is actually giving two different interpretations of the 1937-38 bear market in this book. Perhaps he recognized the correct interpretation as the book was going to press and made some quick references to his new thoughts on the first and final pages. On the other hand, perhaps he had the correct interpretation at the time of writing but inadvertently included his previous incorrect notes when he inserted Chapter IX, describing additional formations, into Collins' manuscript.

⁵ In nearly the last words of the book, Elliott correctly concludes that the March 31, 1938 low was only wave A of a large A-B-C bear market. This interpretation properly forecasts the lower low in 1942.

X

THE WAVE PRINCIPLE IN OTHER FIELDS

For years the word "cycle" has been in common use, but always in a rather loose manner implying merely a broad upward and downward movement. Thus, as concerns the course of trade in the United States, some economists refer to the period 1921-1932 as a completed cycle; others say that the period contained three cycles of lesser or greater intensity — the movement from early 1921 to mid-1924, from 1924 to late 1927, and from 1927 to mid-1932. In general, the cycle has been recognized in a rough way, largely for the reason that, in its extreme aspects, it necessarily intrudes on our plans and opinions, but the underlying law of the cycle has eluded the observer.

This treatise, using the stock market as but one illustration, has dealt with the law of the cycle, and in the disclosure has shown how one cycle becomes but the starting point of another, or larger, movement that, itself, is a part of and subject to the same law as the lesser movement. This is entirely consonant with every study of Nature, for we know that She has ever unfolded in an upward direction, but always in an orderly progression. Underlying this progression, however, in whatever field, is a fixed and controlling principle, or the master rule under which Nature works. It has been the purpose of this volume, first to present the law and then to show its practical application in one of the most baffling fields of analytical research.

Merely as cursory examples of the operation of the Wave Principle in other fields, we have presented some graphs herein, chosen at random, which readily illustrate that the law is at work wherever motion exists (see charts 69 through 78). It is recommended that this subject be given further attention by students in fields of activity outside the stock market, as it should simplify and clarify their particular work.

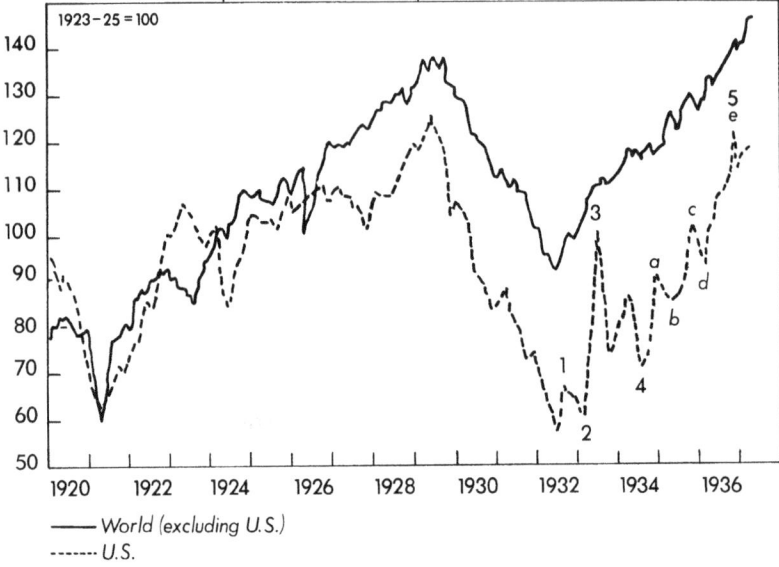

Figure 69

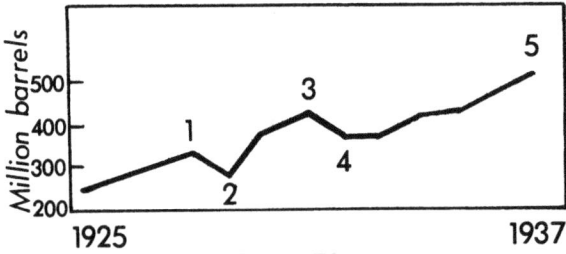

Figure 70

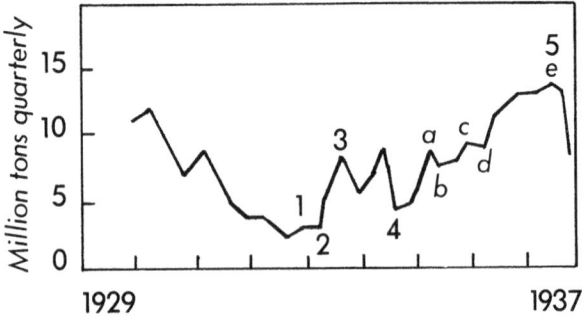

Figure 71

Prices of farm products (Bureau of Labor)

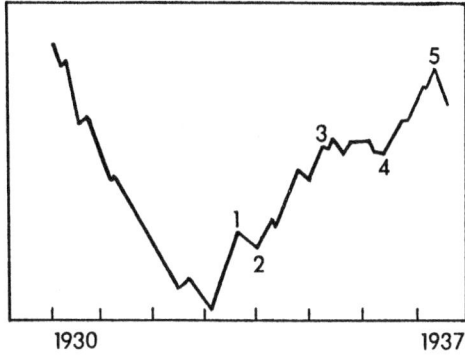

Figure 72

New paid – for life insurance

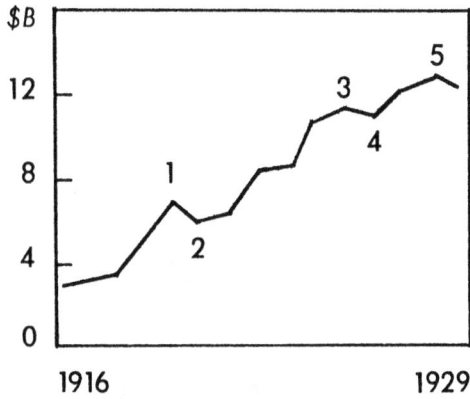

Figure 73

Population movements
from farms to cities

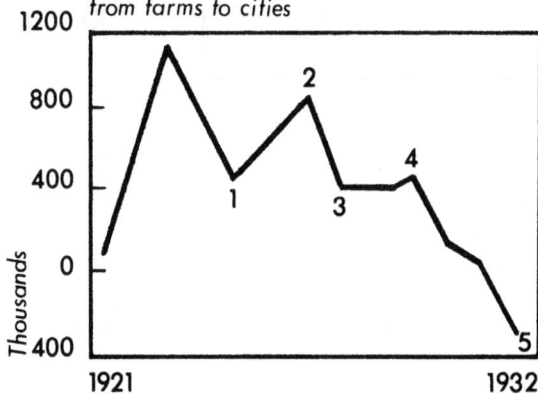

Figure 74

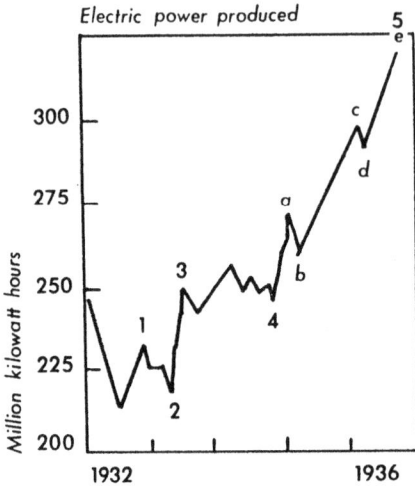

Figure 75

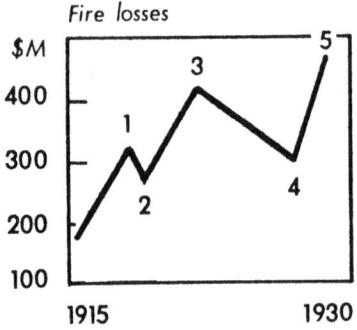

Figure 76

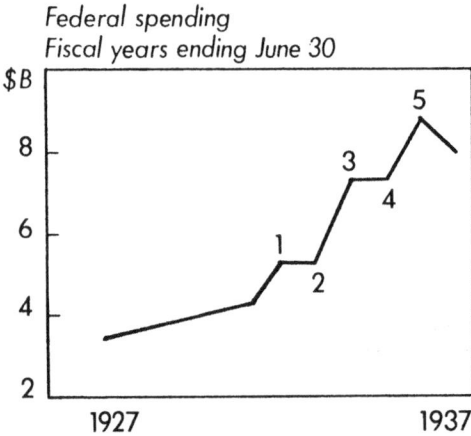

Figure 77

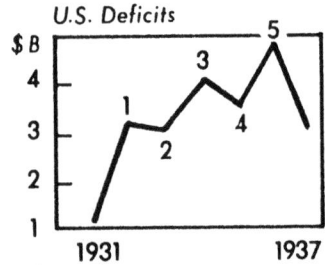

Figure 78

By no means do cycles of different items top and bottom together. Two or more may top together but bottom on widely different dates, or vice versa. A few items are noted below:

	Orthodox Tops	*Bottoms*
Stocks	1928 (not 1929)	1932
Bonds	1928	1932
Production Activity	1920	1933
Commodities	1920	1932/33
Real Estate	1923	1933
Volume Ratio	1928	June 18, 1938
N.Y.S.E. Seats	1928	June 15, 1938

After bottoming in 1932, bonds made an orthodox top in April 1934, at which time stocks would probably have topped likewise but for the N.R.A.[1] Following the orthodox top in 1934, bonds described an immense "irregular" correction with wave "B" topping in December 1936, then bottoming in wave "C" with stocks in March 1938.

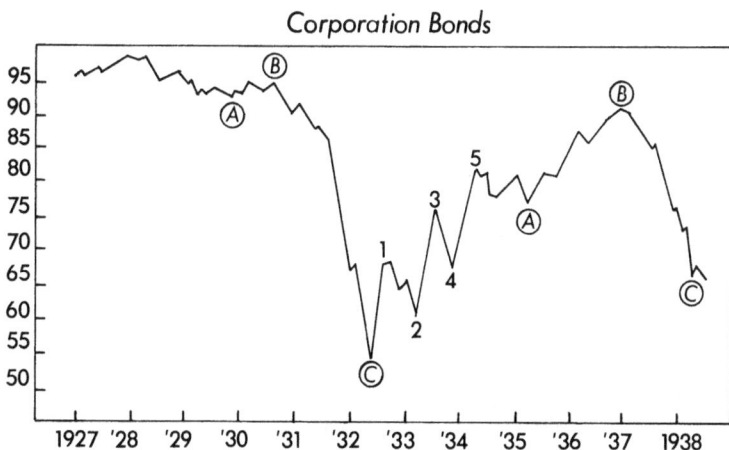

Figure 79

ENDNOTES

[1] N.R.A. refers to the National Industrial Recovery Act, enacted in 1933.

THE FINANCIAL WORLD ARTICLES

ANNOUNCING "THE WAVE PRINCIPLE"

A few months ago Mr. R.N. Elliott presented to us for consideration the results of his studies which led to the discovery of a phenomenon in human activity which may be observed most readily in stock market cycles. Believing that our readers should be informed of new developments in the art of interpretation of stock market movements, we have arranged with him to prepare a series of articles on the principle which he has discovered, the first of which will appear in the next issue of The Financial World. Many years of Mr. Elliott's career were spent in Latin America, where he served as an accountant and in other capacities in the railroading profession, and in 1927 he retired to Los Angeles, California. At that time the stock market attracted his attention. He studied economics and many "systems," charts and theories of market interpretation and forecasting. Expressions current then as now, such as "resistance levels," "double bottoms," "head and shoulders," "trend lines," etc., were examined, but the significance of their applications was found to be limited. However, the possible implications of the word "cycle," which was applied rather vaguely in stock market studies, excited his curiosity. In 1934, he began to notice certain duplications of patterns which were similar in both large and small movements. This eventually resulted in his discovery, which he has named "The Wave Principle."

During the past seven or eight years, publishers of financial magazines and organizations in the investment advisory field have been virtually flooded with "systems" for which their proponents have claimed great accuracy in forecasting stock market movements. Some of them appeared to work for a while. It was immediately obvious that others had no value whatever. All have been looked upon by The Financial World with great scepticism. But after investigation, we became convinced that a series of articles on this subject would be interesting and instructive to our subscribers. We leave to the individual reader a determination of the value of Mr. Elliott's principle as a basis for market forecasting, but believe that it is likely to prove at least a useful check on conclusions based upon economic considerations.

— The Editors

Introducing "The Wave Principle"

By R. N. Elliott

—*Falcofoto*

R. N. Elliott

DURING the past seven or eight years, publishers of financial magazines and organizations in the investment advisory field have been virtually flooded with "systems" for which their proponents have claimed great accuracy in forecasting stock market movements. Some of them appeared to work for a while. It was immediately obvious that others had no value whatever. All have been looked upon by THE FINANCIAL WORLD with great scepticism. But after investigation of Mr. R. N. Elliott's Wave Principle THE FINANCIAL WORLD became convinced that a series of articles on this subject would be interesting and instructive to its readers. To the individual reader is left the determination of the value of the Wave Principle as a working tool in market forecasting, but it is believed that it should prove at least a useful check upon conclusions based on economic considerations.
—The Editors.

SINCE the beginning of time, rhythmic regularity has been the law of creation. Gradually man has acquired knowledge and power from studying the various manifestations of this law. The effects of the law are discernible in the behavior of the tides, the heavenly bodies, cyclones, day and night, even life and death! This rhythmic regularity is called a cycle.

Historical Significance

The first great advance in the scientific application of the law was made in the time of Columbus by Leonardo da Vinci in his illuminating study of the behavior of waves. Other great men followed with special applications: Halley with his comet, Bell with sound waves, Edison with electrical waves, Marconi with radio waves, and still others with waves of psychology, cosmic waves, television, etc. One thing in common that all these waves or forms of energy have is their cyclical behavior or ability to repeat themselves indefinitely. This cyclical behavior is characterized by two forces — one building up and the other tearing down. Today Hitler is said to be timing his conquests in accordance with this natural law as interpreted in the movements of the stars — but the destructive forces are accumulating and at the proper time will become dominant—completing the cycle.

Because of this phenomenon of repetition or rhythmic recurrence, it is possible to apply the lesson learned from other manifestations of the law in a very practical and profitable way. The trade cycle and the bull and bear movements of the stock market are also governed by the same natural law. Some fifty years ago Charles Dow through his observations of the important changes in the stock market gradually built up the Dow Theory, which now is accepted in many quarters as having special forecasting significance. Since Dow's studies, the store of information regarding market transactions has been greatly multiplied, and important and valuable new forecasting inferences can be drawn from certain behavior.

Through a long illness the writer had the opportunity to study the available information concerning stock market behavior. Gradually the wild, senseless and apparently uncontrollable changes in prices from year to year, from month to month, or from day to day, linked themselves into a law-abiding rhythmic pattern of waves. This pattern seems to repeat itself over and over again. With knowledge of this law or phenomenon (that I have called the Wave Principle) it is possible to measure and forecast the various trends and corrections (minor, intermediate, major and even movements of a still greater degree) that go to complete a great cycle.

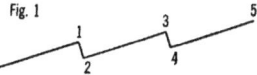

Fig. 1

This phenomenon is disclosed in Figure 1. The full wave or progressive phase of the cycle consists of five impulses: three moving forward and two moving downward. Waves 1, 3 and 5 are in the direction of the main trend. Wave 2 corrects Wave 1— and Wave 4 corrects Wave 3. Usually the three forward movements are in approximately parallel planes; this may also be true of Waves 2 and 4.

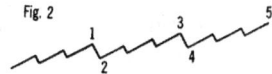

Fig. 2

Each of the three primary waves that together make a completed movement is divided into five waves of the next smaller or intermediate degree. This subdivision is shown in Figure 2. Note carefully that there are five smaller or intermediate waves making

PART I

INTRODUCING "THE WAVE PRINCIPLE"

Since the beginning of time, rhythmic regularity has been the law of creation. Gradually man has acquired knowledge and power from studying the various manifestations of this law. The effects of the law are discernible in the behavior of the tides, the heavenly bodies, cyclones, day and night, even life and death. This rhythmic regularity is called a cycle.

Historical Significance

The first great advance in the scientific application of the law was made in the time of Columbus by Leonardo da Vinci in his illuminating study of the behavior of waves. Other great men followed with special applications: Halley with his comet, Bell with sound waves, Edison with electrical waves, Marconi with radio waves, and still others with waves of psychology, cosmic waves, television, etc. One thing in common that all these waves or forms of energy have is their cyclical behavior or ability to repeat themselves indefinitely. This cyclical behavior is characterized by two forces — one building up and the other tearing down. Today Hitler is said to be timing his conquests in accordance with this natural law as interpreted in the movements of the stars — but the destructive forces are accumulating, and at the proper time will become dominant, completing the cycle.[1]

Because of this phenomenon of repetition or rhythmic recurrence, it is possible to apply the lesson learned from other manifestations of the law in a very practical and profitable way. The trade cycle and the bull and bear movements of the stock market are also governed by the same natural law. Some fifty years ago Charles Dow through his observations of the important changes in the stock market gradually built up the Dow Theory, which now is accepted in many quarters as having special forecasting significance. Since Dow's studies, the store of information regarding market transactions has been greatly multiplied, and important and valuable new forecasting inferences can be drawn from certain behavior.

Through a long illness the writer had the opportunity to study the available information concerning stock market behavior.

Gradually the wild, senseless and apparently uncontrollable changes in prices from year to year, from month to month, or from day to day, linked themselves into a law-abiding rhythmic pattern of waves. This pattern seems to repeat itself over and over again. With knowledge of this law or phenomenon (that I have called the Wave Principle), it is possible to measure and forecast the various trends and corrections (Minor, Intermediate, Major and even movements of a still greater degree) that go to complete a great cycle.

Figure 1

This phenomenon is disclosed in Figure 1. The full wave or progressive phase of the cycle consists of five impulses: three moving forward and two moving downward. Waves 1, 3 and 5 are in the direction of the main trend. Wave 2 corrects wave 1 and wave 4 corrects wave 3. Usually the three forward movements are in approximately parallel planes; this may also be true of waves 2 and 4.

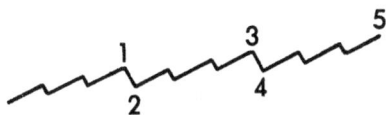

Figure 2

Each of the three Primary waves that together make a completed movement is divided into five waves of the next smaller or Intermediate degree. This subdivision is shown in Figure 2. Note carefully that there are five smaller or Intermediate waves making up the Primary wave 1, five in Primary wave 3, and five in Primary wave 5. The Primary wave 2 corrects the completed Primary wave 1 consisting of five Intermediate waves; wave 4 in turn corrects the five Intermediate waves that make up Primary wave 3.

Each Intermediate forward wave is in turn divided into five Minor waves as shown in Figure 3. When the fifth Minor wave of the fifth Intermediate phase of the fifth Primary movement has spent its force, a formidable top has been constructed. Upon completion of a movement of this magnitude, the destructive forces become dominant; the Primary trend turns downward and a bear market is in progress long before the economic, political or financial reasons for the change in outlook are clearly apparent.

Figure 3

ENDNOTES

[1] The "destructive forces" were evidenced by the bear market, which ended in 1942 and which coincided with the nadir in the fortunes of the Allies in World War II.

PART II

In the preceding discussion of the Wave Principle as applied to the forecasting of stock price movements, it was pointed out that a completed movement consists of five waves, and that a set of five waves of one degree completes the first wave of the next higher degree. When wave 5 of any degree has been completed, there should occur a correction that will be more severe than any previous correction in the cyclical movement.

Completed Movement

The rhythm of the corrective phases is different from that of the waves moving in the direction of the main trend. These corrective vibrations, or waves 2 and 4, are each made up of three lesser waves, whereas the progressive waves (1, 3 and 5) are each composed of five smaller impulses. In Figure 4, the completed movement is shown, being identical to Figure 3 except that waves 2 and 4 of the "zig-zag" pattern are shown in greater detail. These waves 2 and 4 are thus shown to consist each of three component phases, but as these two waves are also "completed movements," they are also characterized by five-wave impulses; that is, the "a" and "c" phases (the first and third movements of the correction) are also each composed of five smaller waves, while "b" (the correction of the correction) is composed of three lesser waves. This question of corrections will require more extended discussion later on, as some forms and types are so complicated in structure that their presentation at this stage might be confusing.

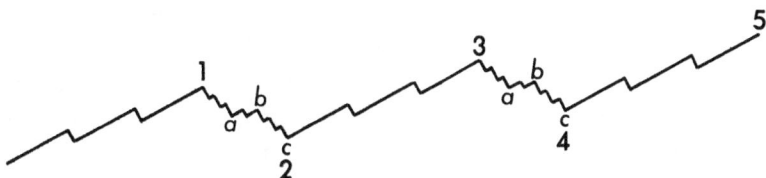

Figure 4

The student using the Wave Principle to forecast price changes does not require confirmation by a companion average, inasmuch as the Principle applies to individual stocks, to various groups (steels, rails, utilities, coppers, oils, etc.) and also to commodities and the various "averages," such as those of Dow-Jones, Standard Statistics, New York Times, New York Herald Tribune, the Financial Times of London, etc. At any given time it will be found that some stocks are advancing and others are declining, but the great majority of individual stocks will be following the same pattern at the same time. It is for this reason that the wave pattern of the "averages" will correctly reflect the cyclical position of the market as a whole. The larger the number of stocks included in an average, the more sharply outlined the wave impressions will be. This means that if stocks are widely distributed among a large number of individuals, the response to cyclical influences will be registered more definitely and rhythmically than if the distribution is limited.

Price Ranges Used

No reliance can be placed on "closings," daily or weekly. It is the highest and lowest ranges that guide the subsequent course of the cycle. In fact, it was only due to the establishment and publication by Dow-Jones of the "daily range" in 1928 and of the "hourly range" in 1932 that sufficient reliable data became available to establish the rhythmic recurrence of the phenomenon that I have called the Wave Principle. It is the series of actual "travels" by the market, hourly, daily and weekly, that reveal the rhythmic forces in their entirety. The "closings" do not disclose the full story, and it is for this reason (lack of detailed data) that the phase-by-phase course of the London stock market is more difficult to predict than the New York market.

The complete measurement of the length of a wave is therefore its continuous travel between two corrections of the same or greater degree. The length of a wave of the lowest degree is its travel in one direction without any sort of correction even in the hourly record.[1] After two corrections have appeared in the hourly record, the movement then enters its fifth and last stage, or third impulse. So-called "resistance" levels and other technical considerations have but little value in forecasting or measuring the length or duration of these waves.

Outside Influences

As the Wave Principle forecasts the different phases or segments of a cycle, the experienced student will find that current news or happenings, or even decrees or acts of government, seem to have but little effect, if any, upon the course of the cycle. It is true that sometimes unexpected news or sudden events, particularly those of a highly emotional nature, may extend or curtail the length of travel between corrections, but the number of waves or underlying rhythmic regularity of the market remains constant. It even seems to be more logical to conclude that the cyclical derangement of trade, bringing widespread social unrest, is the cause of wars, rather than that cycles are produced by wars.

ENDNOTES

[1] When minute-by-minute or tick-by-tick records are available, even smaller waves are quite discernible.

PART III

Because after the fifth wave of an advancing movement has been completed the correction will be more severe than any yet experienced in the cycle, it is desirable to determine beforehand where the top of this wave will be. With such knowledge, the investor can take the necessary steps to assume a defensive policy and convert profits into cash under the most favorable market conditions. He will also be in a strong position to repurchase with confidence when the correction has run its course.

The previous article stated that "The complete measurement of the length of a wave is therefore its continuous travel between two corrections of the same or greater degree." By repeatedly measuring the length of these waves as they develop, under a method known as channeling, it is possible to determine at the time of completion of wave 4 approximately where wave 5 should "top."

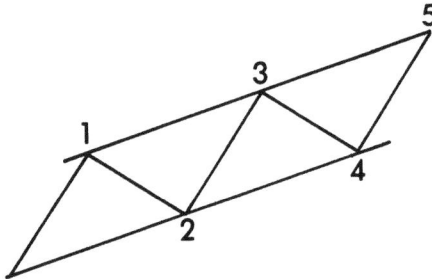

Figure 6

Figure 6 shows a normal completed movement or "cycle," in which waves 1, 3 and 5 each have approximately the same length.[1] Forecasting the ultimate movement by the channeling method must wait until waves 1 and 2 have been completed. At such time it is possible to ascertain the "base line" for the lower limits of the channel by extending a straight line from the starting point of wave 1 through the stopping point of wave 2. This is shown in Figure 7. Wave 3, normally parallel to wave 1, should end in the approximate vicinity of the tentative or dashed upper line of the channel.

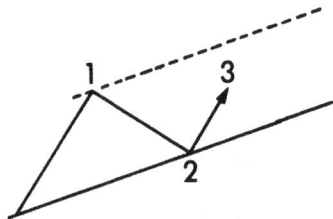

Figure 7

This tentative upper line is drawn parallel to the base line from the top of wave 1 and extended forward. But conditions may be so favorable that wave 3 takes on temporary strength and exceeds the normal theoretical expectation, as shown in Figure 8.

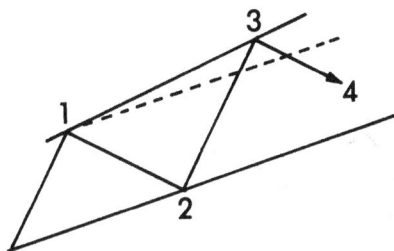

Figure 8

When wave 3 has ended, the actual upper channel line is drawn from the top of wave 1 through the top of wave 3. And for forecasting the bottom of wave 4 reaction, a tentative or dashed base line is drawn from the bottom of wave 2 parallel to the actual wave 1-wave 3 upper channel line. In Figure 9, the theoretical expectancy for termination of wave 4 is shown, as well as the actual termination.

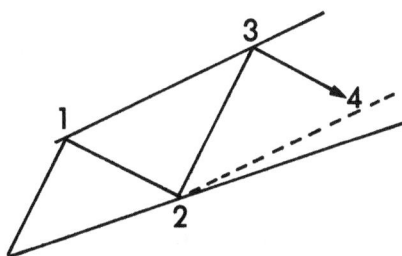

Figure 9

With the second reaction, or wave 4, terminated, the final and all-important channeling step can be taken. The base line of the channel is extended across the stopping points of the two reactionary phases (waves 2 and 4), and a parallel upper line is drawn across the top of wave 3. Wave 1 is disregarded entirely, unless wave 3 was exceptionally strong.[2] When the base and upper parallel lines are drawn as suggested, the approximate termination of wave 5 will be forecast, as shown in Figure 10.

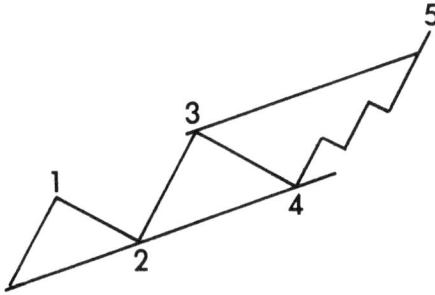

Figure 10

This channeling method is, of course, subordinate in importance to the rhythm of the various phases that make up the completed movement. Waves 1, 3 and 5 should each be composed of five waves of the next lower degree. Theoretically, wave 5 should wind up at about the intersection with the upper parallel line drawn as above described. Sometimes, however, wave 5 develops excessive strength. Patterns in which this "throw-over" should occur will be discussed in subsequent articles.

ENDNOTES

[1] By error of omission, no chart labeled "Figure 5" appeared in the articles, possibly due to editing by the magazine.

[2] Elliott seems to be referring to a phenomenon I have noticed whereby when wave three is abnormally strong, almost vertical, the correct channel for marking the end of wave five is constructed by drawing an upper channel line that touches the peak of wave one and *cuts through* wave three. This idea is illustrated in *Elliott Wave Principle.*

PART IV

A completed price movement has been shown to consist of five waves, with the entire movement representing the first wave of the next larger degree. By classifying the degree of the various phases, it is possible to determine the relative position of the market at all times as well as the economic changes that should follow.[1]

The longest reliable record of American stock prices is the Axe-Houghton Index (published in *The New York Times Annalist*) dating from 1854. Long range forecasting under the Wave Principle must therefore start with the completion of the bear market that terminated in 1857. The great tidal movement that commenced in 1857 and ended on November 28, 1928 (the orthodox top) represents one wave of a cycle of the largest degree. Whether this extended movement was the First, Third or Fifth wave of the Grand Super Cycle necessarily depends upon what happened previous to 1857. By breaking this historic wave down into its component series of five-wave movements, and by breaking in turn the fifth wave of the next smaller degree into its five waves, the student will have actual examples of the various degrees that markets traverse. To avoid confusion in classifying the various degrees of market movements, it is suggested that the names and symbols devised below be used in their respective order (see table, next page).

The longest of these waves lasted for over seventy years and included a long series of "bull" and "bear" markets. But it is the combination of the smaller hourly, daily and weekly rhythms that complete and measure the important Intermediate and Primary cycles that are of great practical importance to every investor.

When the Dow-Jones Industrial Average reached 295.62 on November 28, 1928, the price movement completed the fifth Minuette impulse of the fifth Minute wave of the fifth Minor phase of the fifth Intermediate movement of the fifth Primary trend in the fifth Cycle of the fifth Super Cycle in wave 1, 3 or 5 of the Grand Super Cycle. For that reason, although the actual top of 386.10 was not reached until September 3, 1929, the point reached on November 28, 1928, is designated as the "orthodox" top. This may sound confusing to most readers, but the patterns in which "irregular tops" higher than "orthodox tops" occur will be discussed in due course.

```
   Degree            Symbol
     of               and
  Movement          Wave No.                    Duration

Grand Super Cycle: gsc I (?)............1857-1928

                      ⎧ sc I..................1857-1864
                      ⎪ sc II.................1864-1877
Super Cycle......⎨ sc III................1877-1881
                      ⎪ sc IV.................1881-1896
                      ⎩ sc V..................1896-1928

                      ⎧ c I...................1896-1899
                      ⎪ c II .................1899-1907
Cycle............⎨ c III................1907-1909
                      ⎪ c IV..................1909-1921
                      ⎩ c V...................1921-1928

                      ⎧ ((I)).....June, 1921-Mar., 1923
                      ⎪ ((II))....Mar., 1923-May,  1924
Primary..........⎨ ((III))...May,  1924-Nov., 1925
                      ⎪ ((IV))....Nov., 1925-Mar., 1926
                      ⎩ ((V)).....Mar., 1926-Nov., 1928
```

```
Intermediate... (I)-(V) ⎫   ⎧ Price movements illus-
Minor..............I-V  ⎪   ⎪ trating the Intermedi-
Minute.............1-5  ⎬   ⎨ ate  and  smaller  de-
Minuette...........A-E  ⎪   ⎪ grees will be discussed
Sub-Minuette.......a-e  ⎭   ⎩ in subsequent articles.
```

ENDNOTES

[1] Only a true technician would make this comment.

PART V

The scope and duration of any price movement are influenced by what happened in the previous cycle of similar or larger degree. The movement that started in 1896 and took 33 years to complete, culminating on September 3, 1929 at 386.10, was so dynamic that the corrective bear cycle was correspondingly severe.

Orderly Decline

Within less than three years, prices were reduced to 10.5 per cent of the peak level. Despite its high speed, the downward course of the bear cycle followed a well-defined and rhythmic pattern of waves. Furthermore, it kept within the limits of the pre-measured channel. It was, therefore, possible to determine beforehand approximately where the bear market would end and the new bull market begin. Because of the amplitude of the previous cycles, the new bull market would necessarily be of a large degree, lasting for years. When taking a position for such a movement, the long term investor would be warranted in maintaining his investments until the end of the fifth Major wave was in measurable sight. From that point he should be extremely careful.

Previous discussions have dealt with the fundamental theory of the Wave Principle. It is now appropriate to show the application of the theory to an actual market. In Figure 11, the completed five-wave movement of the extreme monthly price ranges of the Dow-Jones Industrial Average from July 8, 1932 to March 10, 1937 is charted arithmetically. The series of Minuette, Minute, Minor and Intermediate waves all resolved themselves — in the monthly, weekly, daily and hourly records — to form and complete each of the five Primary waves. Waves ((I)), ((III)) and ((V)) were each composed of [five distinct phases, and waves ((II)) and ((IV)) of][1] three distinct phases, as shown by the A-B-C patterns. The extent and duration of each important phase are shown in the accompanying table.

When wave ((IV)) is finished and wave ((V)) is under way, much closer attention to the market is required. Accordingly, the channel was carefully noted. A base line was drawn from the bottom of wave ((II)) through the bottom of wave ((IV)), and an upper line parallel thereto was extended forward from the top of wave ((III)). See the accompanying table and chart.

Phases of the Primary Movement 1932-1937

Wave ((I)) from 40.56 July 8, 1932 to completion of
Wave ((V)) at 195.59 on March 10, 1937. (Dow Jones
Industrial Monthly Averages).

WAVE	FROM			TO		
((I)).....	40.56	July	8, 1932-	81.39	Sept.	8, 1932
((II))....	81.39	Sept.	8, 1932-	49.68	Feb.	27, 1933
A......	81.39	Sept.	8, 1932-	55.04	Dec.	3, 1932
B......	55.04	Dec.	3, 1932-	65.28	Jan.	11, 1933
C......	65.28	Jan.	11, 1933-	49.68	Feb.	27, 1933
((III))...	49.68	Feb.	27, 1933-	110.53	July	18, 1933
((IV))....	110.53	July	18, 1933-	84.58	July	26, 1934
A......	110.53	July	18, 1933-	82.20	Oct.	21, 1933
B......	82.20	Oct.	21, 1933-	111.93	Feb.	5, 1934
C......	111.93	Feb.	5, 1934-	84.58	July	26, 1934
((V)).....	84.58	July	26, 1934-	195.59	Mar.	10, 1937

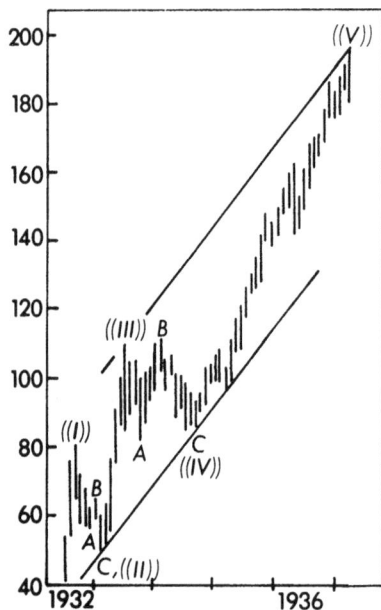

Figure 11

Bearish Indication?

In November 1936, immediately after the President was reelected by an overwhelming majority vote, external conditions appeared to be so favorable for the bull market that it was extremely difficult even to think of being bearish. Yet according to the Wave Principle, the bull market even then was in its final stage. The long term movement that started in 1932 had by November 12, 1936 reached 185.52, and the various five-wave advances of the preceding 53 months were in the culminating stage of the Primary degree. Note how close the price level was to the upper part of the channel at that time. Yet it required another four months to complete the pattern.

The final and relatively insignificant wave, necessary to confirm that the end was at hand, developed during the week ended Wednesday, March 10, 1937. In that week both the industrial and rail averages moved forward on huge volume to a moderately higher recovery level, and according to one of the most widely followed market theories thereby[2] "reaffirmed that the major trend was *upward*."

The industrials reached 195.59 — compared with the November 1929 panic bottom of 195.35 and the February 1930 rally top of 196.96.[3] In that week the advancing prices met the top of the channel. The President's remarks about prices for copper and steel being too high did not take place until April, and by that time the bear movement was well under way.

ENDNOTES

[1] I added the words in brackets, as they appeared to be missing.

[2] I.e., the Dow Theory.

[3] Elliott recognized this type of support/resistance level in the averages. The market often chooses levels around which to turn continually or to break only dramatically. Usually these levels have something to do with Fibonacci relationships. Look closely at the 740 level, the 780 level, the 847 level and the 995 level on a chart of the recent history of the Dow.

PART VI

In the 1932-1937 Primary bull movement (see Figure 11, Part V), waves ((I)) and ((III)) ran at high speed. Naturally they terminated in a short time. But wave ((V)) was so gradual and orderly that it lasted longer than the time interval required for the previous four waves combined. In the discussion of this movement, it was stated that by November 1936 it was evident that the bull market was in an extremely advanced stage, but that it required another four months to complete the pattern. Although the largest phases of the Fifth Primary were in the culminating stage, the smallest component phases (Minuette, etc.) were still developing.

Spans of the 5th Wave
of the Several Degrees Indicated

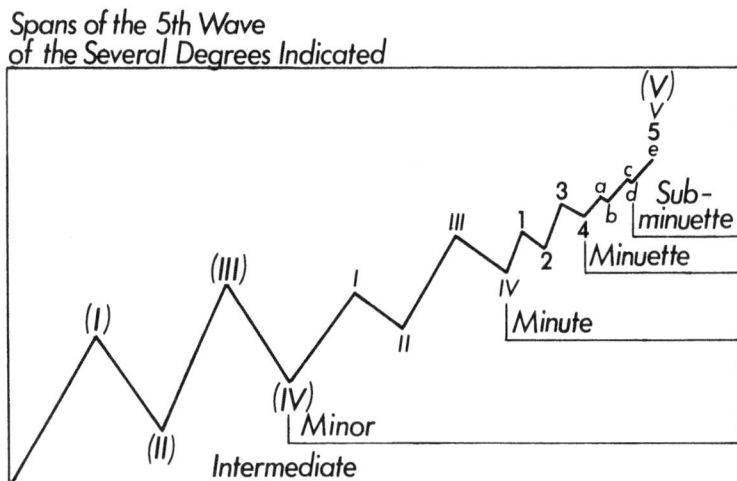

Figure 12

Figure 12 illustrates how the fifth wave of an important degree becomes extended by the development of five waves of the next smaller degree, and five more of a still smaller degree. Thus, an Intermediate trend will end on the fifth Sub-Minuette impulse of the fifth Minuette wave of the fifth Minute phase of the fifth Minor movement of the fifth Intermediate swing. Note that as wave (V) advances, the corrections tend to become smaller and of shorter duration. Compare with 1935-1937. The termination of a fifth wave marks the point at which an entire movement of the same degree is to be corrected by a reverse movement of similar degree.

Confusion in the identification of the waves of the smaller degrees, developing toward the end of the fifth wave of the important degree, is sometimes caused by "throw-overs." A throw-over is a penetration in an advancing movement of the upper parallel line of the channel (see Part III), and in a declining movement of the lower parallel line of the channel. Volume tends to rise on a throw-over, and should be very heavy as applied to the fifth Intermediate wave of a Primary movement. Failure of the fifth wave of any degree to penetrate the channel line, accompanied by indications of a sustained decline, is a warning of weakness. The extent of the weakness depends upon the degree of the wave. Sometimes, such weakness furnishes a new base for the recommencement of the fifth wave. Throw-overs are also caused by the scale of the chart study of the movement. They are more likely to occur in an advancing movement on arithmetic scales, and in declining movements on logarithmic scales.

Sometimes the fifth wave will "stretch" — that is, deploy or spread out. The fifth wave, instead of proceeding in the normal one-wave pattern of the same degree as the movement as a whole, simply stretches or subdivides into five waves of lower degree. In rhythmic forecasting, this stretching applies to the fifth wave itself, rather than to the terminating cycle of which it is a part. Such spreading out is a characteristic of markets that are unusually strong (or weak, if a down movement). An example of stretching occurred in the 1921-1928 upswing, representing the culmination of a 72-year advance.

PART VII

The rhythm of corrective movements is the most difficult feature of the Wave Principle. Intensive study of the detail of the correction will sometimes be necessary in order to determine the position of the market and the outlook. Mastery of the subject, however, should prove extremely profitable. All corrections are characterized by *three* broad waves, but the detail and extent can vary considerably, and thus different patterns are formed. Various factors (time, rate of speed, extent of previous movement, volume, news items, etc.) tend to influence and shape the corrective pattern. Based on the writer's market research and experience, there appear to be four main types or patterns of corrections. These types have been designated as zig-zag, flat, irregular and triangle. Discussion of the triangle, in its various forms, must be presented in a separate article. The other three forms are diagrammed in Figures 13, 14 and 15.

Small corrections that run their course in a comparatively short time are exemplified in Figure 13. Corrections of a larger degree are described in Figure 14. Figure 15 affords a diagram of the market action when the Primary or Intermediate trends turn downward. Some of these corrections, particularly those of the irregular type, may extend over a period of years and embrace movements that are commonly mistaken for "bull markets."

The three-wave or A-B-C formations that characterize the zig-zag, flat and irregular corrections are clearly shown in the accompanying diagrams. The zig-zag type was discussed briefly in Part II (Figure 4). It differs from other corrections in that both the first and third waves (A and C) are composed of five smaller vibrations. The second (B) wave of zig-zag corrections is composed of three impulses. Sometimes, in high-speed movement, the first leg (A) may appear continuous, and resort to the smaller or hourly studies may be necessary to detect the flow.

The first and second waves of both flats and irregulars each consist of *three* vibrations of a degree smaller than that of the previous movement. Of the three movements making up the second or "B" phase of both flats and irregulars, the first and third (a and c) are each composed of *five* still smaller impulses. In a flat, all of the three waves have approximately the same length.

An irregular correction is distinguished by the fact that the second or "B" wave advances to a secondary top higher than the

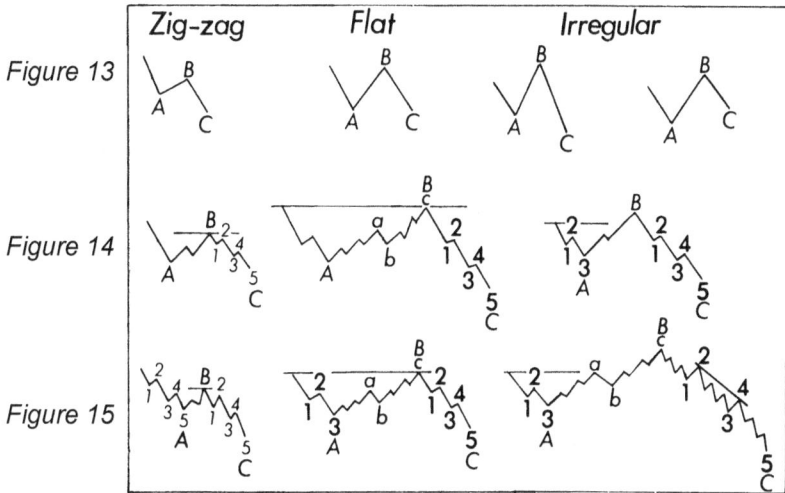

Zig-zag   Flat   Irregular

Figure 13

Figure 14

Figure 15

orthodox top established in the Primary movement. Liquidation in the third or "C" wave is therefore usually more intensive than in the first phase. Normally C terminates below the bottom of A, although there are instances of C, the third phase, being abbreviated. In the larger and important corrections, such as Primary and Intermediate, the "C" or third phase of the irregular correction may consist of *three smaller five-wave sets*, as shown in Figure 15.

By analyzing and placing the type of correction that is being experienced, the student has a basis for determining both the extent of the correction, and the extent of the following movement. Channeling (see Part III) can help in determining the extent. The application of these corrective patterns to specific markets will be shown and discussed in subsequent articles.

PART VIII

Triangular corrections are protracted trend hesitations. The main movement may have gone too far and too fast in relation to the slower economic processes, and prices proceed to mark time until the underlying forces catch up. Triangles have lasted as long as nine months and have been as short as seven hours. There are two classes of triangles, horizontal and diagonal. These are shown in Figures 16 and 17.

Figure 16

Figure 17

Figure 18

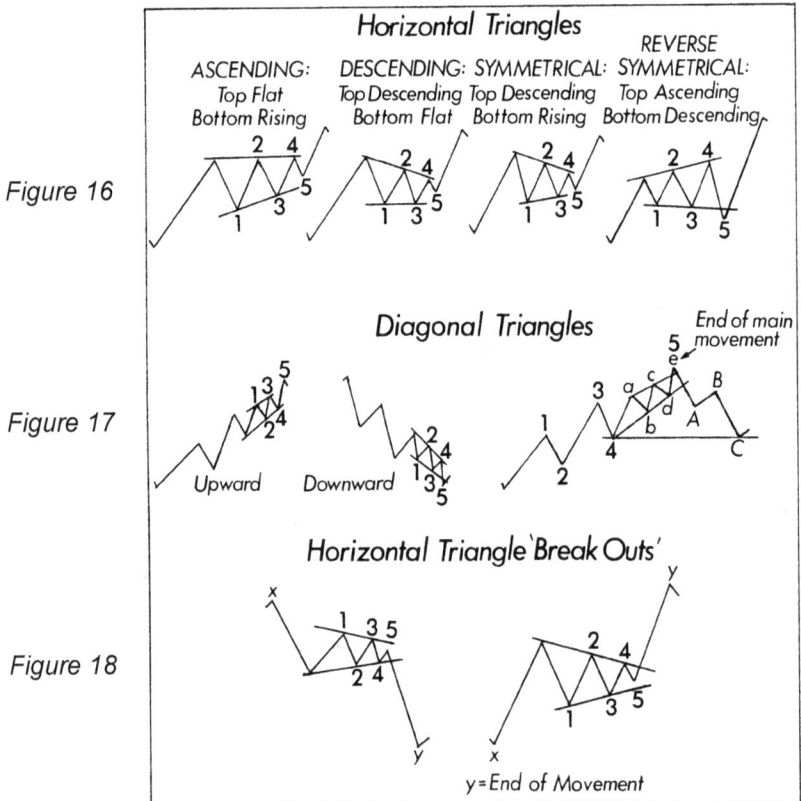

The four types of horizontal triangles are Ascending, Descending, Symmetrical and the rare Reverse Symmetrical. In the last named, the apex is the beginning of the triangular correction. In the other forms the apex is the end of the correction, which, however, may terminate before the apex is actually reached.

All triangles contain five waves or legs, each of which is composed of not more than three lesser waves. Outlines that do not conform to this definition fall outside the law of the Wave Principle. All waves in a triangle must be part of a movement in one direction; otherwise, the "triangle" is only a coincidence.

The entire travel within the triangle represents a wave of the main movement. The horizontal triangle occurs as wave 2 or wave 4. If it occurs as wave 2, the main movement will have only three waves. At the conclusion of a horizontal triangle, the market will resume the trend that was interrupted by the triangle, and the direction of that trend will be the same as that of triangular wave 2. The "break-out" from the horizontal triangle (in the direction of triangular wave 2) will usually be fast and represent the final wave of the main movement, and be followed by reversal of the trend. The extent of the "break-out" will usually approximate the distance between the widest parts of the triangle. The diagrams in Figure 18 illustrate the "break-out" from horizontal triangles.

Diagonal triangles are either upward or downward. They can occur as either wave 3 or wave 5 of the main movement.[1] Usually they occur as wave 5, and are preceded by four main waves. But the completion of the diagonal triangle represents the end of the main movement. The second wave within the diagonal triangle will be in the direction opposite to that of the main movement, and will indicate the direction of the reversal to follow conclusion of the triangle. At the conclusion of the fifth wave in this form of triangle, the rapid reversal of trend will usually return the market to about the level from which the triangle started (see Figure 17, third diagram).

Triangles are not apparent in all studies. Sometimes they will appear in the weekly scale, but will not be visible in the daily. Sometimes they are present in, say, The New York Times average and not in another average. Thus, the broad and important movement from October 1937 to February 1938 formed a triangle in the Standard Statistics weekly range, but was not visible in other averages; the second wave of this triangle pointed downward; the fifth wave culminated on February 23; the drastic March break followed.

ENDNOTES

[1] Based on the discussion of diagonal triangles in *The Wave Principle*, this comment is almost assuredly unintentional. Diagonal triangles never occur as wave three. Third waves are characteristically strong, while fifths are terminal movements. There is some evidence that they sometimes appear as first waves. See *Elliott Wave Principle*.

PART IX

The "extension," though not frequent, is one of the most important market phenomena measurable by the Wave Principle. In an extension the length (and degree)[1] of the wave becomes much larger than normal. It may occur as a part[2] of wave 1 or 3, but is usually a part of wave 5 of the main movement.[3] The extended movement is composed of the normal five-wave phase, followed by a three-wave retracing correction, and then by a second advancing movement in three phases. Of the normal five waves, the fifth vibration is usually the largest and most dynamic of the series,[4] thus becoming, in effect, an extension of the extension.

A warning of the approach of this dynamic phase of wave 5 is conveyed when waves 1 and 3 are short and regular and confined within the channel,[5] and when the first corrective vibration of the extension is completed near the top of the channel. The length of important extensions may be several times the breadth of the original channel.

Channelling is also useful in measuring the travel of the extension. Thus, in Figures 19 and 20, the line "b-d" represents the base line, and the dashed upper parallel line "c-e" measures the normal expectancy for the "first top" of the extension.

The completion of the normal or first five waves of an extension is never the end of the cyclical movement but does constitute a distinct warning that the bull cycle is approaching an end, as only two more broad waves (one down and one up) would fully reflect the maximum force of the bull market.

After the first five waves of the extension have been completed, a severe correction (that is usually in three waves, but may be triangular) sets in. This correction becomes wave A of an irregular cyclical correction. Wave A generally carries the market down (breaking the extension channel) to about the beginning of the extension, although a protracted period of backing and filling may serve to mitigate the severity of this corrective phase. The dashed line marked "X" in Figure 20 indicates the average expectancy for the completion of wave A.

When wave A has been completed, the main or cyclical movement is resumed in three broad phases that carry the market into new high ground — even though "e" in Figures 19 and 20 may have been the "orthodox top" of a Major or Primary

bull movement. But this new top, or "irregular top," is the final
high point for the bull market. This three-wave advancing phase
becomes wave B of the irregular cyclical correction.

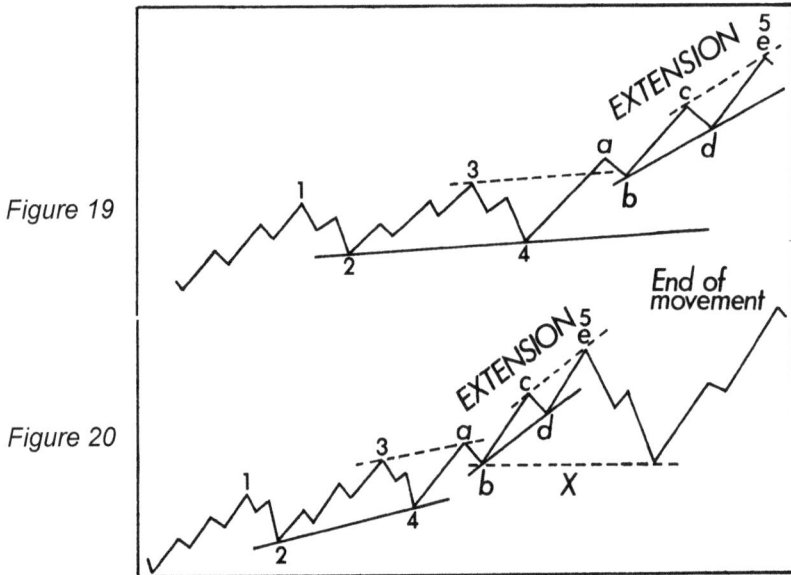

Figure 19

Figure 20

The completion of wave B marks the beginning of wave C
of the irregular cyclical correction, that in this phase is a bear
market of major importance. Wave C should carry the market
down in five fast waves to about the bottom of Primary wave IV
of the preceding bull movement. Example: following the dynamic
extension in 1928; wave A, down from November to December,
1928; wave B, upward to September 1929; wave C, downward to
July 1932.

Extensions also occur in bear markets. Thus, the five waves
of an extension were completed October 19, 1937, with the market
reaching 115.83, followed, in this case, by a broad triangular
correction (instead of the irregular A-B-C pattern) covering
a period of four months, eventually reaching 97.46 on March
31, 1938. Wave 2 of this triangular correction was in the same
direction as the downward cyclical trend.

A tremendous extension occurred in commodity price
movements, particularly that of electrolytic copper, in the spring
of 1937.

In individual stocks, the "orthodox top" of International Harvester was reached at 111-112 in January, 1937; wave A, in a backing and filling movement that reduced the severity of the correction, carried the stock to 109 in April; wave B reached a new cyclical top of 120 in August (the general market topped in March), and wave C brought the stock down to about 53 in November.

ENDNOTES

[1] The *size* of an extended wave is larger, but the *degree* (Minor, Intermediate or Primary) is the same as that of the two non-extended waves.

[2] Here Elliott uses the term "extension" to refer to waves 3, 4 and 5 of the extended wave.

[3] See Endnote 5 in Chapter V of *The Wave Principle* regarding this contention. Fifths often are, but third waves *more* often are, the "largest and most dynamic of a series."

[4] Id.

[5] Since an extension generally occurs in one of the three impulse waves, it follows that when waves 1 and 3 are short and simply constructed (as long as wave 3 is longer than wave 1), wave 5 will likely be extended.

PART X

Following the completion of the bull market from 1932 to 1937 (see Figure 11, Part V), a three-phase cyclical correction was in order. The first phase should and did consist of five large waves. The first phase of this correction was the decline that ran from 195.59 (Dow-Jones Industrial Average) on March 10, 1937, to 97.46 on March 31, 1938.[1] The accompanying Figure 21 shows the weekly range of the market during this period, on an arithmetic scale. Despite the highly emotional nature that prevailed at certain stages, the rhythmic forecasting principle continued to function. The minute details registered in the daily and hourly patterns are, of course, not entirely visible in the weekly range. For this reason, the essential details of price and time of the five big waves making up this first cyclical phase are given:

Cyclical Wave (A) — from 195.59 on March 10, 1937, to 163.31 on June 17, 1937.
Cyclical Wave (B) — from 163.31 on June 17, 1937, to 190.38 on August 14, 1937.
Cyclical Wave (C) — from 190.38 on August 14, 1937, to 115.83 on October 19, 1937.
Cyclical Wave (D) — from 115.83 on October 19, 1937, to 132.86 on February 23, 1938.
Cyclical Wave (E) — from 132.86 on February 23, 1938, to 97.46 on March 31, 1938.

Cyclical wave (A) was composed of five Minor waves, as follows:
1 - 195.59 on March 10 to 179.28 on March 22.
2 - 179.28 on March 22 to 187.99 on March 31.
3 - 187.99 on March 31 to 166.20 on May 18.
4 - 166.20 on May 18 to 175.66 on June 5.
5 - 175.66 on June 5 to 163.31 on June 17.
Wave 3 in Cyclical Wave (A) was composed of five vibrations.

Cyclical wave (B) was composed of three waves, and an "irregular top":
A - 163.31 on June 17 to 170.46 on June 24.
B - 170.46 on June 24 to 166.11 on June 29.
C - 166.11 on June 29 to 187.31 on Aug. 4.

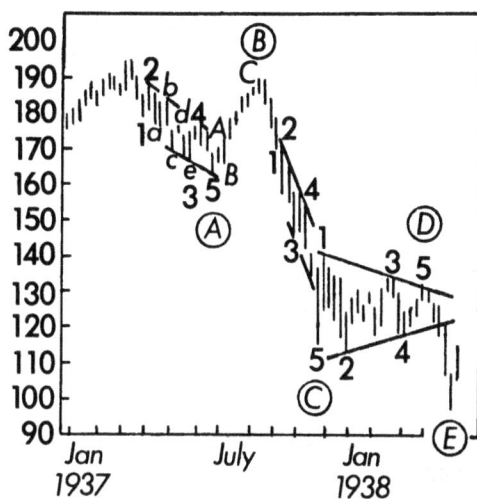

Figure 21

The "irregular top"[2] was completed on August 14, 1937, forecasting a severe cyclical decline.

Cyclical wave (C) was composed of five large waves, with an "extension" developing in the fifth wave. Had it not been for this extension, the normal completion of the first phase of the cyclical correction would probably have been in the neighborhood of 135-140. The analysis of wave (C) is as follows:

1 - 190.38 on Aug. 14 to 175.09 on Aug. 27.
2 - 175.09 on Aug. 27 to 179.10 on Aug. 31.
3 - 179.10 on Aug. 31 to 154.94 on Sept. 13.
4 - 154.94 on Sept. 13 to 157.12 on Sept. 30.
5 - 157.12 on Sept. 30 to 115.83 on Oct. 19.

In Cyclical wave (C), there were three "sets" of five vibrations in the downward trend, with the first, third and fifth Minor waves each being composed of five impulses. Wave 4 was a fairly important upward correction, in the familiar A-B-C formation. The extension that developed in the fifth vibration of wave 5 indicated that the ground thus lost would be immediately recovered, that the secondary decline would carry the market into new low ground for the cyclical correction, that following this secondary decline, the normal protracted period of backing and filling might form a triangle, with the final down thrust[3] completing the first phase of the cyclical correction, and that a very substantial recovery would follow in at least five large waves,[4] thus forecasting the 1938 March-November "bull market."

Cyclical wave (D), as indicated by the "extension" that occurred in wave (C), was composed of a huge triangle:
Triangle wave 1 — in three vibrations (A, B and C), from 115.83 on Oct. 19 to 141.22 on Oct. 29.
A - 115.83 on Oct. 19 to 137.82 on Oct. 21.
B - 137.82 on Oct. 21 to 124.56 on Oct. 25.
C - 124.56 on Oct. 25 to 141.22 on Oct. 29.
2 - 141.22 on Oct 29 to 112.54 on Nov. 23.
3 - 112.54 on Nov. 23 to 134.95 on Jan. 12.
4 - 134.95 on Jan. 12 to 117.13 on Feb. 4.
5 - 117.13 on Feb. 4 to 132.86 on Feb. 23.
None of the "legs" in this triangle was composed of more than three waves. Following the completion of the fifth wave in the triangle, the downward movement of the cyclical correction was resumed.

Cyclical wave (E) was composed of five lesser waves, as follows:
1 - 132.86 on Feb. 23 to 121.77 on March 12.
2 - 121.77 on March 12 to 127.44 on March 15.
3 - 127.44 on March 15 to 112.78 on March 23.
4 - 112.78 on March 23 to 114.37 on March 25.
5 - 114.37 on March 25 to 97.46 on March 31.

The first large phase of the cyclical correction of the 1932-1937 bull market was thus finally completed, and the market was ready for the second important upward phase of the cyclical correction. This correction extinguished 63.3 per cent of the 155.03 points recovered in the 1932-1937 movement.

ENDNOTES

[1] Here Elliott correctly forecasts that the bear market that started in 1937 was not over. The eventual low occurred four years later in 1942.
[2] See Endnote 1 in Chapter IX of *The Wave Principle*.
[3] I.e., wave (E).
[4] I think this should read "*three* large waves."

PART XI

In using the Wave Principle as a medium for forecasting price movements, the student should recognize that there are cycles within cycles, and that each such cycle or sub-cycle must be studied and correctly placed in respect to the broad underlying movement. These sub-cyclical or corrective phases in a bull market are often important enough to be mistaken for "bear markets." The strong but sub-cyclical correction from March 31, 1938 to November 12, 1938 had a "bull pattern" of five important waves making up its first phase,[1] and was (and still is) regarded by many as a real bull market. Broadly speaking, extended rallies or corrections of bear cycles are composed of three phases, and this is also true of extensive bearish corrections of bull movements.

Wave Characteristics

The character of the waves making up an extended movement is affected by a number of factors that may seem irrelevant to the inexperienced. Examination of any completed movement seems to support the fatalistic theory that the extent or objective of the price movement is fixed or predetermined. The time of the entire cycle is also possibly fixed, but the time of the component phases appears to be variable.[2] The variations in the time cycle appear to be governed by the speed or rate of the price movement, and vice versa. Thus, if the market movement has been violent and rapid in one phase, the next corresponding phase is likely to show a marked slowing down in speed.[3] Example: The first Primary wave of the 1932-1937 bull cycle advanced 40 points or 100 per cent in 9 weeks, averaging 4.4 points per week. The second bull phase advanced 60 points or 120 per cent in 20 weeks, averaging 3 points per week. The third or final phase crept forward 110 points or 130 per cent in 138 weeks, averaging 0.8 point per week. High speed at the end of long movements usually generates similar speed in the first wave of the reversal: compare the March 1938 downward movement with the following April reversal.

At certain stages volume seems to play an important part in the price movement, and volume itself will expand or contract to help control and complete the price cycle. Study of the time cycle and volume cycles is sometimes distinctly helpful in clarifying the position of the price spiral.[4] Volume tends to increase in the third wave of the cycle, and to maintain about the same activity in the fifth wave. As the bottom of the volume cycle is approached, erratic price changes in high priced stocks, or inactive stocks with thin markets, can distort the small waves in the trend of the averages to such an extent as to create temporary uncertainties. But these waves of volume are also useful in determining the extent and time for completion of price phases, and also in determining the time and direction and even the speed of the following movement. This is especially true in fast swinging markets like those that characterized 1938. The best results therefore will follow from correlation of the volume and time cycles with the component phases of the broad price movement, as the price patterns and all degrees of volume[5] are governed by precisely the same Wave Principle phenomenon.

To maintain a proper perspective, the student should chart at least two and preferably more broad averages, using the weekly range, the daily range, and the hourly record, and showing the accompanying volume. The weekly range should be sufficient properly to evaluate the broad changes in trend, but the monthly range studies will also undoubtedly appeal to many investors. The daily range, by affording close observation of the smaller changes, is essential in correct interpretation of the cyclical progression, and is quite necessary for determining the precise time of important reversals in trend.

Critical Points

The minute changes recorded in the hourly study not only afford valuable and extensive material for practice in wave interpretation, but are especially useful in times when the market is moving at such high speed that the pattern is not clearly registered in the longer-time charts. Thus, the small triangle that appeared in the hourly record of October 1937 signalled an immediate acceleration or extension of the downward movement; the dynamic October 18-19 "panic" followed. At other critical points the hourly study has also proved valuable, as in locating the "orthodox top" before the final irregular top, thus selecting the time for strategic liquidation near the crest. As the first hourly phase following the break in March 1938 developed in five Minute waves, it thus afforded a strong confirmation that the important trend had actually changed.

ENDNOTES

[1] Here Elliott correctly forecasts that one more new high will be made (which it was in late 1939) before the final bear market low (which occurred in 1942).

[2] This contention is not tenable, since every wave is itself both an "entire cycle" and a "component."

[3] This is another aspect of the rule of alternation.

[4] Here Elliott uses the word "spiral," reflecting the subjective feeling one gets while tracking waves. The theory of the logarithmic spiral as a model for the Wave Principle had not occurred to him.

[5] My studies do not support this assertion.

PART XII

Previous articles have discussed the theory of The Wave Principle and its application to broad market movements. The broader the category, the more clearly the wave impressions are outlined. The wave pattern of the comprehensive stock price averages such as the Dow-Jones, The New York Times, or Standard Statistics averages will correctly reflect the cyclical position of the market as a whole. Therefore, purchases and sales of a diversified list of representative stocks in accordance with the movements of the averages will result in profits, as their aggregate market value will swing in sympathy with the general market. But for the seeker of maximum profits consistent with safety, it is not enough to buy or sell a group of stocks without separate analysis of each individual stock. These individual studies may reveal that some companies are experiencing a cycle differing greatly from that of the market as a whole. A prominent example was the case of American Can in the spring of 1935.

The accompanying charts depict the analysis of American Can[1] by The Wave Principle. In Figure 22, the complete monthly price range history is shown from June, 1932 — the beginning of the bull movement — to June 1935, the time when the "orthodox top" occurred. The action of the stock from that point on to completion of the cyclical correction in December 1937 is shown in "trend lines." This monthly record condenses the weekly and daily details into the five broad Primary waves that complete a cyclical movement. These relatively broad charts also help materially in maintaining the proper perspective.

When the important fifth Primary wave of the cycle commenced in May 1934 — or in other words, when the Primary wave ④ reaction was completed — it became necessary to study the market action more closely. Hence Figure 23, which shows the weekly price record of the fifth Primary wave. After this Primary wave had progressed through Intermediate wave 4, it became important to follow the daily price ranges, as shown in Figure 24. The fifth Intermediate wave started in March 1935, and five Minor waves were completed by June 1935. This signalled the "orthodox top"[2] of the main bull movement in American Can at 144.

Following the "orthodox top" of the bull cycle in American Can, there developed a reaction to 136-137 in August 1935, forming wave Ⓐ. Then a rally to 149-150 in October 1935 forming

Figure 22   Figure 23   Figure 24

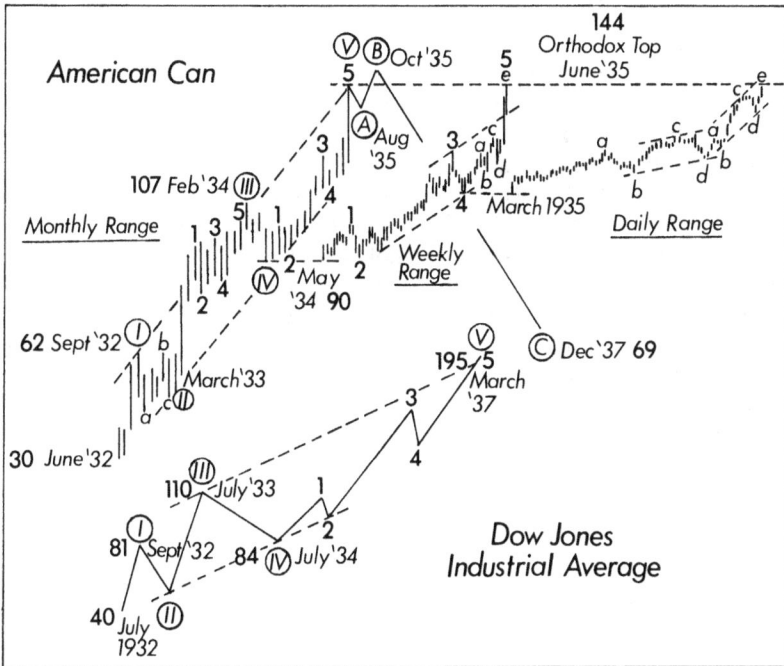

Figure 25

wave Ⓑ, the irregular but final top. From this point developed the long wave Ⓒ, in five Intermediate movements, terminating at 69 in December 1937.

At the time of the "orthodox top" in American Can, the investor would have observed the striking difference between the cyclical positions of that stock and of the general market. See Figure 25, which outlines the trend lines of the important Primary waves of the Dow-Jones Industrial Averages. In March 1935, American Can was in the final stages of a bull cycle (Fifth Intermediate wave of the Fifth Primary). On the other hand the general market was just commencing the Fifth Primary wave, and still had to experience five upward Intermediate waves. By June 1935, the long term investor in American Can would have realized that any further appreciation in that stock would be highly uncertain, and that much greater profits were available in the general market with minimum risks. From that point the general market advanced nearly 80 points or 65 per cent.

ENDNOTES

¹ In Figure 22, the correct count, avoiding overlapping and fulfilling third wave requirements, would be to place the (II) where Elliott has a, and (within wave (III)) 1 where he has b, 2 where he has c, and 3 where he has 1. Wave 4 of (III) then takes an a-b-c count, and the rule of alternation is still satisfied.

² In Figure 24, Elliott ignores the overlapping and the insufficient third wave (labeled "c"). From the description of the supposed (A) and (B) waves that follow, it seems highly likely that the third wave of the final wave 5 of (5) simply extended, thus eliminating the imperfect count. Elliott's a and b are all right, but his c could be reserved for the first peak within the supposed (B) (thereby completing an extension from the low at b), the d for the next small reaction (his b of (B)), and the e for the actual high. As previously discussed, Elliott calls several tops "irregular" that might be better explained by third-wave extensions.

SELECTED ESSAYS
1940-1942

THE BASIS OF THE WAVE PRINCIPLE[1]

OCTOBER 1, 1940

Civilization rests upon change. This change is cyclical in origin and characteristics. A rhythmic series of extreme changes constitutes a cycle. When a cycle has been completed, another cycle is started. The rhythm of the new cycle will be the same as that of the previous cycle, although the extent and duration may vary. The cycle progresses in accordance with the natural law of movement.

The behavior of cycles has been studied extensively by puzzled economists, bankers and business men. In this connection, the conservative *London Economist* in a recent issue, commenting upon the results of a long study of trade cycles made by Sir William Beveridge, the noted British economist, said:

> Sir William's researches have emphasized once again that the more the trade cycle is studied, the more it seems to follow the pressure of forces which, if they are not wholly beyond the reach of human control, have at least enough of the inexorable in their nature to make the policies of governments resemble the struggles of fish caught in the tides. Sir William pointed out that the trade cycle ignores politics; he might have added that it overrides economic policies.

The causes of these cyclical changes seem clearly to have their origin in the immutable natural law that governs all things, including the various moods[2] of human behavior. Causes,[3] therefore, tend to become relatively unimportant in the long term progress of the cycle. This fundamental law cannot be subverted or set aside by statutes or restrictions. Current news and political developments are of only incidental importance, soon forgotten; their presumed influence on market trends is not as weighty as is commonly believed.

This law of natural change is inevitable, and applies to the seasons and the movements of the tides and planets. It has truly been said that change is the only "immutable thing in life." Being a natural phenomenon, it necessarily governs all human activities, even the relatively static sciences of biology and botany. Even time and mathematics appear to be amenable to the application of this law of rhythm, from the small unit of hours to the great intervals of decades, centuries and millennia. Measuring the behavior of cycles should therefore offer a reliable means of forecasting changes, regardless of the cause,[4] and thus yield handsome profits.

In an independent study of the available data, extending over a period of many years, the writer has observed certain recurring behavior of change in movement. Apparently these changes follow a natural law that inevitably influences the mass. Finally there evolved certain principles, which were carefully tested back over a long period of years.

By 1934, I was able to resolve the various trends[5] of changes in stock prices to a rhythmic series of component waves, which[6] I called a "cycle." This cyclical rhythm has occurred regularly and repeatedly not only in the available records of the various stock exchanges, but also in commodities, industrial production, temperature, music, variation in color, electric output, population movements to and from cities, etc. In fact, it is manifest so widely, not only in human activities but also in the workings of nature itself, that I have termed this discovery "The Wave Principle."

Understanding of this law enables the close student to forecast the terminations of cycles by means of the market itself. The Wave Principle is not a "market" system or theory. The forecasting principle involved goes far beyond the concept of any known formula.

The number of waves and the extent and duration of movements seem clearly to be allied with the principle of mathematics and with the passage of time, but the number of waves never varies except under certain recognizable conditions of a cyclical nature. The *length* of a wave may possibly be affected by emotional news, but the *number* of waves is clearly not affected by such transient developments. This Principle forecasts and at the same time measures the extent, corrections and reversals of the various trends and cycles long before any supporting statistical evidence is available. A feature of unusual merit is the fact that the experienced student knows at all times the current position of the market in each cycle and therefore is forewarned of the approach of reversals. By means of this rhythmic analysis, the end of a movement is known as it approaches, and the type of the next movement is also known. It is therefore possible to predict with confidence when a bull market is terminating and a bear market is beginning, or vice versa.

The Wave Principle has now been used successfully for several years in the management of investment funds, and in forecasting the important major and intermediate trends. A series of articles, revealing the broad workings of The Wave Principle, was published in *The Financial World* during June, July and August 1939.

How The Wave Principle Works,
and Its Correlation With Mathematical Laws

[7]The Fibonacci Summation Series is the basis of The Wave Principle. The numbers thereof are as follows:

1 - 2 - 3 - 5 - 8 - 13 - 21 - 34 - 55 - 89 - 144, etc.

The sum of any two adjoining numbers equals the next higher number. For example: 3 + 5 = 8. The waves of every movement coincide with these numbers.

Any one of these numbers is approximately 61.8% of the next higher number. The ratio of one wave to its companion is approximately 61.8%.

Figure 1 shows three graphs of a stock market cycle, including the constructive phases of a bull market and the destructive phases of a bear market. The number of waves in a cycle is also compared with the mathematical principles laid down centuries ago by Pythagoras and Fibonacci.

The graph at the top outlines the fundamental or largest waves of a complete cycle. There are five waves in the bull market and three waves in the bear market.

In the middle graph, these same eight fundamental waves are amplified to show their component waves, totaling 34. Note the constancy of the "five-three" rhythm. This graph shows the Intermediate stages of a cycle.

The third graph is simply a more detailed analysis of the same 8 fundamental, or 34 intermediate, waves of a cycle, including the 89 minor waves of a bull market and the 55 minor waves of a bear market. The total is 144. Again the "five-three" relationship holds true. A corrective phase of the cycle will occasionally vary the rhythm slightly for the minor waves, and in such instances, the count will be 7 or 11,[8] according to the type or pattern, which indicates what is happening.

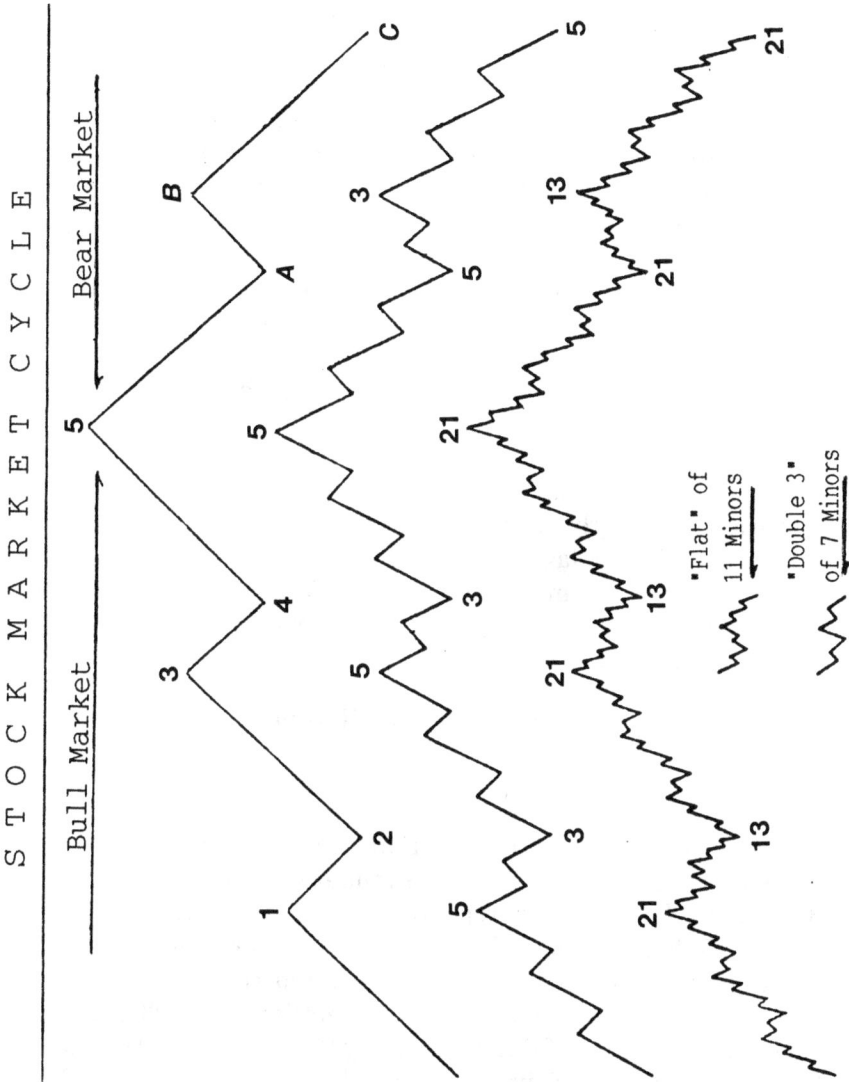

Figure 1

The basis of The Wave Principle is very old. Pythagoras in the sixth century B.C., Fibonacci in the thirteenth century and many other scientists, including Leonardo da Vinci and Marconi, have all shown that they were aware to some extent of this phenomenon. Fibonacci was an Italian mathematician, also known as Leonardo da Pisa. His "Summation Series of Dynamic Symmetry" agrees in every respect with the rhythmic count of the Wave Principle, and the number of waves is the same.

Fibonacci apparently derived his Summation Series from the famous Pythagorean diagram of a pyramid, consisting of ten units, beginning with one and ending with four.[9] This diagram, Pythagoras said, was the "Key to the Secret of the Universe." Not only can this diagram be applied to the seasons of the year, but also to the great inner cycles of the well-known ten-year cycle.[10]

The similarity of The Wave Principle, the Fibonacci Summation Series and the Pythagorean diagram is shown in the tables on the next page.

It should be noted that when I discovered The Wave Principle action of market trends, I had never heard of either the Fibonacci Series or of the Pythagorean Diagram. It is naturally gratifying to me that these old mathematical principles that were laid down centuries ago simply substantiate the validity of a present day application of basic law to practical use.

As to the conformance of the time element, or duration, of market trends with the rhythm of The Wave Principle, many "coincidences" can be cited.

Duration or Time Element[11]

In the analytical discussion of the basis of the Wave Principle, the composition of the waves of varying degrees was shown to be identical with the numerical relationships of the units making up the Fibonacci Summation Series of Dynamic Symmetry. This series is repeated, as follows: 1, 2, 3, 5, 8, 13, 21, 34, 55, 89, 144, etc. These relationships are very useful in identifying and measuring every wave and the extent of each movement, and when used in conjunction with The Wave Principle are also useful in forecasting the duration of trends in the various periods of time (days, weeks, months or years). The time element as an independent device, however, continues to be baffling when attempts are made to apply any known rule of sequence to trend duration.

The Wave Principle

Graphs	Degree	Number of Waves in Bull Market	Bear Market	Total Cycle	Fibonacci Summation Series	Pythagorean Diagram	My elaborations of the Diagram
Top	Primaries	5	3	8	1+2 = 3	• • • • = 1,2,3,4	1 2 3 4 5 6 21 7 8 9 10 34 55
Middle	Interme-diates	5 3 5 3 5 21	3 3 5 13		2+3 = 5 3+5 = 8 5+8 = 13 8+13 = 21	1 2 3 4 5 6 7 8 9 10 = 1 2 3 4 10	
Bottom	Minors	21 13 21 13 21 89	21 13 21 55	34 144	13+21 = 34 21+34 = 55 34+55 = 89 55+89 = 144		2 3 5 8 13 21 34 55 89 144

Figure 2

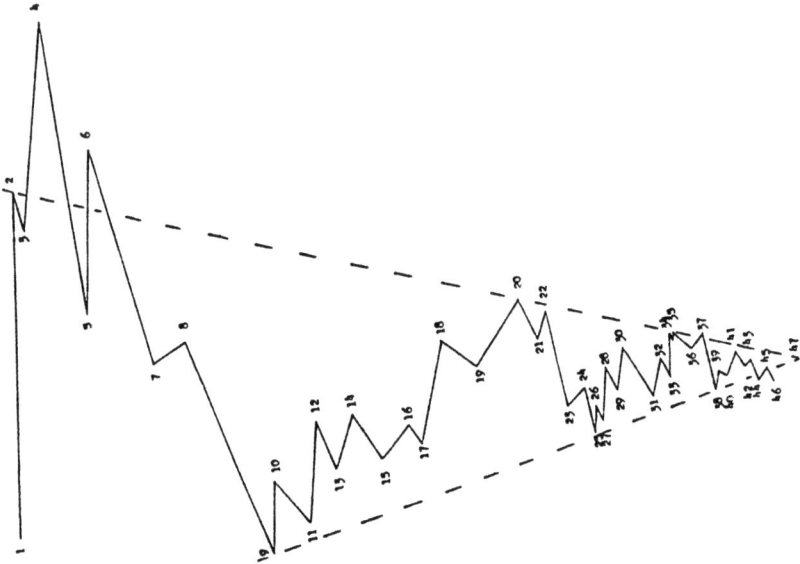

Figure 3

An example of the use of the time element in conjunction with The Wave Principle is given in the accompanying graph of *The New York Times* average of 50 Combined Stocks, arithmetic scale, from August 1921 to May 1941. The various wave reversal points in this twenty-year period are listed in Table A, while the duration between reversal points is set forth in Table B.

The time relationship can also be applied, in conjunction with wave analysis, to other indices, such as trends in corporate bonds in the graph below. The numbers 13, 21 and 55 represent the number of months duration of waves, as indicated by arrows. (The five-wave bull market in long-term government bonds lasted 89 months, measured from January 1932 to June 1939.)

In studying the time element, it should be noted that a movement may start and end near the beginning, middle or end of a month, and for that reason the actual time elapsed, when measured by the day or week equivalent to the summation series of months, can terminate in a month next higher or lower than the series of months indicated.

Table "A"
Numbers at reversal points

No.	Month	Year	No.	Month	Year
1	Aug.	1921	25	Mar.	1938
2	Nov.	28	26	Apl.	38
3	Dec.	28	27	May	38
4	Sep.	29	28	Jul.	38
5	Nov.	29	29	Sep.	38
6	Apl.	30	30	Nov.	38
9	Jul.	32	31	Apl.	39
10	Sep.	32	32	Aug.	39
11	Mar.	33	34	Sep.	39
12	Jul.	33	35	Oct.	39
13	Oct.	33	36	Jan.	40
14	Feb.	34	37	Apl.	40
15	Jul.	34	38	May	40
16	Jun.	35	39	Jun.	40
17	Mar.	35	40	Aug.	40
18	Nov.	35	41	Nov.	40
19	Apl.	36	42	Nov.	40
20	Mar.	37	43	Jan.	41
21	Jun.	37	44	Feb.	41
22	Aug.	37	45	Apl.	41
23	Oct.	37	46	May	41
24	Feb.	38	47	Oct.	41

Table "B"

Numbers From	To	Duration Months	Years	Numbers From	To	Duration Months
1	2	89		20	23	8
1	4		8	20	24	
2	47		13	20	25	13
3	4	8		20	47	55
4	9	34		23	24	5
4	47	144		25	30	8
5	6	5		30	31	5
9	12	13		31	34	5
9	20	55		35	36	3
12	15	13		35	47	
20	25	13		36	37	3
20	21	3		37	46	13
20	22	5		41	46	5

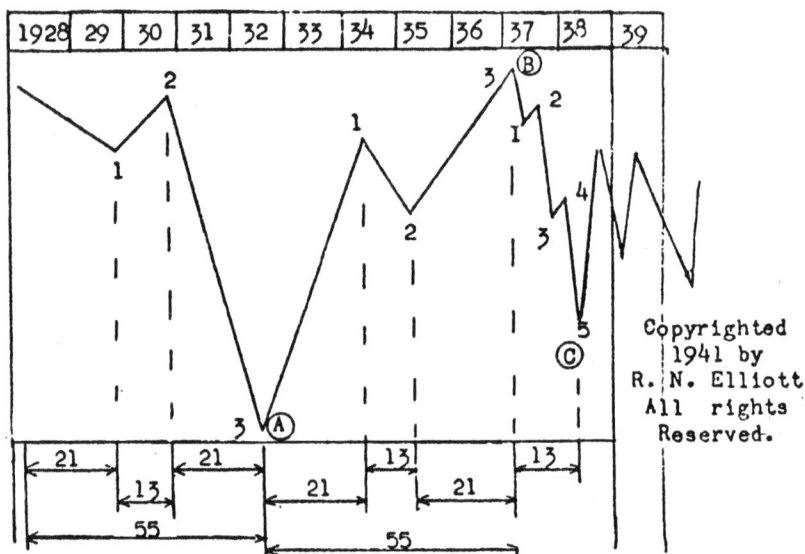

Figure 4

ENDNOTES

¹ This essay includes sections from a page issued in September or October 1938 and from Educational Bulletin A, issued in late December 1939 or early January 1940.

² This is Elliott's only use of any variation of the term *mood*. The phrase "moods of human behavior" doesn't have a clear meaning. This is the closest he skates to the "social mood" of socionomics.

³ He means events that are presumed to be causes.

⁴ Id.

⁵ This would better read, "patterns."

⁶ He means, "...a complete up-and-down sequence of which...."

⁷ The first three paragraphs of this essay are from Interpretive Letter No. 26, "The Ruling Ratio of Waves," dated January 11, 1943.

⁸ As noted on the graph.

⁹ See the "Pythagorean Diagram" on the next page and the picture of Pythagoras in *Nature's Law*, Chapter XXV.

¹⁰ He is probably referring to the Decennial Pattern. This and the next paragraph beg for elaboration. See the discussion in *Elliott Wave Principle*.

¹¹ This section is from Interpretive Letter No. 18, dated August 27, 1941.

MARKET APATHY —
CAUSE AND TERMINATION[1]

AUGUST 11, 1941

The total yearly volume of stock transactions on the New York Stock Exchange has been declining for five consecutive years, and apathy has been most pronounced since October 1939. The causes of this apathy can be traced to cyclical influences and measured mathematically. Sustained market activity expands or

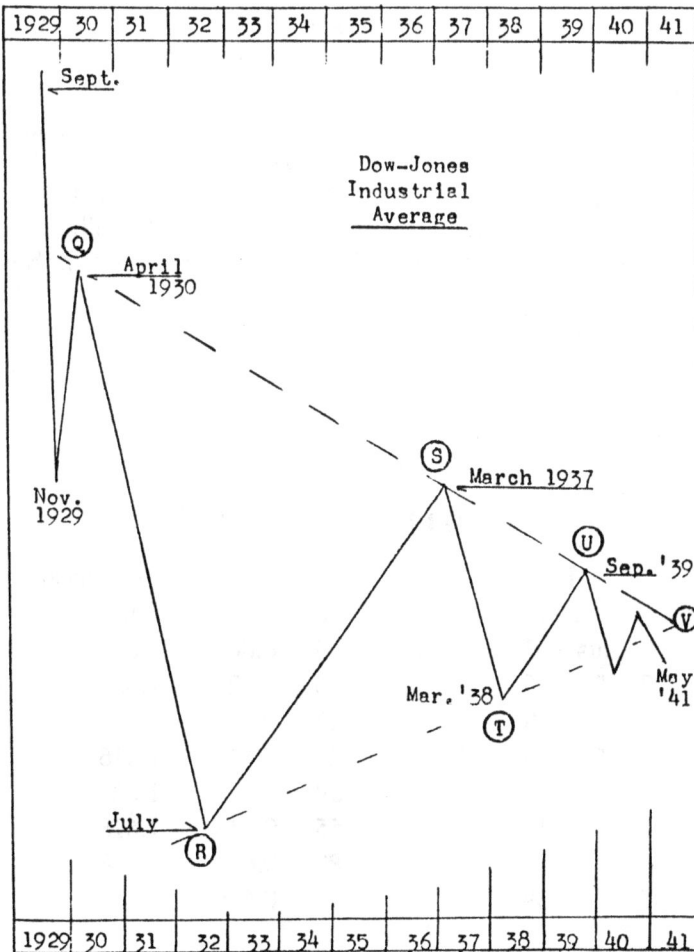

Figure 5

contracts with the length of the price trend. The longer the trend, the greater the public interest and turnover in stocks, and vice versa. During recent years, the swings in the price trend have become progressively shorter, as is characteristic of movements within an orthodox triangle.

The swings of the Dow Jones Industrial monthly average, as shown in the accompanying chart, afford a clear explanation for this lack of confidence and resulting apathy. The two dashed lines, Q - V (drawn across the falling tops of April 1930, March 1937, and September 1939) and R - V (drawn across the rising bottoms of July 1932 and March 1938), form a triangle of gigantic area. Each completed swing of the pendulum within this triangle has become progressively shorter in accordance with the geometric ratio of 0.618, as regards both extent and duration.

The triangular outline is therefore also a "ratio triangle," and as such, differs in important respects from the "wave triangle" described in my Treatise, *The Wave Principle*.[2] The ratio of 0.618 and its reciprocal, 1.618, stem directly from the ratio of the circumference of a circle to the diameter, or 3.1416.[3] This ratio is also the basic characteristic of the Fibonacci Summation Series, which is identical in numerical count with the structure of The Wave Principle. This similarity is discussed fully in a circular, "The Basis of The Wave Principle." The Fibonacci Series, the ratio of each term to the next term, and the reciprocal value, are revealed in the following:

Table of Relativity

First Term			Second Term	Ratio	Reciprocal Ratio
2 plus	3	equals	5	0.60	1.67
3 "	5	"	8	0.625	1.60
5 "	8	"	13	0.615	1.63
8 "	13	"	21	0.619	1.616
13 "	21	"	34	0.617	1.62
21 "	34	"	55	0.618	1.618
34 "	55	"	89	0.618	1.618
55 "	89	"	144	0.618	1.618

These ratios and series have been controlling and limiting the extent and duration of price trends, irrespective of wars, politics, production indices, the supply of money, general purchasing power, and other generally accepted methods of determining stock values. *That this statement is true is verified* by the following tabulation of important movements since April 1930:

The Cyclical Relativity of Market Trends

Wave No.	Dates From	To	Points From	To	Change			Ratio
R	April 1930	July 1932	296.0	40.5	255.5			
S	July 1932	March 1937	40.5	196.0	155.5	155.5/	255.5=	60.9%
T	March 1937	March 1938	196.0	97.0	99.0	99.0/	155.5=	63.6%
U	March 1938	Sept. 1939	97.0	158.0	61.0	61.0/	99.0=	61.6%
								Avg. 62.0%

This feature proves that current events and politics have no influence on market movements.

Since the causes of this phenomenal market behavior originate in the relativity of the component cycles compressed within the triangular area, it is distinctly encouraging to be able to point out that the rapidly approaching apex of the triangle should mark the beginning of a relatively long period of increasing activity in the stock market.

With the Wave Principle, the fact that all five measures (the ratio of cyclical trends, the relative time for the movement, the mathematical nature of a triangle, and the Fibonacci Summation Series all stemming from the common source) point to an approaching culmination of a tremendous thirteen-year cyclical correction is extraordinary.

ENDNOTES

[1] This treatise is an excellent innovative analysis and a correct conclusion.

[2] The difference Elliott points out is, in fact, crucial. Apparently a ratio triangle may appear apart from a wave triangle. Thus, the 13-year triangle is not a required interpretation despite the Fibonacci relationships.

[3] See discussion in Chapter 3 of *Elliott Wave Principle*.

TWO CYCLES OF AMERICAN HISTORY[1]

AUGUST 25, 1941

1776 - 1857, 81 years
1857 - 1941, 84 years

The earliest available stock record is the Axe-Houghton Index, dating from 1854. The essential "change" characteristics of the long movement from 1854 to September 1929 are shown in the accompanying graph. The wave from 1857 to 1929 may be either Cycle wave I, III or V, depending upon the nature and extent of development of the country before 1854. There is reason to believe, however, that the period from 1857 to 1929 can be regarded as Cycle wave III.[2] In the first place, the broad periodicity of approximately eighty years connects the Revolutionary Period, the Civil War Period and World War II that has been in progress during the past decade. Secondly, the market since 1929 has outlined the pattern of a gigantic thirteen-year triangle of such tremendous scope that these defeatist years may well be grouped as Cycle wave IV. Thirdly, my observation has been that orthodox triangles appear only as the fourth wave of a cycle.

To appreciate the cause of triangular Cycle wave IV, it is necessary to review the previous years, particularly the dynamic span of 1921 to 1929. Attention is therefore invited to component wave 5, shown in the accompanying graph of the Axe-Houghton Index, with this particular wave running from 1906[3] to 1929. The fifth or "e" wave, running from 1921 to the orthodox "extension" top of November 1928, was further subdivided as shown on page 38 of the Treatise. This pattern is referred to in my Treatise as a "half-moon." This movement was extremely dynamic, accompanied by high speed, large volume and wild speculation. Furthermore, it was the culminating phase in the long span from 1857.

A cycle such as that from 1857 to 1929 and containing such a frenzied movement as that from 1921 to 1929 necessarily requires an extensive correction, not only from the standpoint of price change but also in breadth of area or duration. High speed movements in one direction always generate proportionally high speed in the ensuing movement in the opposite direction.[4] The

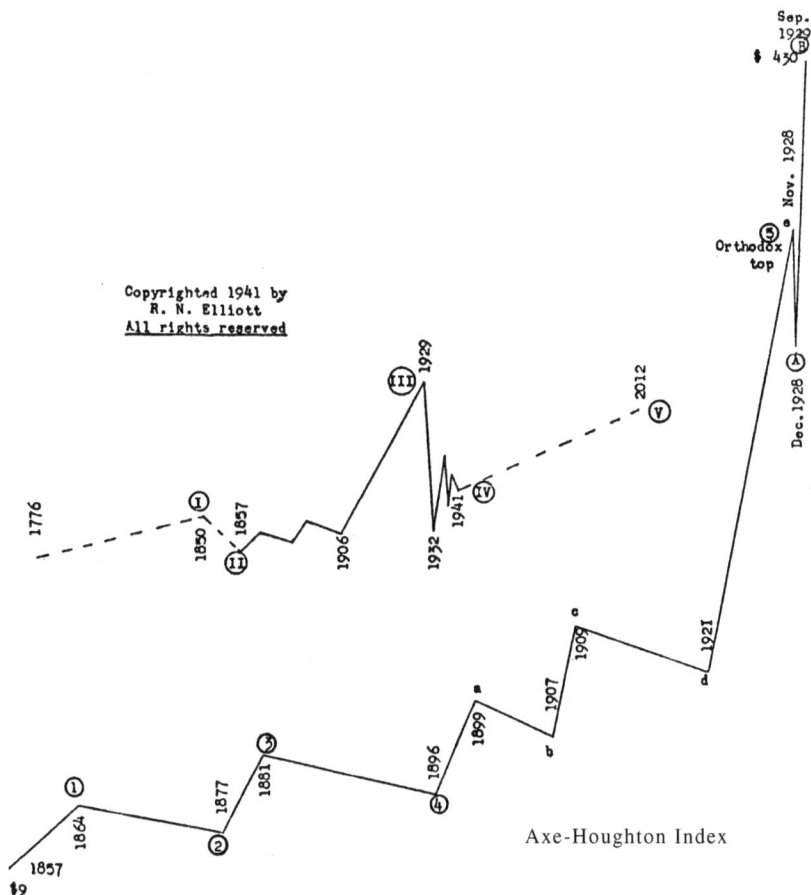

Figure 6

momentum carries over, in corrections, into the subsequent
swings. Similarly, the extent, duration and volume characteristics
are relative, cycle by cycle. In summation, the proportional
arrangement of the necessarily extensive correction of the 1857-
1929 wave called for shorter and shorter movements together
with decreasing speed and volume. Nature's inexorable law of
proportion accounts for the recurrent 0.618 ratio of swing by
swing comparison. The whole movement (or all the movements)
since 1928 (and also from April 1930) form a tremendous triangle,
and this triangle is regarded as Cycle IV of an order dating back
to as early as 1776.[5]

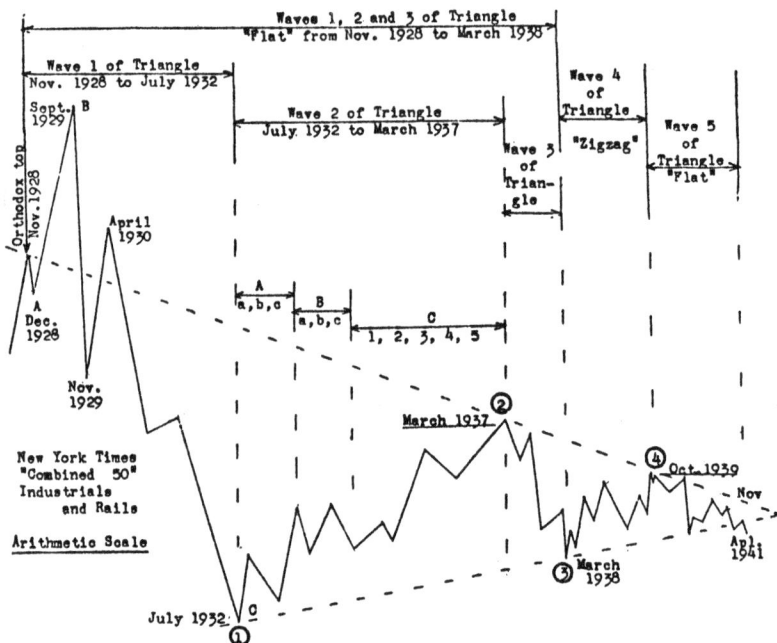

Figure 7

Triangle wave ⑤ is well advanced, and its termination, within or without the area of the triangle, should mark the final correction of the 13-year pattern of *defeatism*. This termination will also mark the beginning of a new Cycle wave V (composed of a series of cycles of lesser degree), comparable in many respects with the long cycle from 1857 to 1929. Cycle V is not expected to culminate until about 2012.[6] (See dashed line in the first graph.)

ENDNOTES

[1] This essay is from Interpretive Letter No. 17.

[2] A remarkable conclusion, fully supported by the discovery of additional data. See the presentation in *Elliott Wave Principle* as well as the updated charts on the next page. The first chart shows the wave count for the Grand Supercycle bull market from 1784 in the Dow Jones Industrial Average *adjusted for inflation* (i.e., using constant dollars), which shows a legitimate triangle in the wave (IV) position from 1929

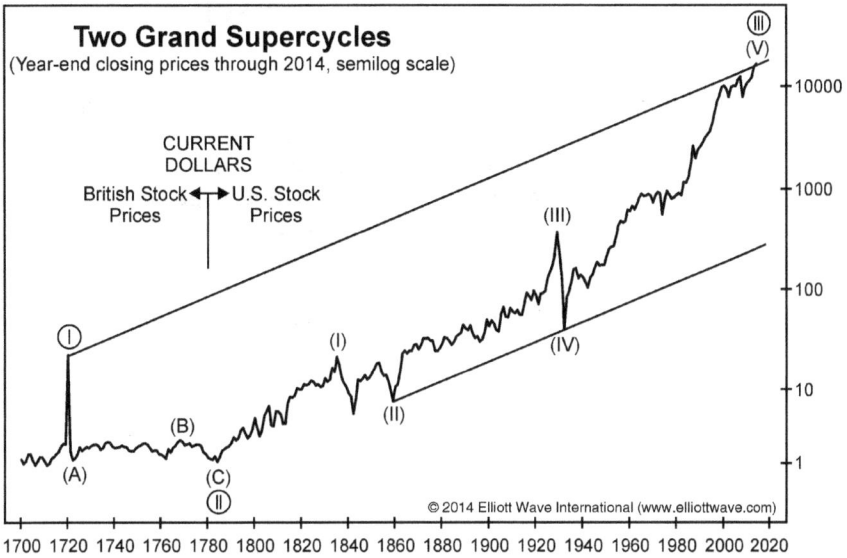

Two Grand Supercycles
(Year-end closing prices through 2014, semilog scale)

CURRENT
DOLLARS

British Stock ◄──►U.S. Stock
Prices   Prices

Ⓘ

(B)

(A)   (C)
              Ⓘ

(I)

(II)

(III)

(IV)

Ⓘ
(V)

© 2014 Elliott Wave International (www.elliottwave.com)

10000
1000
100
10
1

1700 1720 1740 1760 1780 1800 1820 1840 1860 1880 1900 1920 1940 1960 1980 2000 2020

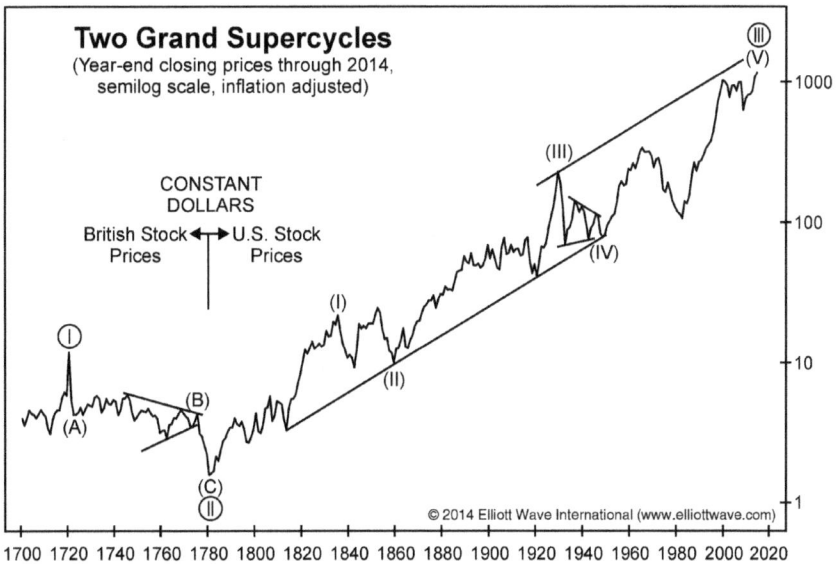

Two Grand Supercycles
(Year-end closing prices through 2014,
semilog scale, inflation adjusted)

CONSTANT
DOLLARS

British Stock ◄──►U.S. Stock
Prices   Prices

Ⓘ

(A)   (B)

(C)
Ⓘ

(I)

(II)

(III)

(IV)

Ⓘ
(V)

© 2014 Elliott Wave International (www.elliottwave.com)

1000
100
10
1

1700 1720 1740 1760 1780 1800 1820 1840 1860 1880 1900 1920 1940 1960 1980 2000 2020

to 1949 and a long fifth wave carrying so far into 2015, just 3 years
past Elliott's estimate of 2012. The second chart shows the count in
current dollars, by which measure the bull market has lasted 83 years
from 1932.

[3] He means 1896.

[4] While such behavior is common in commodity prices, it is not
always true in the stock market. In fact, the opposite often occurs.

[5] Good call. The record shows the low in 1784 in British stock prices.

[6] This estimate is based on a length equivalent to the 1857-1928 (orthodox top) advance, as he states in the next essay, "The Future Pattern of the Market." Thrusts, as he points out elsewhere, are normally short and sharp; but this time it wasn't. He incorporates this idea in an otherwise identical forecast in the final pages of *Nature's Law* but suggests a thrust that is too brief. Regardless, his call for a multi-decade advance in the midst of the pervasive gloom of 1942 is stunning in its accuracy and foresight, made possible only because he ignored all the news and exclusively examined the pattern.

THE FUTURE PATTERN OF THE MARKET [1]

OCTOBER 26, 1942

The pattern of the past 21 years (1921-1942) furnishes a basis which may be used for forecasting that of the next 70 years, as well as estimating what the record may have been between 1776 and 1850.

Graph 1 below covers the entire period from 1776 to 2012 and shows five waves of large degree. A Wave Principle cycle is always composed of five waves up and three waves down, regardless of the degree or size.

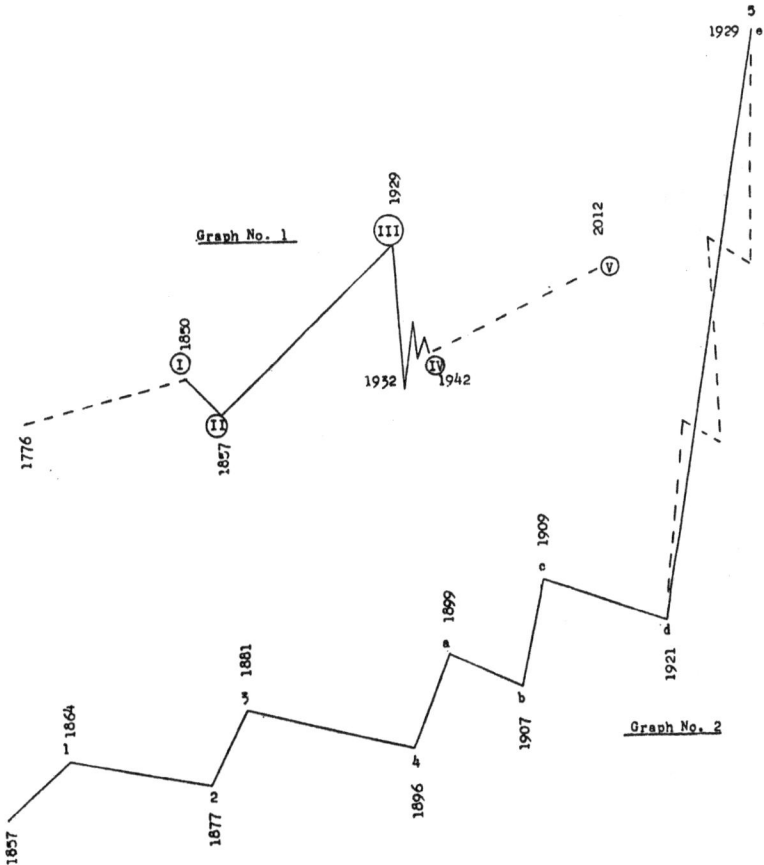

Figure 8

Waves 2 and 4 are always corrections. *Triangles may appear as wave 4, never as wave 2 insofar as I have observed.* Therefore, the pattern of the period from 1929 to 1942, being a triangle, is wave ⒾⓋ of a Supercycle.[2] Wave Ⓥ is about to start, and based on the duration of wave Ⓘ (1857-1929), it should terminate about the year 2012.[3]

Having established that wave ⒾⓋ started in 1929, wave Ⓘ obviously ended in the same year.[4] Wave Ⓘ of Graph 1, from 1857 to 1929, is detailed in Graph 2, using the Axe-Houghton Index.

The 5th wave of Graph 2 started in 1896. It subdivided into five waves, and its subdivided 5th wave, *starting in 1921, extended. Extensions never appear twice in a cycle.* Therefore, no extension of this degree should appear between 1942 and 2012.[5] Doubtless, neither did one appear in wave Ⓘ, previous to 1850, for which period I have no record. For these reasons, the two dashed lines in Graph 1,[6] previous to 1850 and following 1942, are sound conclusions.[7]

Wave Ⓥ of Graph 1 will embrace three bull markets and two intervening bear markets. The amplitude of waves (percentagewise) and volume will resemble those of the period between 1857 and 1909, as depicted in Graph 2. No one now living will witness a "New Era" of the 1920s type.[8]

ENDNOTES

[1] Elliott's analysis here (from "Educational Bulletin O") is a repeat of the analysis in the preceding essay, updated at a time when he knew that the market had passed its Supercycle wave (IV) bottom. The overall analysis remains a remarkable feat and was shown to be correct with the new availability of past data, as presented in *Elliott Wave Principle*.

[2] Should read "Grand Supercycle."

[3] See Endnote 6 of the preceding essay.

[4] This sentence and the next three, as well as Graph 2, reveal that on at least this occasion, Elliott interpreted 1921-1929 as a straightforward "five," a conclusion with which I entirely agree. 1929-1932 is then a straightforward A-B-C. His "irregular top" thesis is unnecessary, as he himself reveals in this passage. History shows that the stock market almost invariably traces out one simple pattern after another, despite the feeling one gets occasionally in real time that the market is playing some new "trick." As a pattern nears its end, missing clarity always returns in a flash of recognition.

[5] Elliott's example suggests that within a five wave structure, typically only one subwave will contain an extension in one of its impulse subwaves, whereas actually the correct guideline is that usually only one impulse wave within a five wave structure *will be* an extension. There is no reason why an extension should not appear as a *subwave* of each impulse wave in a five wave sequence. In fact, it nearly always does.

[6] Elliott was sometimes careless with his drawings. Wave (V) in graph 1, for instance, was clearly intended to climb to a new high. Neither did the 1932 low fall below the peak of wave (I).

[7] Elliott's historical wave count is brilliant and accurate. His conclusion, made only six months after the 1942 low, was entirely correct that that low would not be exceeded prior to a multi-decade advance. His conclusion regarding the rise into the beginning of his data in 1850 was similarly accurate, although wave (I) began in 1784 and ended in 1836 (the correction was a flat, with an intervening high in 1852).

[8] The fifth wave of Cycle degree that accelerated in 1982 and carried through the 1990s has been a "New Era" wave (i.e., founded on hope) and has been analogous to the 1920s at Supercycle (though not Grand Supercycle) degree.

NATURE'S LAW
THE SECRET OF THE UNIVERSE

by

R.N. Elliott

REFERENCE INDICATIONS[1]

Reference to chapters, pages, diagrams, etc. will be indicated as follows:

(C)   Chapter. For example, "C 24" means Chapter No. 24.

(D)   Diagram. For example, "D 4" means Diagram No. 4.

(FSS) Numbers of the Fibonacci Summation Series

(OT)   Orthodox top.

(G)   Graph. For example, "G X" means "Graph X".

(P)   Page. For example, "P 5" means Page 5.

(PD)   "P2 D4" means Page 2, Diagram 4.

(PG)   "P3 G6" means Page 3, Graph 6.

(PPD) "P4 P6 D8" means Page 4, Paragraph 6, Diagram 8.

(R)   Ruling ratio of the Fibonacci Summation Series, such as .62 or reciprocal 1.62.

Publisher's Note: In the original monograph, nearly every sentence was treated as a separate paragraph and numbered. We have taken the liberty of condensing the style of arrangement for easier reading. The references to text areas by codes as described above have been eliminated.

ENDNOTES

[1] Elliott's talent for ordering and labeling comes out even here.

NATURE'S LAW

THE SECRET OF THE UNIVERSE

By R. N. ELLIOTT

❦

Vitally Important for

Traders in Securities, Commodities, etc.; Investors; Customers'
Brokers; Market Technicians; Bankers; Business Managers;
Economists; Trusts.

✦

Of Interest to

Artists, see page 9; Botanists, see pages 9, 51; Egyptologists, see
pages 7, 8, 51; Inventors, see pages 38, 39; Mathematicians, see
pages 7, 9, 29, 31, 51; Philosophers, see page 4; Physicians, see
page 55; Psychologists, see pages 7, 24; Pyramidists, see pages
7, 8, 29, 51, 59; Pythagoreans, see pages 7, 8, 56, 57, 58; Students of
Dynamic Symmetry, see pages 8, 9, 10, 11.

INTRODUCTION

RHYTHM IN NATURE[1]

No truth meets more general acceptance than that the universe is ruled by law. Without law it is self-evident there would be chaos, and where chaos is, nothing is. Navigation, chemistry, aeronautics, architecture, radio transmission, surgery, music — the gamut, indeed, of art and science — all work, in dealing with things animate and things inanimate, under law because nature herself works in this way. Since the very character of law is order, or constancy, it follows that all that happens will repeat and can be predicted if we know the law.

Columbus, maintaining that the world was round, predicted that a westward course from Europe must eventually bring his ships to land and despite scoffers, even among his own crew, saw his prediction realized. Halley, calculating the orbit of the 1682 comet, predicted its return which was strikingly verified in 1759. Marconi, after his studies in electrical transmission, predicted that sound could be conveyed without wires, and today we can sit in our homes and listen to musical and other programs from across the ocean. These men, as have countless more in other fields, learned the law. After becoming thus posted, prediction was easy because it became mathematical.

Even though we may not understand the cause underlying a particular phenomenon, we can, by observation, predict that phenomenon's recurrence. The sun was expected to recurrently rise at a fixed time thousands of years before the cause operating to produce this result was known. Indians fix their month by each new moon, but even today cannot tell why regular intervals characterize this heavenly sign. Spring plantings are witnessed the world over because summer is expected as next in order; yet how many planters understand why they are afforded this constancy of the seasons? In each instance the rhythm of the particular phenomenon was mastered.

Man is no less a natural object than the sun or the moon, and his actions, too, in their metrical occurrence, are subject to analysis. Human activities, while amazing in character, if approached from the rhythmical bias, contain a precise and natural answer to some of our most perplexing problems. Furthermore, because man is subject to rhythmical procedure, calculations having to do with his activities can be projected far into the future with a justification and certainty heretofore unattainable.

Very extensive research in connection with what may be termed human activities indicates that practically all developments which result from our social-economic processes follow a law that causes them to repeat themselves in similar and constantly recurring serials of waves or impulses of definite number and pattern. It is likewise indicated that in their intensity, these waves or impulses bear a consistent relation to one another and to the passage of time. In order to best illustrate and expound this phenomenon it is necessary to take, in the field of man's activities, some example which furnishes an abundance of reliable data and for such purpose there is nothing better than the stock exchange.

Particular attention has been given to the stock market for two reasons. In the first place, there is no other field in which prediction has been essayed with such great intensity and with so little result. Economists, statisticians, technicians, business leaders, and bankers, all have had a try at foretelling the future of prices over the New York Stock Exchange. Indeed, there has developed a definite profession with market forecasting as its objective. Yet 1929 came and went, and the turn from the greatest bull market on record to the greatest bear market on record caught almost every investor off guard. Leading investment institutions, spending hundreds of thousands of dollars yearly on market research, were caught by surprise and suffered millions of dollars loss because of price shrinkage in stock holdings that were carried too long.

A second reason for choosing the stock market as an illustration of the wave impulse common to social-economic activity is the great reward attendant on successful stock market prediction. Even accidental success in some single market forecast has yielded riches little short of the fabulous. In the market advance from July 1932 to March 1937, for illustration, an average of thirty leading and representative stocks advanced by 373%. During the course of this five-year movement, however, there were individual stocks whose per cent advance was much larger. Lastly, the broad advance cited above was not in a straight upward line, but rather by a series of upward and downward steps, or zig-zag movements of a number of months' duration. These lesser swings afforded even greater opportunity for profit.

Despite the attention given the stock market, success, both in the accuracy of prediction and the bounties attendant thereto, has necessarily been haphazard because those who have attempted to deal with the market's movements have failed to recognize the extent to which the market is a psychological phenomenon. They have not grasped the fact that there is regularity underlying the fluctuations of the market, or, stated otherwise, that price movements in stocks are subject to rhythms, or an ordered sequence. Thus market predictions, as those who have had any experience in the subject well know, have lacked certainty or value of any but an accidental kind.

But the market has its law, just as is true of other things throughout the universe. Were there no law, there could be no center about which prices could revolve and, therefore, no market. Instead, there would be a daily series of disorganized, confused price fluctuations without reason or order anywhere apparent. A close study of the market, however, as will be subsequently disclosed, proves that this is not the case. Rhythm, or regular, measured, and harmonious movement, is to be discerned. This law behind the market can be discovered only when the market is viewed in its proper light, and then is analyzed from this approach. Simply put, the stock market is a creation of man and therefore reflects human idiosyncrasy. In the pages which follow, the law, or rhythm, to which man responds will be disclosed as registered by market movements that fluctuate in accordance with a definite wave principle.

Nature's Law has always functioned in every human activity. Waves of different degrees occur whether or not recording machinery is present. When the machinery described below is present, the patterns of waves are perfected and become visible to the experienced eye. This machinery is:

A. Extensive commercial activity represented by corporations whose ownership is widely distributed.
B. A general market-place where buyer and seller may contact quickly through representatives.
C. Reliable record and publications of transactions.
D. Adequate statistics available on all matters relating to corporations.
E. Daily high and low range charted in such a manner as will disclose the waves of all degrees as they occur.

The daily range of stock transactions was inaugurated in 1928 and the hourly record in 1932. These are necessary in order to observe the Minor and Minute waves, especially in fast markets.

Contrary to teachings of the Dow Theory, a popular device for gauging stock market movements, "Nature's Law" does not require confirmation by two averages. Each average, group, stock or any human activity is interpreted by its own waves.

ENDNOTES

[1] Except for minor revisions, this Introduction is the same as Chapter I of *The Wave Principle*.

CHAPTER I

THE GREAT PYRAMID GIZEH

Many years ago I endeavored to ascertain the meaning of the word "cycle," but no one could define it. Curiosity led to a study of graphs, and I discovered rhythm in fluctuations (as disclosed in my Treatise published in 1938). Later I found that the basis of my discoveries was a law of Nature known to the designers of the Great Pyramid Gizeh, which may have been constructed five thousand years ago.

There are several pyramids in Egypt and elsewhere, but Gizeh is the original, and the only one that discloses symbols. Other pyramids were subsequently built to serve as crypts for the bodies of kings and their families. As early as 820 B.C., Al Mamoun, a Turkish Caliph, erroneously supposed that Gizeh housed the bodies of former pharaohs and that hoards of gold might be found. This proves that even at that early date the symbols of Gizeh were unknown. The period of Gizeh's construction was not only pre-literary but pre-hieroglyphic. Hieroglyphics are present in other pyramids but not in Gizeh.

Immense sums of money have been expended to learn the symbols of Gizeh, especially during the past fifty years. Their definitions are remarkably correct insofar as today's knowledge permits an understanding. Much of this knowledge is comparatively recent and indicates that the scientific symbols embodied in Gizeh must have been supernatural or that previous civilizations existed which equalled or exceeded today's development. It is possible that a high degree of civilization previously existed on the Western Hemisphere, especially from Mexico to Argentina. The Bible mentions giants and quite recently jaws of giants have been found that may have weighed four or five hundred pounds.[1]

Insofar as I have been able to learn, Egyptologists overlooked certain important symbols contained in the Great Pyramid, such as the ratio of the elevation to the base of the pyramid which is 61.8% and the number of inches of the elevation which is 5,813. (Note the numbers 5, 8, and 13, mentioned below in the Summation Series.) The unit of measurement in Egypt was, and is, the "inch" as we know it today.

The outlines of a side view is that of a cycle, that is, **3** lines; in a pyramid there are **5** surfaces, four above ground and one at the bottom; from the apex **8** lines are visible; total surfaces and lines: **13**.

Fibonacci, an Italian mathematician of the thirteenth century, visited Egypt and on his return disclosed a summation series as follows: 1 2 3 5 8 13 21 34 55 89 144.... Any two adjoining numbers equal the next higher — for example, 5 + 8 = 13. The ratio of any number to the next higher is 61.8%. (The lower numbers produce a ratio slightly at variance). Therefore *the elevation to the base of the pyramid provides a ratio that rules the entire series.*

The seeds of a sun flower are located in curved rows that intersect each other. The highest number of intersections is 144. This is also the number of Minor waves in a complete cycle of the stock market (bull and bear markets). Numbers of the series are present in the human body, botany, production, animals, music and waves of human activities including the stock market.

Pythagoras, a Greek philosopher of the fifth century, B.C., visited Egypt and on his return disclosed the diagram and title shown in Chapter 2.

ENDNOTES

[1] Since proved to be otherwise, of course!

CHAPTER II

NATURE'S LAW

Nature's Law was known at least five thousand years ago. Egypt was "in flower" by at least 1,500 B. C. and is the oldest of today's list of nations. It is not known when the Egyptian pyramids were built. The Great Pyramid Gizeh was constructed at least five thousand years ago. Some students advance evidence that it existed before the threat of floods that prompted Noah to build the ark. Other students believe that it may be thirty thousand years old.

In *Life* magazine (December 3, 1945) there appears a very interesting article entitled "The Building of the Great Pyramid." Mr. Bel Geddes prepared models of different stages of construction and pictures of them are shown. The report was prepared for the *Encyclopedia Britannica*. It says that the total weight of material used was 3,277,000 tons, whereas the material used in the Empire State Building, the tallest building in the world, weighs only 305,000 tons.

The marvelous ingenuity, skill, time and labor expended by the designers and builders of the pyramids to erect a perpetual symbol demonstrates the supreme importance of the messages they desired to convey to posterity. That era was pre-literary and pre-hieroglyphic, therefore symbols were the only means of recording.

For centuries the pyramids have been exhaustively investigated, especially during recent years. Insofar as I have observed, Egyptologists overlooked an important, perhaps the most important symbol. I refer to the outer lines of the pyramid Gizeh.

Pythagoras was a renowned Greek philosopher of the fifth century, B. C. The older cyclopedias give a very detailed description of his activities. The *Encyclopedia Britannica* shows a diagram and cryptic title which may be the only record he left. It was made after he returned to Greece following a prolonged visit to Egypt. The diagram and title appear in Figure 1. It is fair to assume that the Pythagoras diagram refers to a pyramid.

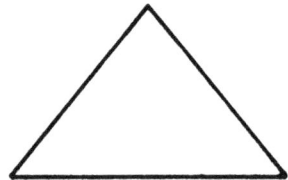

The Secret of the Universe

Figure 1

The original measurements of the Great
pyramid of Gizeh are estimated to have been:
base 783.3 feet, elevation 484.4 feet, ratio
61.8%. The elevation, 484.4 feet, equals 5,813
inches (5-8-13 FSS).

Looking at a pyramid from any one of the
four sides, **3** lines are visible. The diagram
in Figure 2 is a complete cycle. Viewing the
pyramid from any one of the four corners as in Figure 3, **5** lines
are visible. A pyramid has **5** surfaces — four above ground and
the bottom. From the apex, a pyramid shows **8** lines, as shown
in Figure 4.

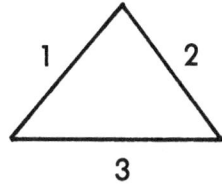

Figure 2

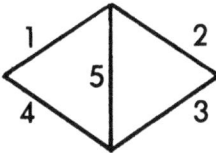

Figure 3

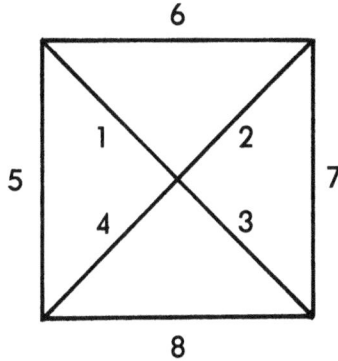

Figure 4

Fibonacci was an Italian mathematician of the thirteenth
century, A. D. He was better known in his day as Leonardo de
Pisa. He visited Egypt and Greece, and on his return to Italy
disclosed what is known as a summation series. This series of
numbers follows: 1 2 3 5 8 13 21 34 55 89 144....

Any two adjoining numbers equal the next higher number,
for example, 5 + 8 = 13. Any number divided by the next higher
number gives a ratio of .618, for example, 8/13 = .618. Any number
divided by the next lower number gives a reciprocal of 1.618. In
the lower numbers the ratios are not exact, but close enough for
practical purposes. To simplify reading, I will hereafter refer to
the former as .62 and the latter as 1.62.

Note that the first five numbers of the Summation Series, 1,
2, 3, 5, and 8, are shown in the complete diagram of a pyramid.

The late Jay Hambidge, an American artist, visited Egypt, Greece and Italy and wrote several very important and interesting books. By permission of Yale University Press, I quote pages 27 and 28 of his book entitled *Practical Applications of Dynamic Symmetry*:

Botanists use the disk of the sunflower as a sort of general illustration of the law of leaf arrangement. It exhibits the phenomenon in nearly two-dimensional form. The seeds are distributed over the sunflower disk in rhomboidal shaped sockets and the complex of these sockets forms a design of intersecting curves, the pattern being something like the old-fashioned chasing on watchcases. This pattern of curves is the interesting feature of the sunflower seed arrangement.

First. The curve itself is a definite kind of curve. As a matter of fact it is quite like the curve of shell growth. It is regular and possesses certain mathematical properties. These properties are a necessary consequence of uniform growth as will be explained presently.

Second. When these curves are counted it will be found that a normal sunflower disk of five or six inches in diameter has 89. Winding in one direction there are 55 and in the other direction there are 34. That is to say, the normal head exhibits 55 curves crossing 34. The two numbers are written 34 + 55. Below the apex flower of the stalk there are usually secondary flowers, smaller in size. The curve-crossing numbers for these are generally 21 + 34. Lower of the stalk may be tertiary flowers of late development. The curve-crossing numbers of these are 13 + 21.

At Oxford, in England, sunflowers have been nourished to produce abnormal disks and the curve-crossing numbers have increased from 34 + 55 to 55 + 89. Professor Arthur H. Church, a leading modern authority on this fascinating subject, tells us of a gigantic disk raised at Oxford whereon the curve-crossing numbers were 89 + 144.

Around the seed complex of the flower disk there is an arrangement of florets. Like the seeds, these exhibit curve-crossing numbers. They are usually 5 + 8.

If we begin at the bottom of the plant stalk and count the actual number of leaves up to the flower disk, we are likely to find, as we wind our progress around the stalk, that we pass a certain number of leaves before we find one imposed directly over the one first counted, and that this number and the number of revolutions about the stalk, are constant between each leaf imposition. These will represent curve-crossing numbers belonging to the same series of numbers exhibited by the seeds and florets.

The numbers we have mentioned belong to what is called a summation series, so called because each number represents a sum of preceding numbers of the series, in this case 2. This series of numbers is: 1, 2, 3, 5, 8, 13, 21, 34, 55, 89, 144, etc. Each member of this series is obtained by adding together the two preceding numbers.

If we take any two members of this series and divide one into the other as, say 34 into 55, we obtain a ratio, and this ratio is constant throughout the series; that is to say, any lesser number divided into any greater number which immediately succeeds it produces the same ratio. This ratio is 1.618 plus, a number with a never ending fraction. If we reverse the operation and divide 55 into 34, we obtain the number .618 plus. It will be noticed that the difference between these two results is 1 or unity.

It will also be noticed that when we make these two divisional operations that there is a slight error. This is due to the fact that the series is not quite accurate when expressed in whole numbers. There should be a very small fraction. But as the error is within that of observation in the growing plant, the whole number is retained to facilitate checking.

It is an extraordinary coincidence that this ratio of 1.618 or .618 is a ratio which fascinated the ancient Greeks exceedingly. Extraordinary, because they could have had no suspicion that it was connected with the architecture of plants. It was called by them extreme and mean ratio.

During the middle ages it was given the name Divine Section and in fairly recent time, Golden Section.

From experience I have learned that 144 is the highest number of practical value. In a complete cycle of the stock market, the number of Minor waves is 144, as shown in the following table and in Figure 7, Chapter 4:

Number of Waves	Bull Market	Bear Market	Total (complete cycle)
Major	5	3	8
Intermediate	21	13	34
Minor	89	55	144

All are Fibonacci numbers and the entire series is employed. The length of waves may vary, but not the number. Note the FSS numbers in the following:

— The bodies of humans follow the numbers 3 and 5. From the torso there are 5 projections — head, two arms and two legs. Each leg and arm is subdivided into 3 sections. Legs and arms terminate in 5 toes and fingers. The toes and fingers (except the big toe) are subdivided into 3 sections. We have 5 senses.

— The monkey is the same as a human except that his feet are the same as his hands, that is, his big toe is the same as his thumb. Most animals have 5 projections from the torso — head and four legs, total 5. Birds have 5 projections from the torso — head, two feet and two wings.

— Music: The best example is the piano keyboard. "Octave" means eight. Each octave is composed of 8 white keys and 5 black keys, total 13.

— Chemical elements: There are approximately 89 primary elements.

— Colors: There are 3 primary colors. Blending produces all other colors.

Miscellaneous Observations:

— The Western Hemisphere is composed of 3 subdivisions, North, Central and South America.

— In the Western Hemisphere there are 21 Republics, all of which are members of the Pan-American Union. North America is composed of 3 countries, Canada, Mexico and the United States. South America is composed of ten Republics and three European colonies, total 13. Central America was, previous to the Panama Canal, composed of 5 Republics.

— The United States was originally composed of 13 states. Today there are 55 subdivisions as follows: 48 states, District of Columbia, Philippines, Panama Canal Zone, Puerto Rico, Alaska, Hawaiian Islands and the Virgin Islands.

— On the Declaration of Independence there are 56 signatures. The original number was 55. The last was added later.

— Main branches of the Federal Government: 3.

— Highest salute of the Army: 21 guns.

— Voting age: 21 years.

— The Bill of Rights contains: 13 points.

— The colors of the national flag are: 3.

— The Washington Monument in Washington, D. C. (The cornerstone was laid July 4, 1848.):

Total cost, $1,300,000.	13
Height of shaft, 500 feet.	5
Height of capstone, 55 feet.	55
Base of shaft, 55 feet square.	55
Top rim of shaft, 34 feet.	34
Steps of foundation (number):	8
Windows (two on each side):	8

The capstone is in the form of a pyramid with a base 34 feet square and a height 55 feet (ratio .618).

— The Axis was composed of 3 partners. Germany dominated 13 countries in rapid succession but stalled on the fourteenth, Russia. Mussolini served as dictator for 21 years.

— In 1852 Commodore Perry paid a courtesy visit to Japan and invited the "Son of Heaven" to abandon absolute isolationism. In 1907, 55 years later, Japan seriously threatened the United States. In 1941, 34 years later, and 89 years from 1852, Japan attacked Pearl Harbor.

CHAPTER III

HUMAN ACTIVITIES

The expression "human activities"[1] includes such items as stock prices, bond prices, patents, price of gold, population, movements of citizens from cities to farms and vice versa, commodities prices, government expenditures, production, life insurance, electric power produced, gasoline consumption, fire losses, price of seats on the stock exchange, epidemics, and real estate. The main item of interest is the price of securities, which everyone should understand, at least to some degree.

It behooves us to prepare for the "rainy day." Permanent improvements, such as for example, the construction of buildings, conservation projects, roads, bridges, factories, homes, etc. should await cyclical lows for the double purpose of low cost to the owner and employment of labor. Fluctuations in economic welfare are as unfailing as the earth's revolution.

ENDNOTES

[1] See the charts in the final pages of *The Wave Principle*.

CHAPTER IV

DISTINCTIVE FEATURES
OF HUMAN ACTIVITIES

All human activities have three distinctive features —
pattern, time and ratio — all of which observe the Fibonacci
Summation Series. Once the waves can be interpreted, the
knowledge may be applied to any movement, as the same rules
apply to the price of stocks, bonds, grains, cotton, coffee and all
the other activities previously mentioned.

The most important of the three factors is pattern. A pattern
is always in process of formation. Usually, but not invariably,
the student is able to visualize in advance the type of pattern.
This facility is furnished by the type of pattern that preceded.
See Chapter 8, "Alternation."

A perfect diagram of a stock market cycle is shown in Figures
5, 6 and 7. It is divided primarily into "bull market" and "bear
market." Figure 5 subdivides the bull market into five Major[1]
waves and the bear market into three Major waves. The diagram
of the bull market in Figure 6 subdivides Major waves ①, ③
and ⑤[2] into five Intermediate waves each. Figure 7 subdivides
Intermediate waves 1, 3 and 5 into five Minor waves each.

In Figure 5, the bear market is subdivided into three
Major waves indicated by the letters Ⓐ, Ⓑ and Ⓒ. In Figure 6,
downward waves Ⓐ and Ⓒ are subdivided into five Intermediate
waves. Wave Ⓑ upward is divided into three Intermediate waves.
In Figure 7, the Intermediate waves are subdivided into five
Minor waves.

In other words, a bear market is the reverse of a bull market,
except that a bear market has three Major waves down, whereas
in a bull market there are five Major waves upward. Corrections
in both bull and bear swings are more difficult to learn.

As the discoveries disclosed herein are original, new
expressions had to be coined. In order to explain the patterns and
their corresponding expressions, perfect diagrams are shown in
various degrees. The word "degree" means relative importance,
so to speak. For example, "Major" degree refers to those waves
in Figure 5. "Intermediate" degree refers to waves in Figure 6.
"Minor" degree refers to waves shown in Figure 7. See Chapter
2 for numbers of waves.

Bull Market   Bear Market

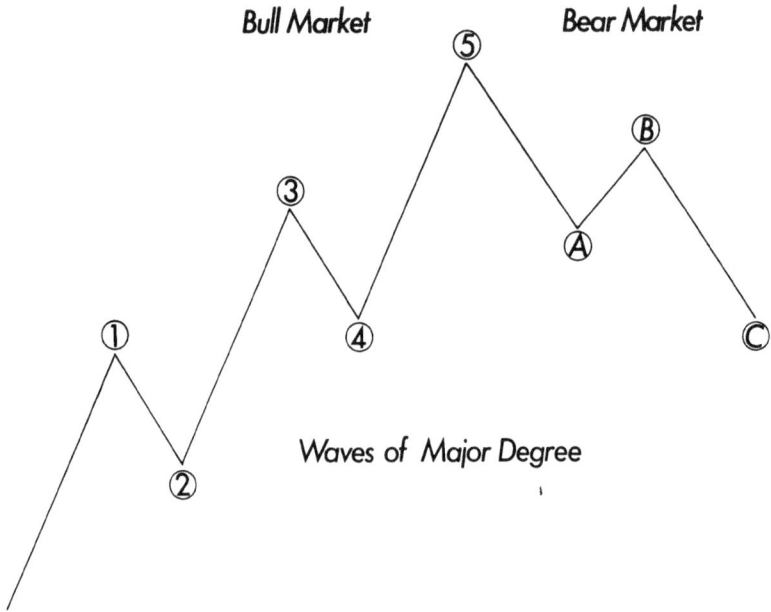

Waves of Major Degree

Figure 5

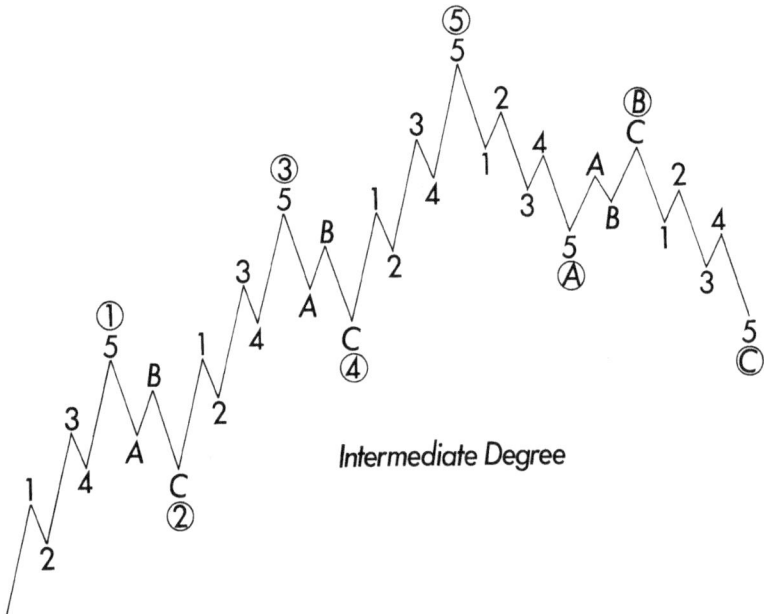

Intermediate Degree

Figure 6

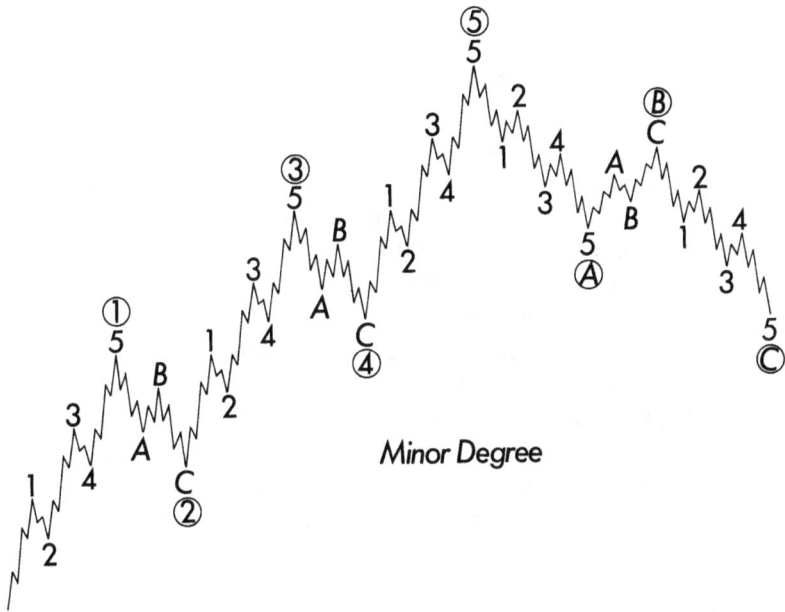

Figure 7

ENDNOTES

[1] The term "Major" is used throughout the next several chapters as a substitute for the term "Primary," which was introduced in the first monograph.

[2] Elliott has improved the wave labeling system used in the first monograph.

CHAPTER V

CORRECTIONS

Patterns of corrections are the same, regardless of their direction or size. In a bull swing, corrections are downward or sidewise. In a bear swing, corrections are upward or sidewise. Therefore, corrections will be diagramed for both bull and bear swings. The diagrams first shown apply to upward swings. Diagrams underneath apply to downswings and will be "inverted." Therefore, whenever the expression "inverted" appears, it applies to the downward main trend.

In Figures 5, 6 and 7 it will be noted that there are three degrees of waves: Major, Intermediate and Minor. Likewise there are three degrees of corrections, as is natural.

There are three types of corrections: Zig-zag,[1] Flat and Triangle.

Zigzags

Figures 8, 9 and 10 are corrections of an uptrend.

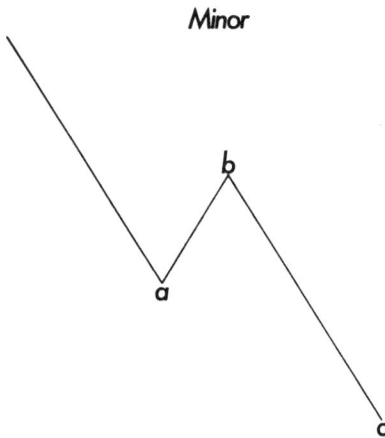

Figure 8

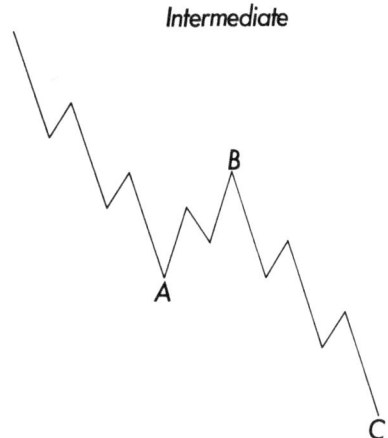

Figure 9

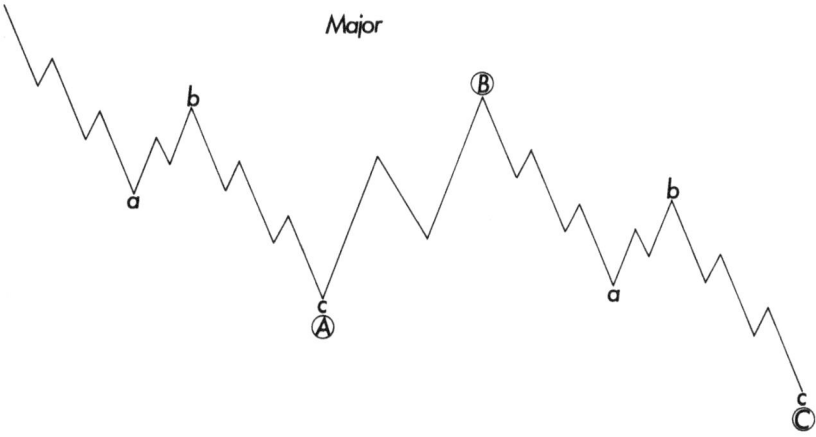

Figure 10

Figures 11, 12, and 13 are inverted (corrections of a downtrend).

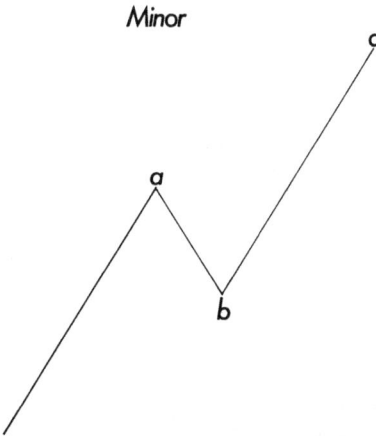

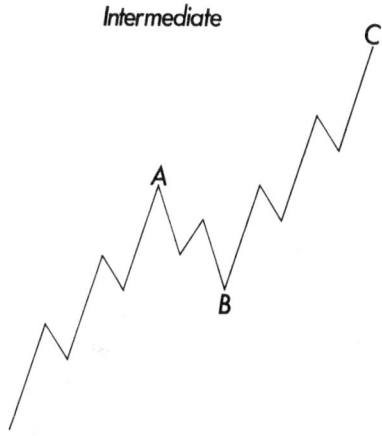

Figure 11

Figure 12

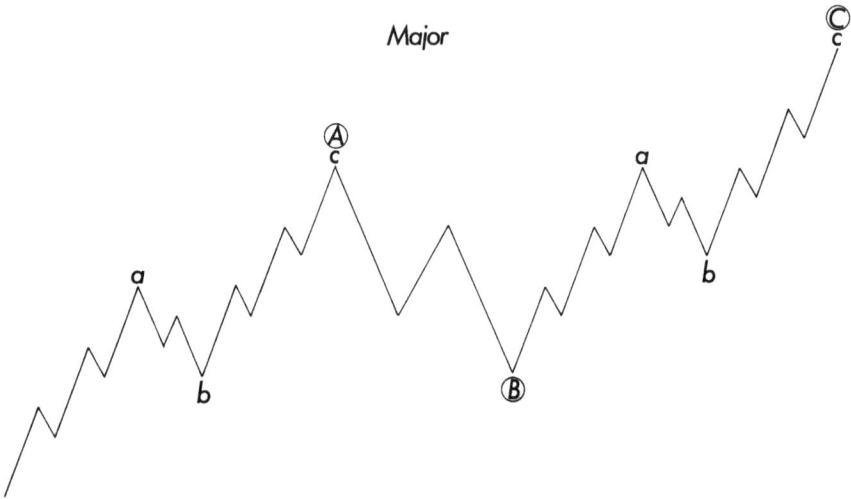

Figure 13

Flats

The next illustrations are flats of Minor, Intermediate and Major degree, both ordinary (Figures 14, 15 and 16) and inverted (Figures 17, 18 and 19). These diagrams are given the name "flat" for the reason that their usual appearance is flat. At times, they slant downward or upward.

As a matter of fact, these patterns might be called "3-3-5." In the last analysis, they are three wave patterns, i.e., A, B and C, whereas a bull pattern is a "5-3-5-3-5" for waves 1, 2, 3, 4 and 5.

The pattern of a human being is "5-3-5-3." There are 5 projections from the torso (head, two arms and two legs); the arms and legs are subdivided into 3 sections; the ends of arms and legs are subdivided into 5 fingers or 5 toes; each finger and toe is again subdivided into 3 sections.

Whether or not wave C of an inverted flat is elongated or not it still remains corrective. It is possible, however, to know when an elongated wave C will occur by reading carefully Chapter 8, "Alternation."

Minor

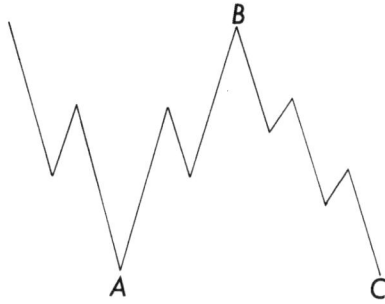

Figure 14

Intermediate

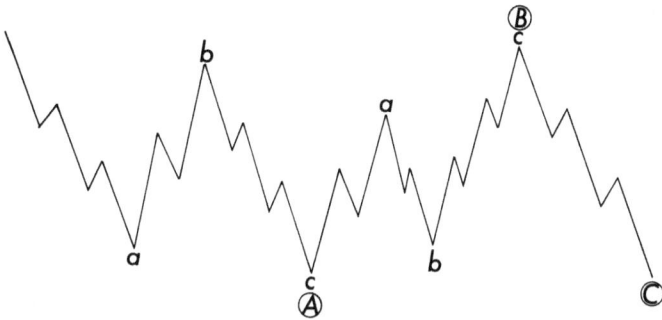

Figure 15

Major

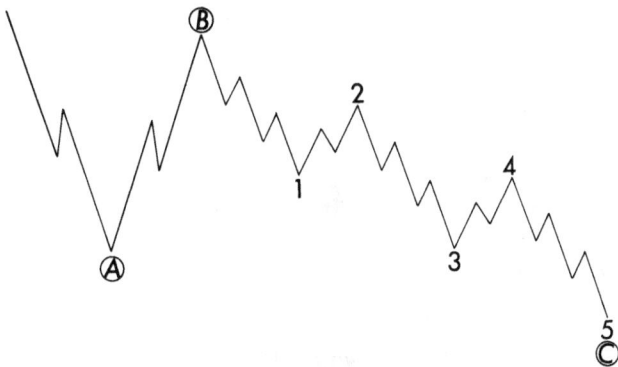

Figure 16

Minor

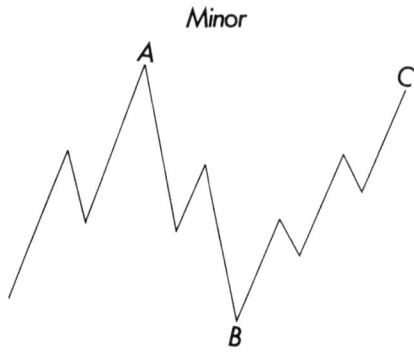

Figure 17

Intermediate

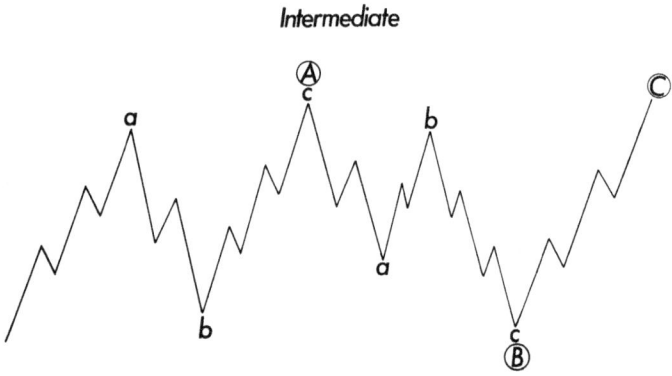

Figure 18

Major

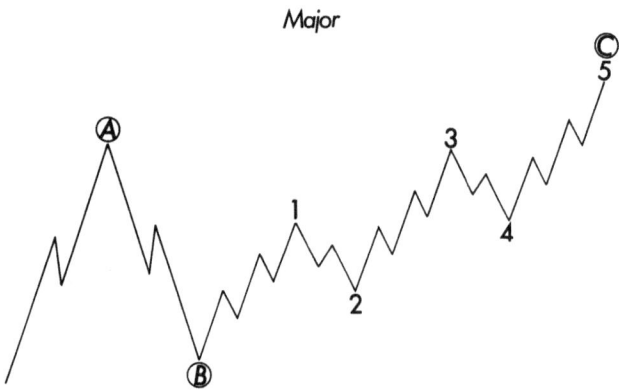

Figure 19

Complex Corrections

A Minor correction would be composed of three waves down, as in Figures 20 and 21.

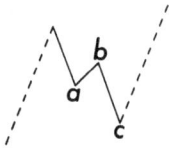

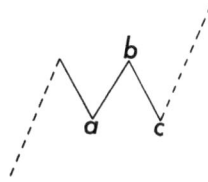

Figure 20   Figure 21

A double sidewise correction would be composed of seven waves as in Figure 22. A triple sidewise movement would have eleven waves sidewise as in Figure 23.

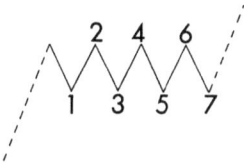

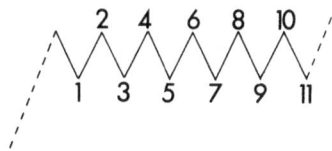

Figure 22   Figure 23

In other words, a sidewise correction to an up trend always ends in a down wave[2], whether it is composed of one, three, seven or eleven waves. They are named as follows: three waves is a "single three," seven waves is a "double three" and eleven waves is a "triple three."

The same number of waves upward are corrective, as in Figures 24, 25 and 26.

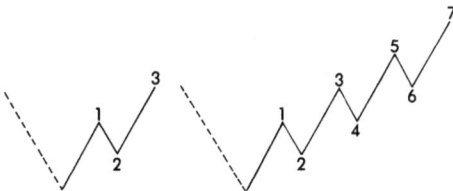

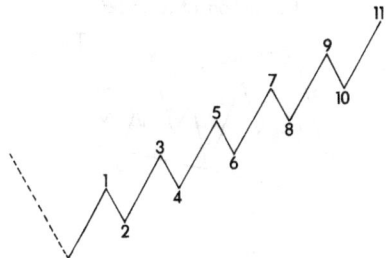

Figure 24   Figure 25   Figure 26

Occasionally these threes are mixed in upward and sidewise, or downward and sidewise, as in Figures 27 and 28 (double threes mixed),[3] and 29 and 30 (double threes upward).

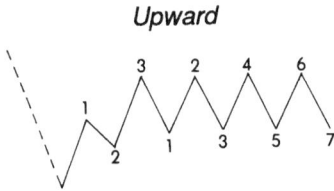

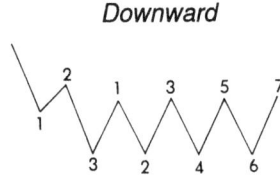

Figure 27   Figure 28

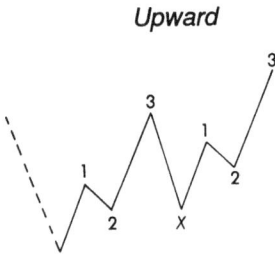

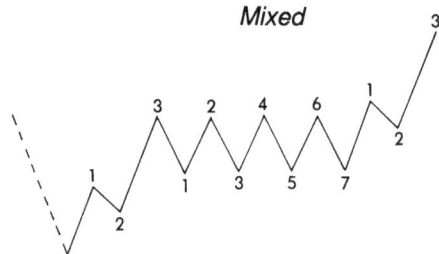

Figure 29   Figure 30

Triangles

Triangles are composed of five waves, or better said, five legs. In the larger types, each leg will be composed of three waves each as shown in Figures 31 and 32.

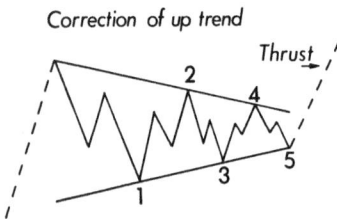

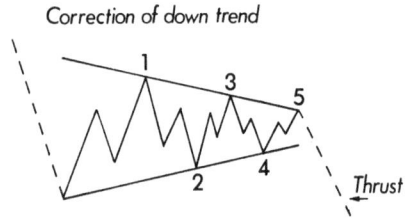

Figure 31   Figure 32

In medium sized types, the fourth and fifth legs may be composed of one wave each, as in Figure 33. In the very small types, the legs are often composed of just one wave. The main guide to the formation of a triangle is the outline, that is, the straight lines drawn across the tops and bottoms. The student cannot be certain that a triangle is forming until the fifth wave has started.

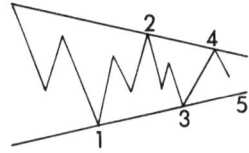

Figure 33

There are three types of triangles,[4] shown in Figure 34.

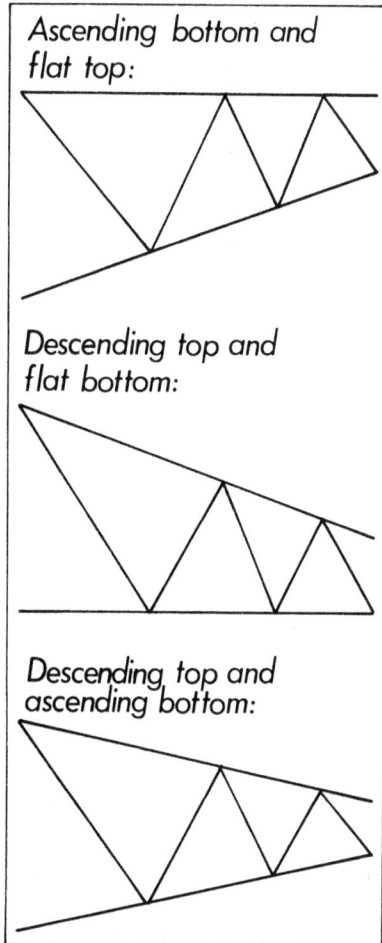

Ascending bottom and flat top:

Descending top and flat bottom:

Descending top and ascending bottom:

Figure 34

The fifth leg may terminate within or without the outline of the triangle,[5] as in Figures 35 and 36.

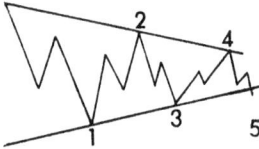

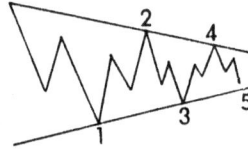

Figure 35   *Figure 36*

The fifth wave should be composed of three waves unless the triangle is very small. On one occasion a triangle consumed only seven hours. The largest triangle occurred between November 1928 and April 1942, thirteen years.[6] This latter movement will be discussed in other chapters.

The movement subsequent to the fifth leg of a triangle is called a "thrust." It will be composed of five waves and in the direction of legs 2 and 4 of the triangle.

Triangles are infrequent. When they appear, their position has always been wave 4 of a movement of any degree, up or down, as shown in Figures 37 and 38.[7]

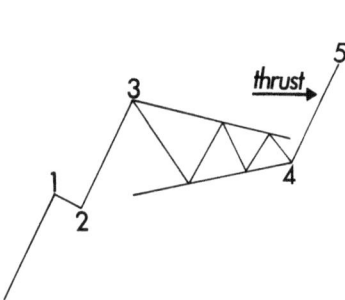

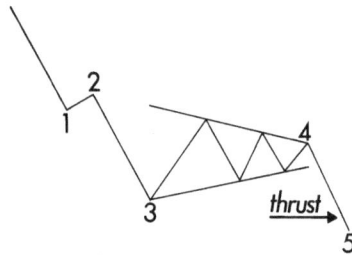

Figure 37   *Figure 38*

The fifth wave, which follows a triangle, is called a "thrust" and is composed of five waves similar to those of waves 1 and 3. As shown above, the fifth wave exceeds the top of wave 3, as in Figure 37, or the bottom of wave 3, as in Figure 38.

ENDNOTES

¹ Figures 10 and 13 are actually drawings of "double zigzags," which Elliott displays in Chapter VI. Either Elliott mis-drew his illustrations here or he decided that double zigzags were more common in Major degree than regular zigzags. For an illustration of a true zigzag of Major degree, refer to the Ⓐ-Ⓑ-Ⓒ section of Figure 7, as well as Figure 15 in the *Financial World* articles and Figure 27 in *The Wave Principle*.

² Elliott overlooked this statement when drawing the illustrations in Figures 27 and 28. He inadvertently left out an additional "three" in each correction, which cannot therefore serve to reinstate the trends previously in motion.

³ Id.

⁴ The illustrations depict ascending, descending and symmetrical (all contracting) triangles. For reasons not stated, Elliott omits discussion of the reverse symmetrical (expanding) type.

⁵ The fifth triangle wave may terminate beyond the triangle boundary but not beyond the level of termination of the third triangle wave.

⁶ See Endnotes 1-8 in Chapter XI.

⁷ They are also found in the B-wave position.

CHAPTER VI

EXTENSIONS

An extension may appear in any one of the three impulses, i.e., waves 1, 3 or 5, but never in *more* than one, as shown in Figures 39, 40 and 41 (upward) and Figures 42, 43 and 44 (inverted).

Figure 39　　　　Figure 40　　　　Figure 41

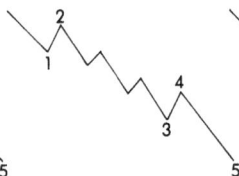
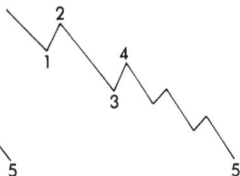

Figure 42　　　　Figure 43　　　　Figure 44

It will be noted that in each instance there are a total of nine waves, counting the extended wave as five instead of one. On rare occasions, an extended movement will be composed of nine waves, all of equal size, as illustrated in Figures 45 and 46.

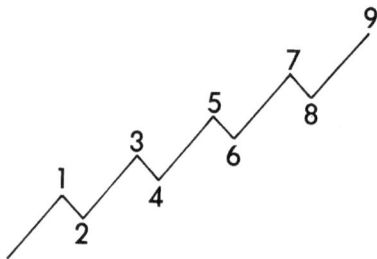
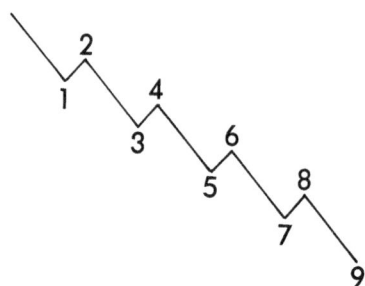

Figure 45　　　　　　　　Figure 46

Extensions occur only in new territory of the current cycle. That is, they do not occur as corrections.

Extensions of Extensions

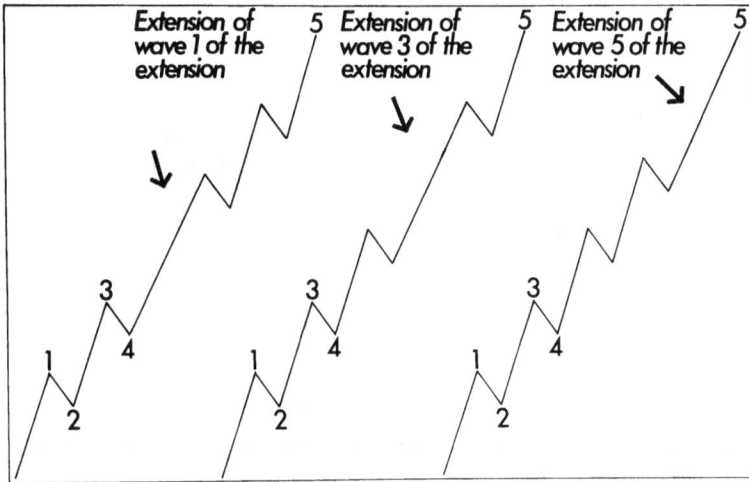

Figure 47

Extension in Wave 5 and Double Retracement

Extensions are "double retraced," that is, a correction will pass over the same ground twice, down and up. It is not necessary to give any consideration to this feature when the extension occurs in the first or third wave, *but only* when the extension occurs in the fifth wave. If the extension occurs in the first wave, the double retracement will be taken care of automatically[1] by waves 2 and 3. If the extension occurs in the third wave, double retracement will be taken care of by waves 4 and 5. See Figure 48 for illustration of an extension in wave 5 and subsequent double retracement.

If an extension is of small degree, retracement will occur immediately. But if it is of Intermediate or Major degree, double retracement may not occur until the entire advance has been completed.[2] When a movement occurs at high speed, the same territory is retraced at almost the same speed in reverse.

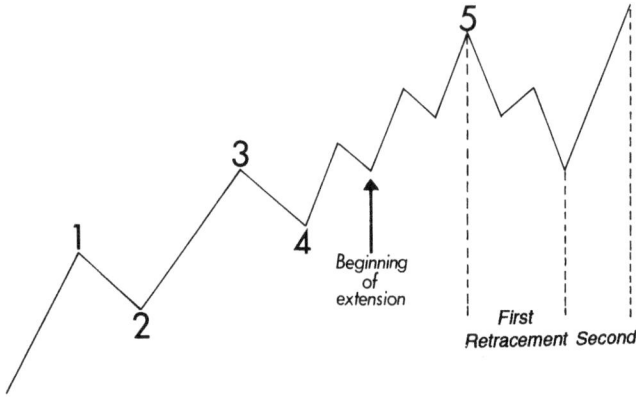

Figure 48

Erroneous Counting

The three impulse waves, 1, 3 and 5, are seldom of the same length. One of the three is usually considerably longer than either of the other two. It is important to note that wave 3 is never shorter than both[3] waves 1 and 5. For example, when wave 3 is shorter than either[4] wave 1 or 5, as in Figure 49, the correct method of counting is as in Figure 50.

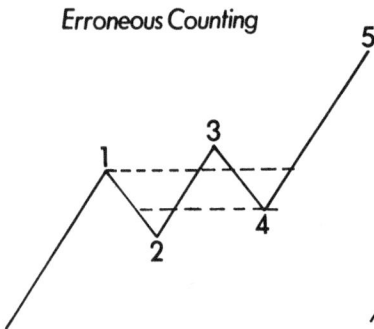

Figure 49

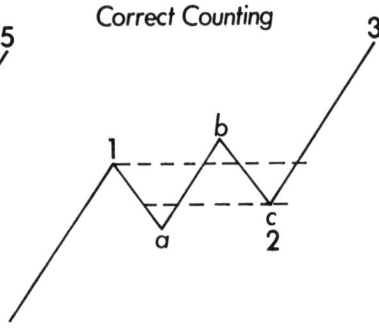

Figure 50

Note that wave 4 overlapped wave 1, which it should not do. Overlapping means that the end of wave 4 was lower than the top of wave 1. Inverted, the example would appear as in Figures 51 and 52.

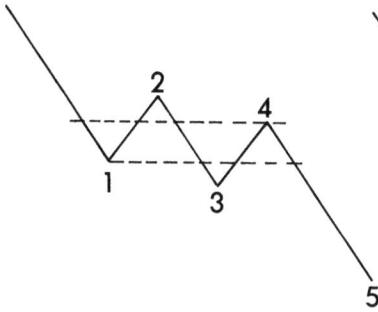

Figure 51

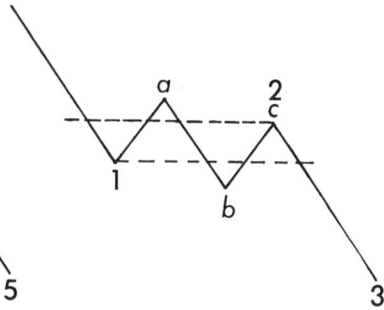

Figure 52

Overlapping within "complex" waves merits careful study. Occasionally complex waves develop into "double threes" or "triple threes," as diagrammed in Chapter 5.

Enlargement of Corrections

It is important to graph a movement in the daily range in order to know whether or not the first upward movement is composed of three or five waves. The weekly range might not disclose this fact. For example, in Figures 53 and 54, an inverted flat is shown in both daily and weekly range.[5] Note that in the weekly range, the precise composition of the first wave up is not disclosed, and the student might erroneously assume that it was composed of five waves in the daily. The weekly range of an inverted flat would appear as being composed of seven waves,

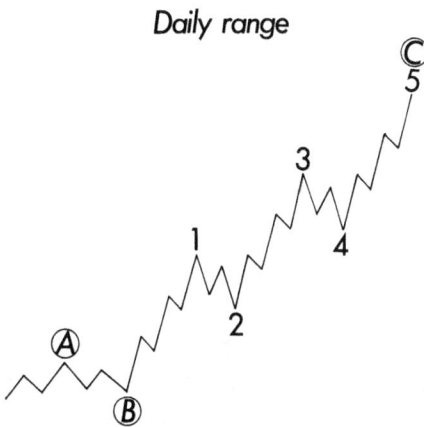

Figure 53

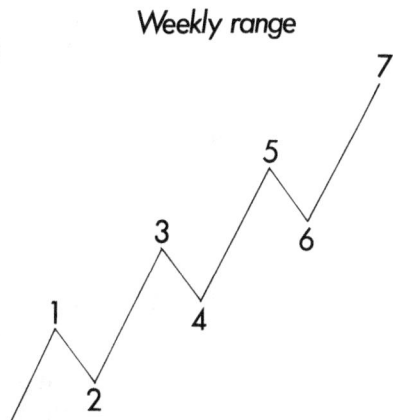

Figure 54

whereas it would be an inverted flat, i.e., A, B, (1, 2, 3, 4, 5) C, as shown in Figure 53.

Similar behavior may occur in zig-zags. A zig-zag does not elongate, but it may enlarge or double, so to speak, as illustrated in Figures 56 and 57. Whether a zig-zag is single or double, its corrective character remains the same.

Daily Range-Single

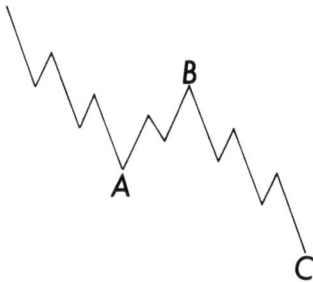

Weekly Range-Double

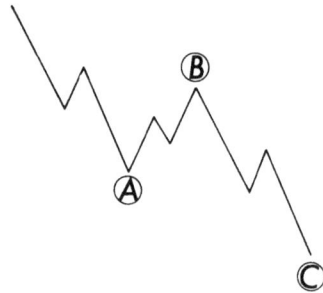

Figure 55

Figure 56

Daily Range-Double

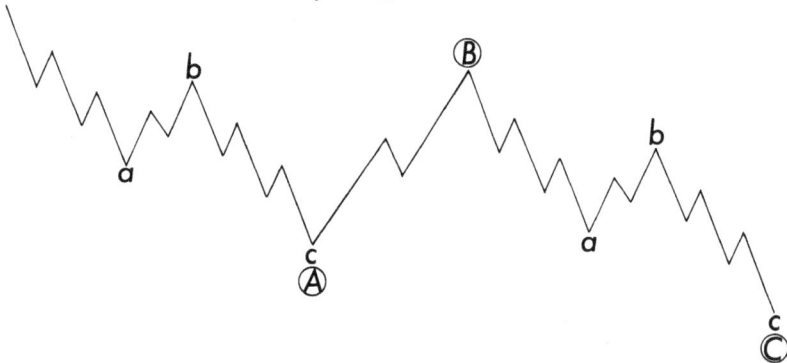

Figure 57

Sidewise Movements

As will have been noted, all corrective movements regardless of the degree are composed of three waves. Sidewise movements follow the same behavior, and are of the same character, corrective. Figure 58 shows two types of sidewise movements[6] following an advance. In Figure 59, the main trend is downward.

Main Trend Upward

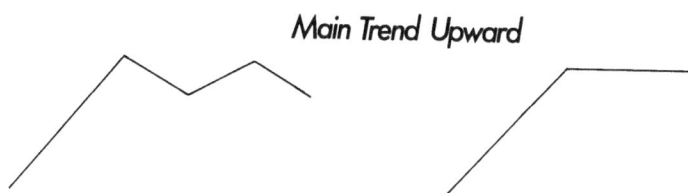

Figure 58

Main Trend Downward

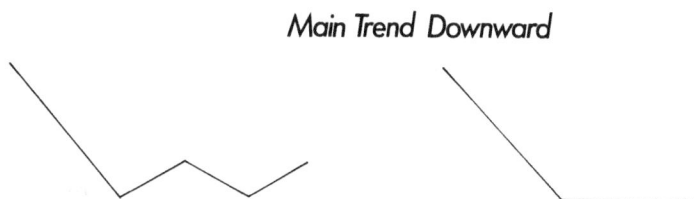

Figure 59

ENDNOTES

[1] Certainly *part* of an extension in the first or third wave will be retraced, but it will not be retraced in the same manner as those within fifth waves. Only after fifth waves will the first retracement return as far back as the low of wave two of the extension.

[2] Degree does not affect patterns. This statement is a reference to an irregular top that is supposedly *followed* by double retracement. It results from Elliott's odd interpretation of the 1928-1930 period.

[3] He means, "shorter than wave 1 and shorter than wave 5."

[4] Id.

[5] These figures are hardly flat in appearance. The overall outline suggests a double zigzag. This discussion probably results from Elliott's tendency to count extended fifth waves when in fact the third wave is extended, thereby leaving a couple of "extra" waves at the end that he counted as A and B.

[6] The first illustration in each of Figures 58 and 59 is a flat. The second merely shows the look of any flat when the data filter is not small enough to show its subdivisions.

CHAPTER VII

IRREGULAR TOPS

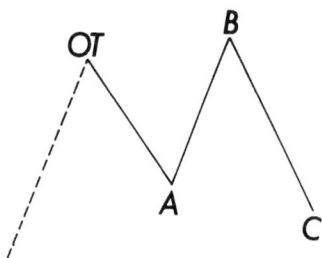

Figure 60

A movement that exceeds the top of a fifth wave (the orthodox top) is an "irregular" top (see Figure 60).[1] Suppose that the five waves up in Figure 61 are of Major degree. The top of the fifth wave would be the "orthodox" top (OT). The first movement from point "5" down would be composed of three waves and lettered "A." The second movement would be upward and exceed the top of 5. This movement would be lettered "B." Like wave A, it would be composed of three waves. The next movement would be composed of five waves down and lettered "C."

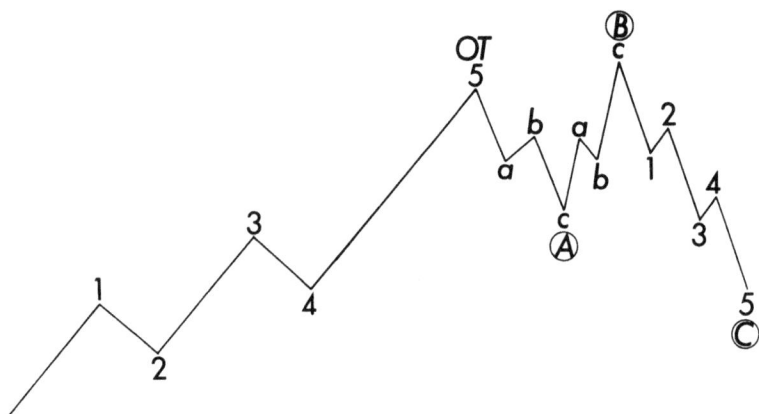

Figure 61

Waves A, B and C all constitute *one* correction, notwithstanding the fact that the end of wave B may be higher than wave 5. This occurred between November 1928 and July 1932.[2] A perfect understanding of this feature is important.

If wave A is a simple zig-zag, wave B will be an inverted flat. This is a case where the law of Alternation gives a warning. "Alternation" is the subject of the next chapter.

ENDNOTES

[1] An "irregular top" is simply the higher price recorded by wave B of an irregular flat correction.

[2] See Endnote 5 in Chapter IV of *The Wave Principle*.

CHAPTER VIII

ALTERNATION

According to the dictionary, alternation is "occurrence or action of two things or series of things, in turn." Alternation is a law of nature. For instance, leaves or branches usually appear first on one side of the main stem and then on the opposite side, alternating their position. The composition of the human body follows the same rule: 5-3-5-3. An endless list of examples could be cited, but the object of this discussion is the habit of alternation in human activity.

Bull and bear markets alternate. A bull market is composed of five waves and a bear market of three waves. Thus, five and three alternate. The same rule governs in all degrees.

A bull movement is composed of five waves. Waves 1, 3 and 5 are upward. Waves 2 and 4 are downward or sidewise. Thus, the odd numbers alternate with even numbers.

Waves 2 and 4 are corrective. These two waves alternate in pattern. If wave 2 is "simple," wave 4 will be "complex," and vice versa. A "simple" correction in the smaller degrees is composed of one wave downward. The "complex" is composed of three waves downward or sidewise. See Figures 62 and 63.

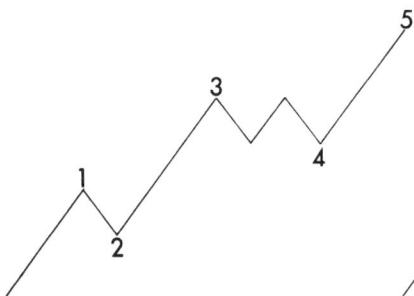
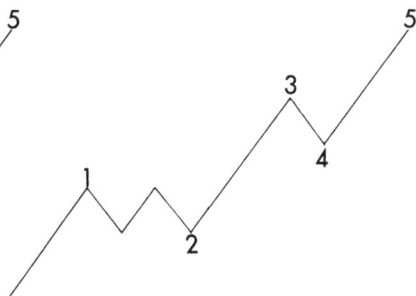

Figure 62   Figure 63

In the larger degrees, such as complete bull and bear markets, the corrective waves are correspondingly larger. Preparation for the final downswing is often tedious. First there is a downward movement of some importance, which I letter with a capital A.

This is followed by an upward swing and designated as wave B. The third and last movement downward is wave C. Wave A may be a zig-zag pattern. In this event, wave B will be a flat, inverted. If wave A is a flat, wave B will be a zig-zag, inverted. (In any event, wave C will be composed of five waves down. It may be severe and approach the starting point of the previous bull market.) Thus, waves A and B alternate.

The thirteen-year triangle furnishes another example of alternation. From November 1928 to March 31, 1938 is a flat.[1] From March 31, 1938 to October 1939 is a zig-zag, inverted. From October 1939 to May 1942 is a flat.[2]

An irregular top is one in which wave B exceeds the top of the fifth wave of the previous bull market, as explained in Chapter 7. Even these alternate. The top of 1916 was irregular, 1919 regular, 1929 irregular, 1937 regular.

Up to 1906, the Rails led upward movements. For 34 (FSS) years, from 1906 to 1940, the Industrials led upward movements. Since 1940, the Rails have been leading.

ENDNOTES

[1] See Endnotes 4 and 5 in Chapter XI of *Nature's Law*.

[2] Actually, this period is either a "five" *or* contains the last part of a triangle for wave B, then a five-wave C. Either count completes the A-B-C from 1937. See Endnote 8 in Chapter XI of *The Wave Principle*.

CHAPTER IX

SCALES

To employ either semi-logarithmic or arithmetic scale and not the other as a general practice is erroneous and deprives the student of their value and utility. The arithmetic scale should always be employed unless and until log scale is demanded.

In a movement of five waves upward, a "base line" is drawn against the ends of waves 2 and 4, then a "parallel line" against the end of wave 3. Figure 64 shows the example.

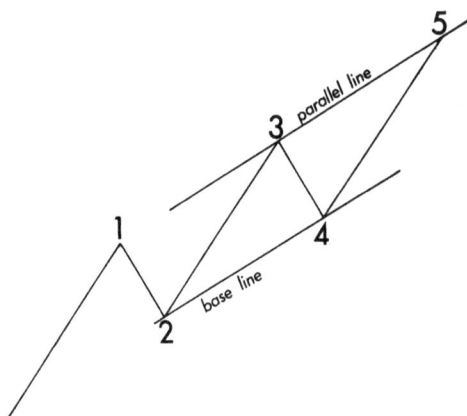

Figure 64

Usually wave 5 will end approximately at the parallel line when arithmetic scale is used. However, if wave 5 exceeds the parallel line considerably, and the composition of wave 5 indicates that it has not completed its pattern, then the entire movement from the beginning of wave 1 should be graphed on semi-log scale. The end of wave 5 may reach, but not exceed the parallel line. For example, if the same figures were graphed on both scales, the pictures would appear as in Figures 65 and 66.

When semi-log scale becomes necessary, inflation is present.[1] If semi-log scale is used and inflation is not present, wave 5 will fail to reach the parallel line by a good margin, as illustrated in Figure 67.

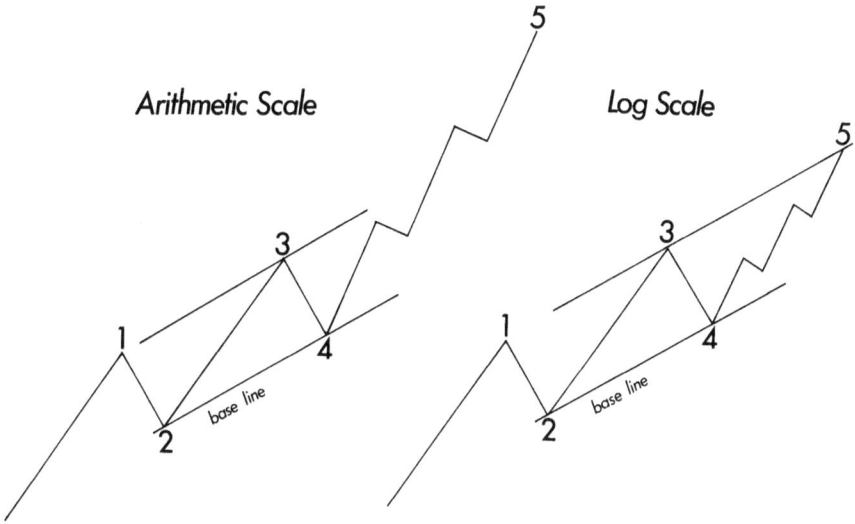

Figure 65

Figure 66

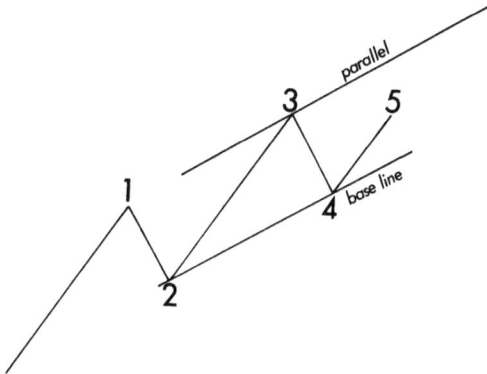

Figure 67

ENDNOTES

¹ "Inflation" as later defined by Elliott in Chapter XII is not monetary inflation as we know the term (see Endnote 1 in Chapter XII). The deciding factor in arithmetic vs. semi-log channeling is probably just the shape of the wave. If arithmetic scale is correct, then the move is developing with reference to *points* advanced. If semi-log scale is correct, the move is developing with reference to *percentage* advanced. Anyone can be given the same starting point and ending point and a specific time frame and draw a perfect Elliott wave on both arithmetic and semi-log scale.

CHAPTER X

EXAMPLES

Demonstrations of Nature's Law in previous pages have been made to facilitate an understanding of the graphs that follow.[1]

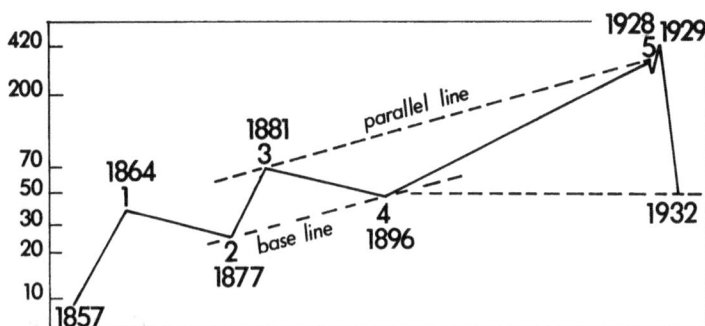

Figure 68

Figure 68 is an outline of the Axe-Houghton-Burgess Index from 1857 to 1932, drawn on semi-logarithmic scale. This is the largest degree for which records are available. Note the five waves from 1857 to November 1928. Note the base line drawn against waves 2 and 4 and the parallel line drawn against wave 3. The end of wave 5 touches the parallel line in November 1928.

The movement as a whole was inflationary; therefore, semi-log is essential. However, arithmetic scale is essential when graphing the several bull markets individually.

Note that the decline to 1932 just reached the beginning of wave 5 in 1896. It was at this 1896 low point that the decline from 1929 to 1932 stopped — in other words, *a normal correction.* Lack of knowledge of past history is the cause of the erroneous use of the expression "The Great Depression," and therefore emphasizes the vital importance of history in this as well as all other activities.

Figure 69 is a detail of wave 5 of Figure 68, drawn on semilog scale. It is divided into five waves of the next lower degree.

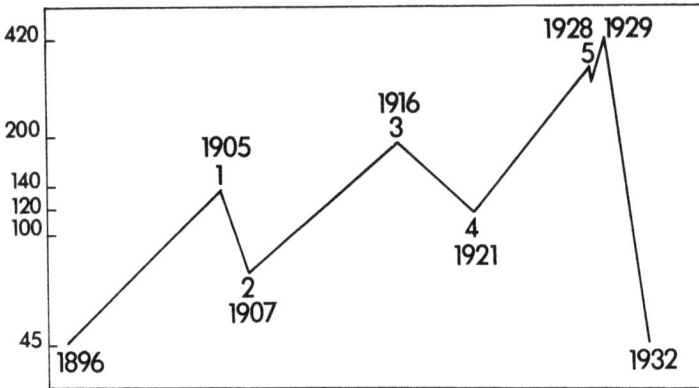

Figure 69

Figure 70 is a graph of the Dow-Jones Industrials for the period 1921 to 1928, drawn on semi-log scale. Note the base line drawn against waves 2 and 4, the parallel line drawn against wave 3, and that wave 5 just touches same.

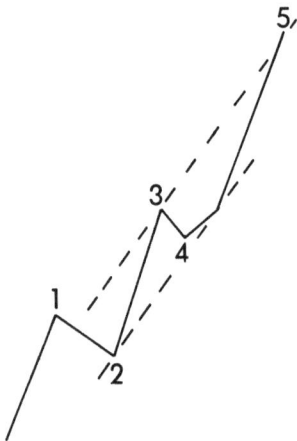

Figure 70

The movement from 1857 to November 1928 is composed of five waves, as shown in Figure 68. The fifth wave from 1896 is subdivided into five waves, as shown in Figure 69. The fifth wave of this movement, starting from 1921, is again subdivided into five waves, as shown in Figure 70. In other words, the entire movement from 1857 is subdivided three times.

In Figure 71, the Dow-Jones Industrial Average is drawn on arithmetic scale and again[2] the amplitude of waves 1 and 3 is 62% of wave 5.

From 1857 to 1928, there were seven bull markets and six bear markets, total 13 (FSS).[3] All bull markets from 1857 to 1928 were *normal* in extent. Remember that from 1921 to 1928 there were three bull markets and two bear markets, not one bull market. The two bear markets were *sub-normal*.

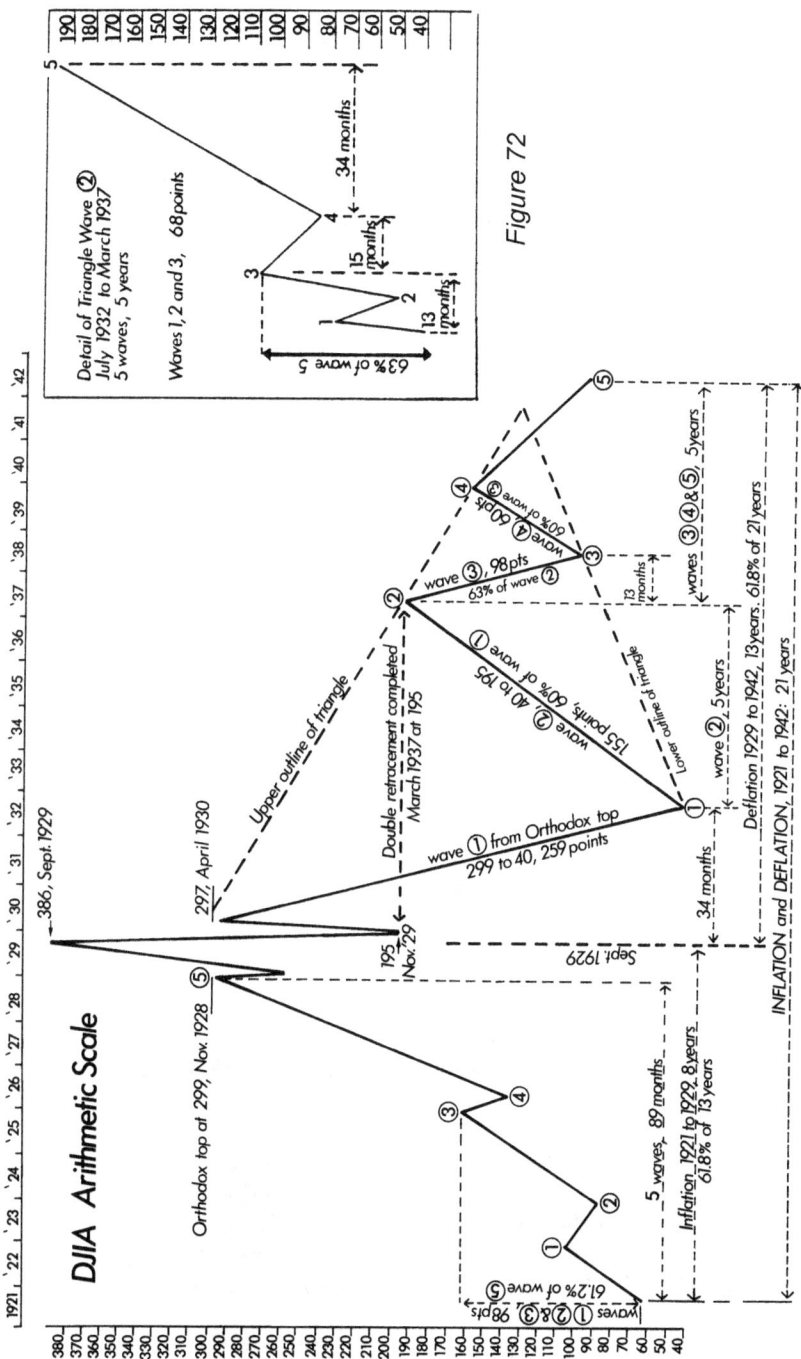

Figure 72

Detail of Triangle Wave ②
July 1932 to March 1937
5 waves, 5 years

Waves 1, 2 and 3, 68 points

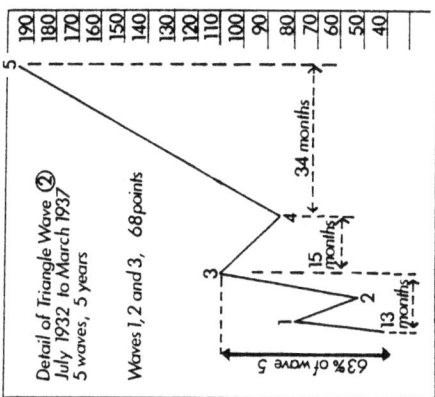

Figure 71

The time factor is important because it usually confirms and conforms to the pattern. For example, from 1928 to 1942 is 13 (FSS) years. From 1937 to 1942 is 5 (FSS) years. Both periods end simultaneously. The entire movement from 1928 to 1942 is one pattern, a triangle. Each wave of the triangle is 62% of its predecessor. All three factors — pattern, time and ratio — are perfect, and in accordance with the Fibonacci Summation Series. See Figure 71.

In the previous pages, Nature's Law has been explained. The numbers of the FSS apply in three ways: number of waves, time (number of days, weeks, months or years), and ratio of the FSS numbers, 62%.

ENDNOTES

[1] For a look at the Grand Supercycle, see Figure 1 of "The Future Pattern of the Market" in the Selected Essays section of this book, as well as Figure 98 in the final pages of *Nature's Law*.

[2] "Again," meaning as in the 1896-1928 advance shown in Figure 69 and the 1932-1937 advance shown in Figure 72. This recurrence is remarkable.

[3] Apparently Elliott is counting the first wave up as one bull market and the third and fifth waves up as three bull markets each.

CHAPTER XI

THE THIRTEEN YEAR TRIANGLE[1]

The orthodox top of November 1928 is 299; the bottom of 1932 is 40; net travel: 259 points. The travel from 1932 to 1937 is from 40 to 195, net 155 points. The ratio of 155 to 259 is 60%.

From the orthodox top of November 1928 to July 1932 is wave ① of the thirteen-year triangle. From July 1932 to March 1937 is wave ② of the triangle, as shown in Figure 71. From March 1937 to March 1938 is wave ③ of the triangle.

This index moved to 195 in March 1937 for reasons other than pattern, ratio and time. The advance from 1921 to 1928 was an extension of the fifth wave starting in 1896. As shown in Chapter VI, an extension is "doubly retraced." The decline to 195, from September to November, 1929 was part of the first retracement. The advance from 40 to 195 during 1932 to 1937 completed the double retracement.[2] Note the precise meeting at 195 of November 1929 and March 1937 in Figure 71.

It should be emphasized that the amplitude of the movement from 1932 to 1937 of 155 points is not that of a typical bull market.[3] Its extent was forced by the four powerful technical forces described above, i.e.,

— The necessity of recovering 62% of the down movement from November 1928 at 299 to July 1932 at 40.
— To complete double retracement of the 1921-1928 extension.
— The time element, sixty months or 5 years.
— Pattern.

In fact, the movement complied with four requisites — wave pattern, amplitude, double retracement and time — all of which are based solely on FSS.

The ratio of amplitude of the 1921-1928 period is such that the advance of waves ① and ③ traveled 98 points, or 62% of wave ⑤, 160 points.

Note the horizontal lines across the bottom of Figures 71 and 72:
— 1921 (beginning of inflation) to 1942 (end of deflation): 21 years.
— 1921 to 1929: 8 years (62% of 13 years).

— July 1921 to November 1928: 89 months.
— September 1929 to July 1932: 34 months.
— July 1932 to July 1933: 13 months.
— July 1933 to July 1934: 13 months.
— July 1934 to March 1937: 34 months.
— July 1932 to March 1937: 5 years.
— March 1937 to March 1938: 13 months.
— March 1937 to April 1942: 5 years.
— 1929 to 1942: 13 years (62% of 21 years).

The pattern and description of triangles are shown in Chapter V. The triangle between November 1928 (the orthodox top) and April 1942 is the symmetrical type. It differs from the ordinary type because it is composed of two patterns, flat and zig-zag. First there was a flat, then a zig-zag and again a flat.[4] This was necessary because of its immense size, the alternation of patterns, the necessity of advancing to 195 in 1937 in order to complete a double retracement of the inflationary extension from 1921 to 1928, the necessity of completing its pattern by 1942 (21 years from 1921), the necessity of maintaining the ratio of 62%, and the necessity of retracing the entire fifth wave from 1896 to 1928, all of which is a very large order.

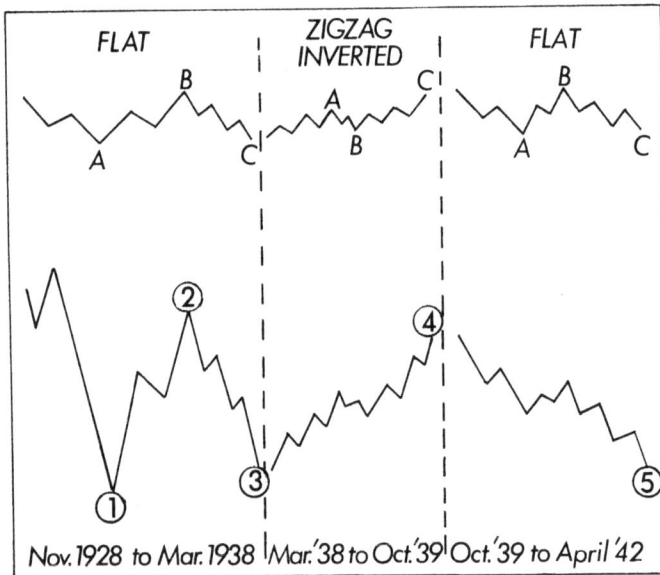

Figure 73

The thirteen-year triangle from 1928 to 1942 was composed of three patterns, as follows:

— November 1928 to March 1938: a flat[5] (triangle waves ①, ②, and ③).
— March 1938 to October 1939: a zigzag, inverted (triangle wave ④).
— October 1939 to April 1942: a flat (triangle wave ⑤).

Note the alternation of patterns: flat, zig-zag and flat. Many other examples of similar nature could be cited. Both the flat and the inverted zig-zag are described in Chapter V. They and the corresponding triangle wave are reproduced in Figure 73.

Figure 74 is a graph on arithmetic scale of the Dow-Jones Industrial Average from November 1928 to April 1942. Each vertical line represents the monthly range.

Triangle wave ① from 1928 to 1932 is composed of waves Ⓐ, Ⓑ and Ⓒ. Wave Ⓐ is composed of three waves down from November to December, 1928. They were fast and therefore visible only in the daily range. Wave Ⓑ is an irregular top in the form of an inverted flat. Wave Ⓒ is composed of five waves down from September 1929 to July 1932 (see numbers on chart), and consumed 34 months.

Triangle wave ② from 1932 to 1937 is a typical bull pattern because it is composed of five waves.[6] However, due to its abnormal size, it may be classed as an inverted flat[7] of very large degree because it forms part of a "corrective." Wave ① consumed 5 years.

Triangle wave ③ was down in five waves from 1937 to 1938 and lasted 13 months. Triangle waves ①, ②, and ③ therefore constitute a flat, from November 1928 to March 1938.

Triangle wave ④, 1938 to 1939, is an inverted zig-zag.

Triangle wave ⑤ from 1939 to April 1942 is a flat.[8] It droops and is very long. Its extreme length was necessary in order to coincide with the overall time period of 13 years from 1928 and 21 years from July 1921.

As stated in Chapter V, the fifth wave of a triangle may or may not be confined within the outline of a triangle. In this case it exceeded the outline.[9] Nevertheless, it is a perfect flat of three waves, marked Ⓐ, Ⓑ, and Ⓒ. Wave Ⓑ is 62% of wave Ⓐ and 62% of wave Ⓒ. In other words, waves Ⓐ and Ⓒ are the same length.

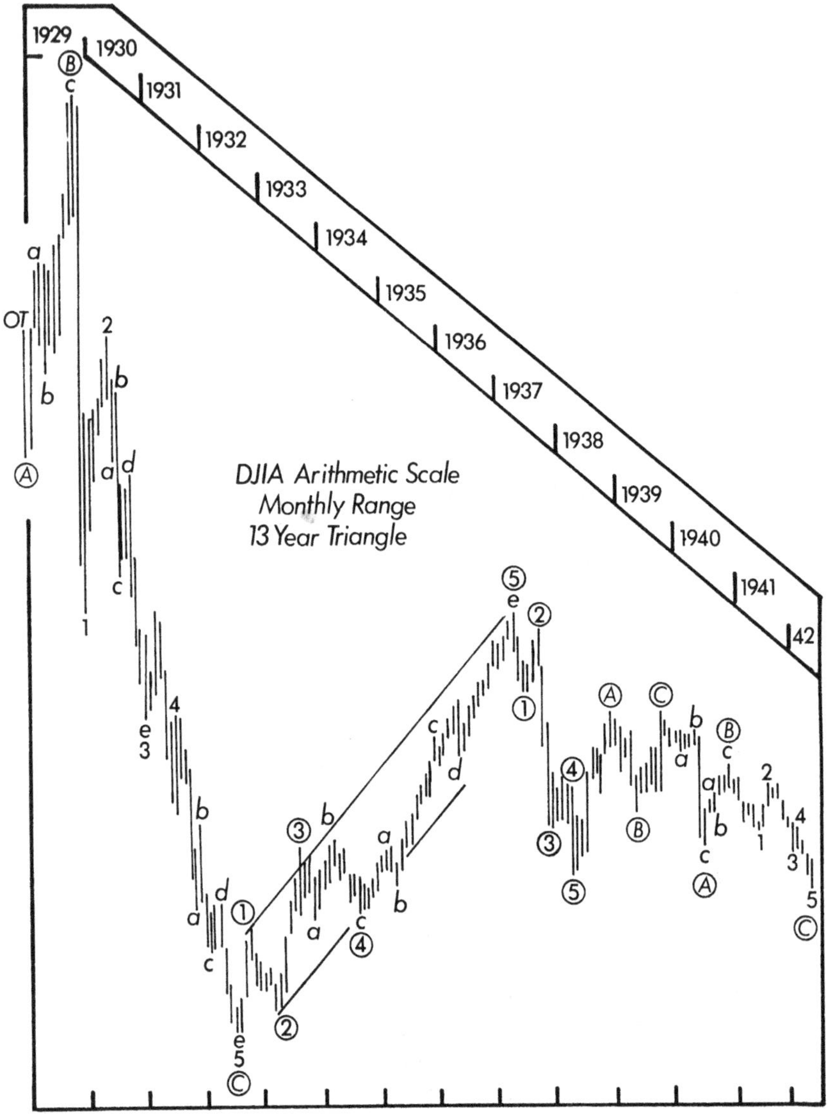

Figure 74

ENDNOTES

[1] Elliott's troubles with interpretation in this volume are due almost entirely to the concept of the thirteen-year triangle. While many of the features in the 1928-1942 period are fascinating, and while the concept helped Elliott call a major low in 1942, the thirteen-year triangle concept as such is invalid. The main problems are that the 1932-1937 rise is a "five" and the 1937-1938 decline is a "five," thus eliminating them as possible triangle legs since all triangle legs must be "threes." The most persuasive argument that a triangle had formed was the series of .618 retracements, all within perfectly converging trendlines, an occurrence that was indeed quite uncanny. However, this phenomenon can occur *across different waves* (as it did from 1976 to 1979), and is not enough justification, *by itself*, to claim that a true triangle is being formed. Unfortunately, Elliott had made up his mind on an irrelevant point outside the Wave Principle, namely that 1929-1932 was too short a time period to correct the previous Supercycle. This assumption led him to the thirteen-year triangle interpretation, which in turn led him into trouble with the basics of wave form, as he tried to fit the subwaves into his predetermined concept. This error of interpretation should not detract from the reader's enjoyment of Elliott's fascinating discoveries and analysis with regard to the period after the 1929 peak.

[2] While these turning points are not coincidence, tying them to the "double retracement" rule, at least as it is stated in theory, seems to be stretching the rule too far. The extension within the *fifth* wave of the 1921-1928 rise *was* doubly retraced as necessary, the top part by Elliott's A and B, and the rest by 1 of C and 2 of C. The reason that the *entire* 1921-1928 rise failed to doubly retrace entirely by means of an irregular correction is that, as Frost and I have concluded, 1921-1929 was not itself an extended wave. The extended wave in the 1857-1929 sequence was the third, as is normal. Therefore the fifth would have no reason to be doubly retraced by an irregular top. The fact that the first retracement covered more than the entire fifth wave is further evidence that the wave was not an extension. Even if we were to consider it an extension, the ensuing fifth Supercycle wave would constitute the second retracement eventually. Still, the action of the market after the 1929 peak is intriguing, and one can see why Elliott considered his double retracement rule satisfied.

[3] True. This is the most dramatic bull market in U.S. history in terms of percentage increase over time.

[4] Elliott is describing all of the first three waves together as a flat because the third wave of the triangle is so undeniably a "five."

[5] Elliott breaks his own rules in this interpretation. If 1937-1938 is the "C" leg of a flat, it must be a "five." If it is a leg of his triangle, it must be a "three." He shouldn't be able to have it both ways.

[6] Absolutely. You will notice that in Figures 72 and 74, Elliott's labels are not consistent with his triangle thesis, but with the correct interpretation.

[7] Frost and I discuss this error in our book. It is possible to rationalize any five-wave move as a "three," but only at the expense of the utility of the Wave Principle and what we call the "right look." Flats are so called because they are *flat*. The B wave of a flat always recedes deep into A-wave territory. In a five-wave move, there is no overlapping of waves, by definition. Therefore the 1932-1937 advance must be classified as a "five."

[8] Again, flats are flat and should not "droop." Actually it is a five-wave decline, with no overlapping, finishing off the zigzag that began in 1937. To count it correctly, put 1 where Elliott has a, 2 where he has b, 3 where he has Ⓐ, 4 where he has Ⓑ and 5 where he has Ⓒ. There is a slightly better count involving a triangle. Beginning at the 1938 low, put Ⓐ where Elliott has Ⓒ, Ⓑ where he has the next Ⓐ, Ⓒ where he has the next Ⓑ, ① where he has 1, and Ⓘ where he has 2. This triangle is wave B of the zigzag from 1937, with the decline from its end then being wave C, which subdivides nicely into a "five." This count is illustrated below.

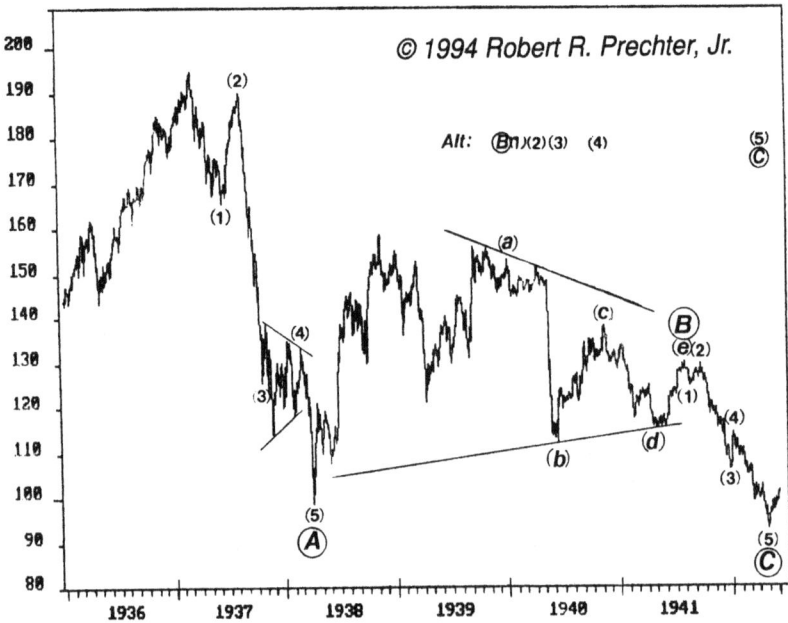

[9] It also exceeded the low of wave three of the triangle, which it should not do.

CHAPTER XII

INFLATION

The term "inflation" is defined in the dictionary as "extension beyond natural limits." One bull market does not exceed "natural limits." A series of bull markets, one above the other, would be "beyond natural limits." One bull market would not be "above another" were it not for sub-normal intervening bear markets.

Inflation[1] occurred during the 'Twenties because of sub-normal bear markets. During this period there were three normal bull markets and two sub-normal bear markets, total five. Warnings of inflation occurred in the following order: normal wave 1, sub-normal wave 2, normal wave 3, sub-normal wave 4, and penetration of the parallel line by wave 5 on arithmetic scale (see Chapter IX, Figure 65).

Figure 75 pictures a normal bull market and a normal bear correction (waves a, b and c) which penetrates the base line substantially. Figure 76 pictures a sub-normal bear correction that barely penetrates the base line.

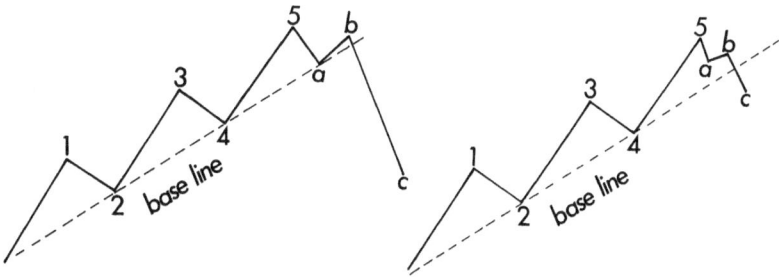

Figure 75   Figure 76

Figure 77 shows the Dow-Jones Industrial Average from 1921 to November 1928 on arithmetic scale. Wave 5 penetrates the parallel line. Penetration of the parallel line demands that the entire picture from 1921 should be graphed on log scale. Figure 78 pictures the same average (monthly range) on log scale. Wave 5 touches but does not penetrate the parallel line.

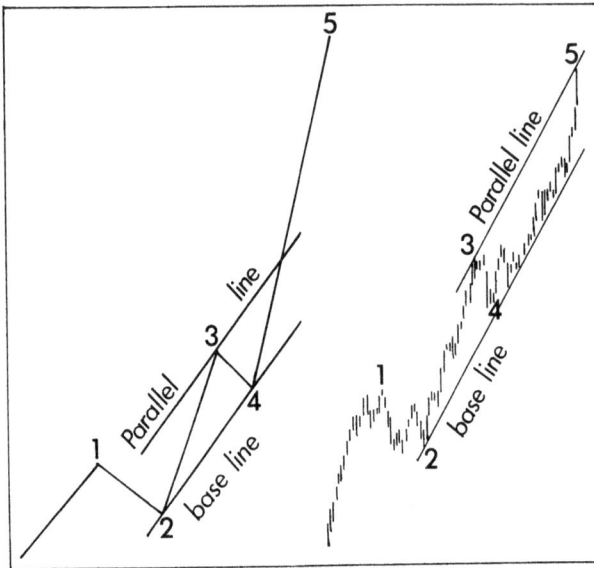

Figure 77   Figure 78

There are three methods of ascertaining in advance at what point, and at what time inflation will terminate: that described above, ratio (described in Figure 71), and time (described in Figure 71).

ENDNOTES

[1] Elliott appears to be correct on this point. One must be careful to look at the monetary aggregates, not commodity, producer or consumer prices, for evidence of inflation. Sometimes (apparently in fourth waves of Cycle degree) inflation drives up commodity prices, and sometimes (apparently in fifth waves of Cycle degree) it drives up investment prices.

CHAPTER XIII

PRICE OF GOLD

Another example of the importance of differentiating between the virtues of arithmetic and log scale is the price of gold. The graph of this item covers one bull market from 1250 to 1939, nearly seven centuries. In Figure 79, wave ② is simple and wave ④ is complex. Note the letters Ⓐ, Ⓑ and Ⓒ of wave ④.

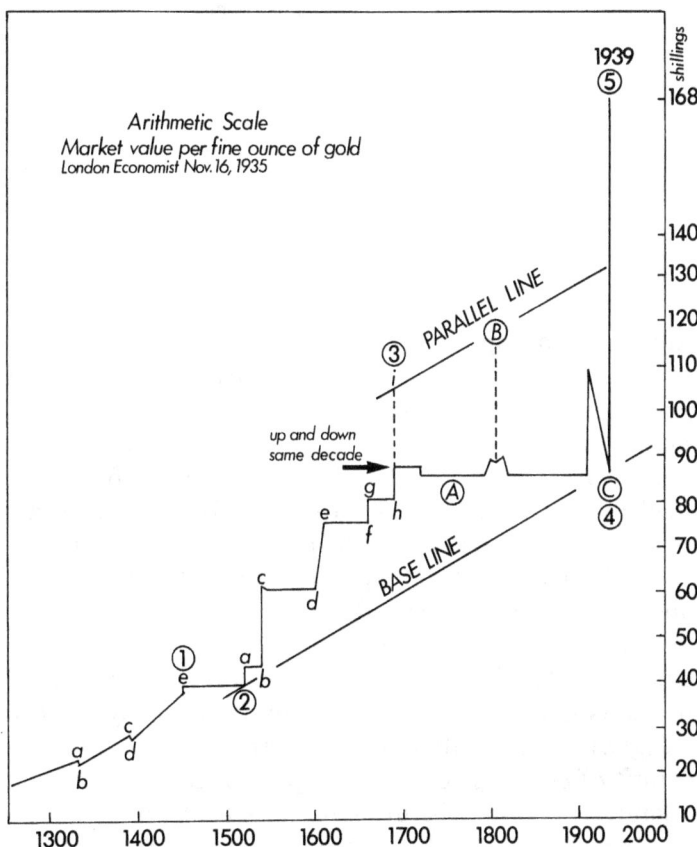

Figure 79

In Figure 79, plotted on arithmetic scale, the price line exceeds the parallel line, therefore semi-log scale is demanded as shown in Figure 80. The parallel line on logarithmic scale

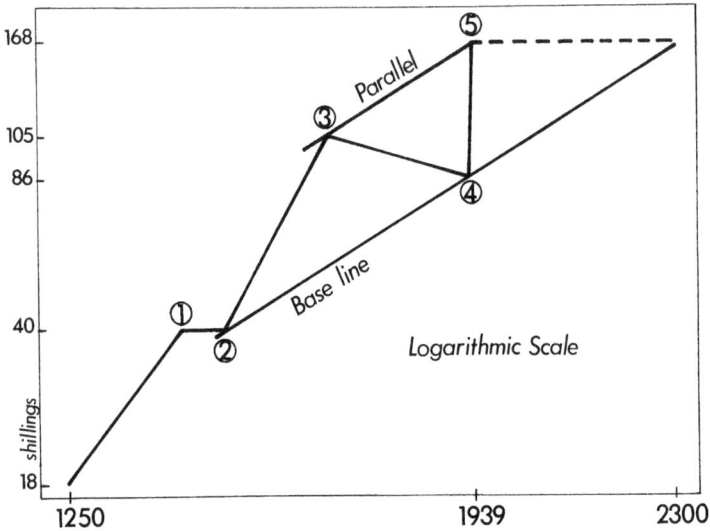

Figure 80

indicates the final top of inflation of any human activity.[1] When an advance of five waves is completed *within* the channel on *arithmetic* scale, inflation does not exist.

The gradual rise of wave ① in Figure 79 suggests that the market price of gold during that period was "free," that is, not fixed by any authority. Thereafter advances were abrupt and corrections sidewise, which indicates that the price was dominated by some authority, presumably political. Corrections may move sidewise, downward, or downward and sidewise as shown in wave ④ of Figure 79.

Under the law herein described, when a pattern has been completed as indicated in Figure 80 on log scale by the contact of wave ⑤ with the parallel line, no further advance in price will occur until *after* the price line has penetrated the base line at some point. Therefore, the probability is that the present price of gold, 168 shillings, will remain stationary, at least until it contacts the base line about the year 2300, as indicated by the junction of the dashed lines at the extreme right of the graph.[2]

ENDNOTES

[1] True, if it is drawn using properly selected wave termination points.

[2] Some people have made a career of deriding Elliott for this conclusion. Perhaps he should have avoided commenting from such sketchy data. Certainly he should have been less dogmatic and described alternative possibilities. Regardless, there is no problem for the Wave Principle or its practice, since the penetration of the upper parallel line immediately suggested an extended third wave in development.

CHAPTER XIV

PATENTS

The expression "human activities" includes every activity, not only the stock market, but production, life insurance, movements from cities to farms and vice versa, etc. as shown in miscellaneous items listed in Chapter III.

Occasionally some rather unusual items present themselves, such as for example patents, which is a human activity but not emotional.[1] Figure 81 is the record of applications for patents from 1850 to 1942. Note the five waves. The fifth wave extended from 1900 to 1929. The Industrial Average followed the same pattern during almost the same period (see Figure 82). Note the "correction" of patents from 1929 to 1942 in three waves, A, B and C. Stocks followed the same pattern during the same period, except that from 1928 to 1942 the "correction" was a triangle instead of three waves A, B and C.

In early days, farming was the principal occupation. Here and there a farmer might own a store or manufacture something as a sideline. Manufacturing was on a piece-work basis and performed in the home. Natural resources, climate, genius and democracy in the United States required the formation of corporations to finance individual initiative. Inventions and the introduction of machinery gradually changed everything. The Louisiana Purchase, the conquest of California, the acquisition of Texas and Oregon, together with settlement of boundaries with Mexico and Canada, added immensely valuable territory.

Genius was (and still is) the principal asset. This is demonstrated by the graph of patent applications from 1850 to 1942. Note that the pattern coincides with that of the stock market. The United States is radically different from any other country in one vital aspect: our ancestors hail from all parts of the world. They were dissatisfied with tyranny and politics of their homelands and came here to enjoy liberty and develop their genius.

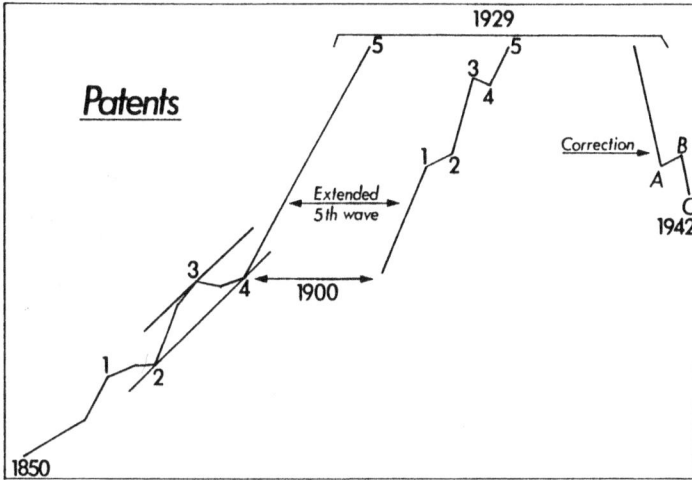

Figure 81

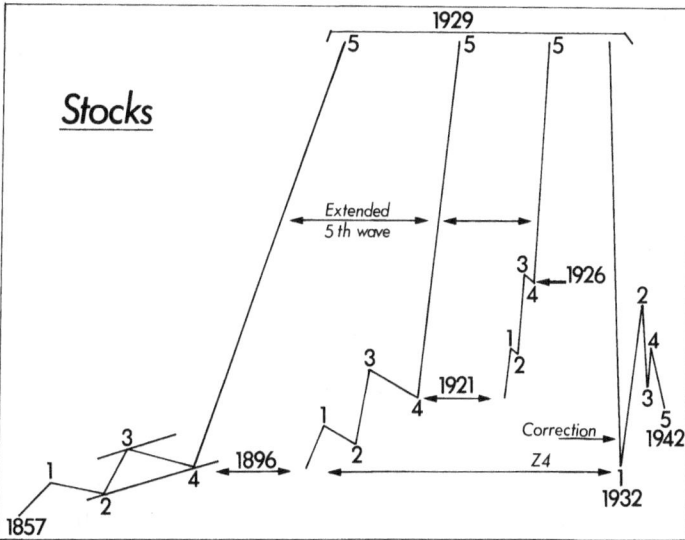

Figure 82

ENDNOTES

[1] The Wave Principle tracks more than emotional phenomena because it is also a record of the progress of society, which is arguably patterned after mankind's collective emotional swings. Socionomics postulates that the moods behind the movement of the averages motivate progress; people produce more and invent more when the dominant mood is "up" rather than "down." For more on this topic, see *Socionomics* (2004).

CHAPTER XV

TECHNICAL FEATURES

The movement of one activity is seldom, if ever, a reliable guide for another. Figure 83 shows graphs of three indices — the London Industrials, the Dow-Jones Industrials and production in the United States. All are plotted from 1928 to January 1943. Production figures are from the Cleveland Trust Company.

The Dow-Jones Industrials (middle graph) registered a five-wave triangle from November 1928 (the orthodox top) to April 1942. The amplitude of each of the second, third and fourth waves of the triangle to its predecessor is approximately 61.8%. The existence of the triangle is proved by its outline, the time element, the composition of each wave, and the uniform ratio of each wave to its predecessor. High speed inflation from 1921 to 1929 (8 years) caused the rapid decline to 1932 (34 months). These, in turn, caused the symmetrical triangle, which simulates a pendulum coming to rest.

The triangle disregarded the following events, which occurred during its 13-year period: reversal from Republican to New Deal administrations, devaluation of the dollar, repudiation of the gold clause in Government bonds, the shattered two-term precedent, the second World War which started in 1939, and the rise in production, the index of which started upward in 1938 and finished its pattern of five waves in June 1941.

The London Industrials (top graph) did not follow New York stocks in 1929. This index registered tops in January 1929 at 140 and in December 1936 at 143. The lows in 1932 and 1940 were the same, 61. From 1940 to January 1943, this index advanced to 131. Between January 26 and July 28 1939, the London Industrial Average formed a triangle.

London stocks invaded the stratosphere in 1720, 1815 and 1899, approximately 89 years (FSS) apart. When and if English stocks should inflate, it does not follow that ours will do so.

A production index prepared by the Cleveland Trust Co. (bottom graph) registered tops in June 1929 at 116 and in 1936 at 112, and a low in 1938 at 63. From 63, a complete advance of five waves finished its pattern in June 1941, before the D-J Industrials started up from the end of the triangle in April 1942.

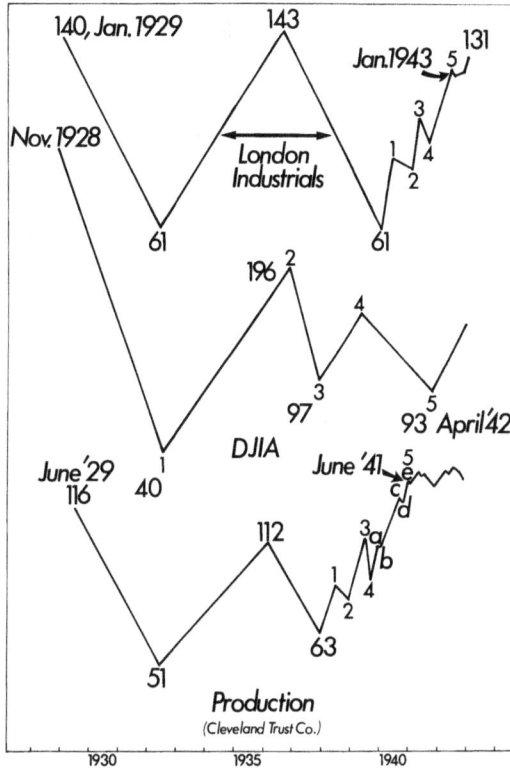

Figure 83

During the period from 1857 to 1928, we participated in three wars, Civil, Spanish and World War I. Nevertheless, the pattern of the Supercycle movement was perfect, as demonstrated elsewhere.

Stocks and commodities have never inflated in unison. Therefore, if commodities explore the stratosphere, it does not follow that stocks will do likewise at the same time. Commodities inflated in 1864 and 1919, 55 years apart.[1]

The worthlessness of news is demonstrated in the next chapter.[2] A financial writer said:

> "The fact that security prices have been advancing on the good news from Salerno and that they reacted in August on similar good news from Sicily leads students to conclude that the August reaction was due chiefly to technical considerations rather than to military happenings."

One day, London experienced a severe "blitz." London stocks advanced and New York stocks declined. Financial writers in both places stressed the blitz as the cause. At the time, London was in an uptrend and New York in a downtrend. Each followed its pattern regardless of the blitz. The same wave behavior occurred following Mussolini's exit on July 25.

The above analysis proves that technical factors govern the market at *all* times.

ENDNOTES

[1] And again in 1974! In terms of years, the Fibonacci number 55 is the length of the so-called Kondratieff wave of economic activity.

[2] Actually, Chapter XVII.

CHAPTER XVI

DOW-JONES RAIL INDEX

An examination of the Rail index is interesting, informative and profitable. Transportation is the most important human factor in our economy because of the great distances between borders since the Louisiana Purchase, the settlement of boundaries with Mexico and Canada, and the additions of Texas and California.

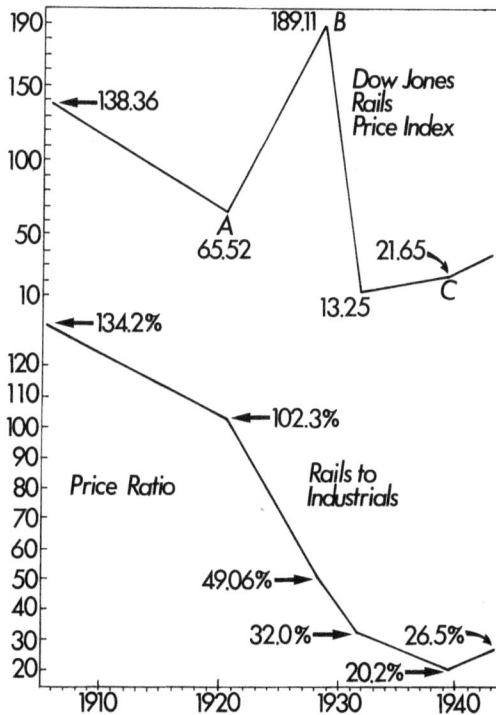

Figure 84

The bottom graph in Figure 84 is the ratio of the Rail index to the Industrial index from 1906 to January 1944. This demonstrates that, in relation to the Industrials, the Rails were persistently weaker from 1906 to 1940 (34 years). The causes of this behavior were the excessive proportion of bonds to common stocks, the Panama Canal which opened for business in 1914

(1906 + 8 = 1914), and the automobile and the airplane. These three factors resulted in weakness of both rail bonds and stocks to such an extent that in 1940, one third of rail mileage was in receivership and another third on the borderline.

The second World War temporarily removed Panama Canal competition and otherwise increased rail revenue, both passenger and freight. The extraordinary revenue that the Rails enjoyed since 1940, especially after Pearl Harbor, enabled the railroad companies to reduce their bonded indebtedness, and in consequence, fixed charges. This benefit is permanent. See Figure 85.

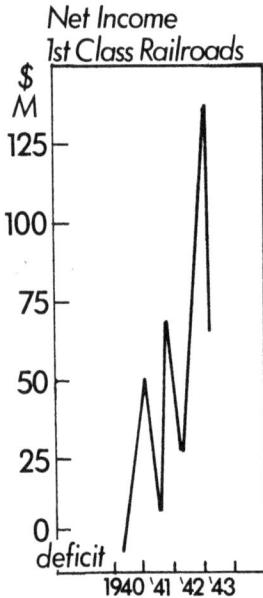

Figure 85

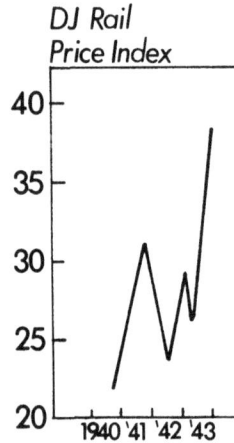

Figure 86

The Rails registered their *ratio* low point in 1940, and from then to July 1943 advanced as shown in Figure 86. The Industrials bottomed two years later in April 1942, at the end of the thirteen-year triangle.

During the 34 (FSS) year period between 1906 and 1940, the Rails reversed downward before the Industrials and reversed upward after the Industrials. Since 1940, this practice reversed; that is, the Rails have been first to reverse upward and last to reverse downward. This practice may continue for some years.

CHAPTER XVII

THE VALUE OF NEWS

Wall Street has an adage that "news fits the market." This means that, instead of the news "making the market," the market foresees and appraises the importance of the underlying forces that later may become news. At best, news is the tardy recognition of forces that have already been at work for some time and is startling only to those unaware of the trend.

The forces that cause market trends have their origin in nature and human behavior and can be measured in various ways. Forces travel in waves, as demonstrated by Galileo, Newton and other scientists. These forces can be computed and forecast with considerable accuracy by comparing the structure and extent of the waves.

The futility in relying on anyone's ability to interpret the value of any single news item in terms of the stock market has long been recognized by experienced and successful traders. No single news item or series of developments can be regarded as the underlying cause of any sustained trend. In fact, over a long period of time the same events have had widely different effects, because trend conditions were dissimilar.

This statement can be verified by a casual study of the forty-five year record of the Dow-Jones Industrial Average. During that period kings have been assassinated, there have been wars, rumors of wars, booms, panics, bankruptcies, New Era, New Deal, "trust busting," and all sorts of historic and emotional developments. Yet all bull markets acted in the same way, and likewise all bear markets evinced similar characteristics that controlled and measured the response of the market to any type of news as well as the extent and proportions of the component segments of the trend as a whole. These characteristics can be appraised and used to forecast future action of the market, regardless of the news.

There are times when something totally unexpected happens, such as an earthquake. Nevertheless, regardless of the degree of surprise, it seems safe to conclude that any such development is discounted very quickly and *without reversing the indicated trend under way before the event.*

One of the safeguards in this respect is the willingness of experienced traders to "sell on good news and buy on bad news," especially when such news runs counter to the prevailing trend. This factor tends to upset the expectancy of the public for the market to react directly and in the same manner to similar news at different times.

Those who regard news as the cause of market trends would probably have better luck gambling at race tracks than in relying on their ability to guess correctly the significance of outstanding news items. Mr. X.W. Loeffler of Westwood, New Jersey, publishes a graph of the Dow-Jones Averages listing the important news events in chronological order (price $1). Examination of this graph shows clearly that the market has advanced and declined on the same kind of news. Therefore, the only way to "see the forest clearly" is to take a position above the surrounding trees.

War starts worldwide forces so powerful that they would seemingly dominate all other considerations and drive the market farther and farther in the same direction. At various times war incidents receive front page display. Sharp breaks in the market during August and September, 1937, again in March, August, and September, 1938, and in March-April 1939 all coincided with war developments. Yet when war was actually declared on September 1, 1939, the market advanced violently on tremendous volume. The only satisfactory explanation for this curious behavior is derived from the technical position of the market cycle at these times.

In 1937, 1938 and early 1939, the market had completed important rallies and was resuming the downward trend at the time of the war incidents. Consequently, these "war scares" were construed bearishly and served simply to accelerate the downward trend. On the other hand, the market was in an entirely different position in September 1939 when the war started. Charts show that a downward phase started in the latter part of July 1939, as a correction of the upward movement from mid-April of that year. This downward phase was *fully completed a week before September 1*, and in fact the market advanced briskly during this short period about ten points from the wave bottom of August.

On the actual announcement of the war, the market fell sharply during the day to a level fractionally below the August bottom and then bounded upward with amazing speed. Those who bought selected stocks at the bottom in August and on the secondary war-scare bottom reaped large profits compared with those who tried to buy stocks in the wild scramble that followed. The late comers in most cases were sorry they had bought, because they paid top prices and sold out at substantial losses. Actually, the peak of the market for the steels and other primary war stocks was reached in less than two weeks after the start of war. Since then, the market has more consistently placed a bearish construction upon the outlook for war stocks and war profits because of the broad bear cycle, which was resumed in the fall of 1939. In contrast, the effect of World War I (1914-1918) was primarily bullish due to the type of price cycle from mid-1913.

When France collapsed early in June 1940, most people felt that the war would be very short and Hitler would inevitably overrun England. Waves, however, had indicated in *May*, when the Dow-Jones Industrial Average reached 110.61, that the worst of the phase was over and that stocks should be bought for a substantial intermediate recovery. Even in the midst of the highly emotional news from Europe during the first half of June, the Average reacted only to 110.41.

At the time of the November 1940 election, sensational news announcements were published regarding huge expenditures to be made for defense and to aid England. Most economists and observers reasoned this would set inflationary forces in motion, and bought stocks. At the same time, however, waves indicated that the inflation would not benefit stocks from a price standpoint, and the upward movement since June having been completed, much lower stock prices would develop. Subsequently, the market declined nearly fifty points.

The general belief that current news affects the market is widespread and even exploited. If current news were responsible for fluctuations, cycles would not occur. Whenever one is inclined to believe in "news," I recommend careful review of the pattern and wave ratios in Figure 71, then recall the events and opinions expressed at numerous times during that twenty-one year period.

CHAPTER XVIII

CHARTING

Students might benefit by detailed suggestions which I have found essential. Model charts are shown in Figure 87.

Accurately observing the lower degrees of waves of a movement requires the daily range of price fluctuations. This high-low range was inaugurated by Dow-Jones in 1928.

The chart spacings recommended for the purpose of emphasizing price fluctuations are a vertical quarter inch for one point of the Industrial Average, a vertical half inch for one point of the Rail Average, and a vertical half inch for one point of the Utility Average. Such spacings on a chart facilitate accurate interpretation. The quarter inch scale is subdivided into fifths, thus eliminating any guesswork as to the exact spot at which to locate the daily range and hourly record.

Likewise it is important to space the distance between days as shown on the model charts. When each vertical line of the chart is employed, instead of every other line, the result is that lines of the price range are too cramped for comfortable reading. Do not leave any space for holidays or Sundays.

Precisely the same scale and forms are recommended for the hourly record — one quarter of an inch horizontally for a session of five hours, or one of the smallest squares for each hour. Do not leave any space following a two hour session on Saturday. Do not show the opening figure. The high-low range for the day should be shown at the end of the last hour of each session. All of these recommendations are portrayed in Figure 87.

Never economize in chart paper at the expense of clarity. When a movement begins on one sheet and terminates on another, clarity is jeopardized. The same is true when a movement is discontinued at the top of the sheet and started again at the bottom.

Chart paper which will properly clarify interpretations of waves is manufactured by Keuffel & Esser, and is for sale by them and by large stationery stores. It is available in these sizes: by the yard 20" wide, in sheets 8 1/2" x 11," and in sheets 10" x 15." Two weights of paper in all three sizes are offered.

It is suggested that charts 10" x 15" be used, and that not more than two averages be charted on one sheet. For example, on one sheet 10" x 15" the daily range of the Industrials and daily volume should be shown, and on another sheet 10" x 15," the daily range of the Rails and Industrials. Use two other sheets 10" x 15," one for the hourly record of the Industrials and the hourly volume of the whole market, and another for the hourly record of the Rails and Utilities, a total of four sheets for the entire program.

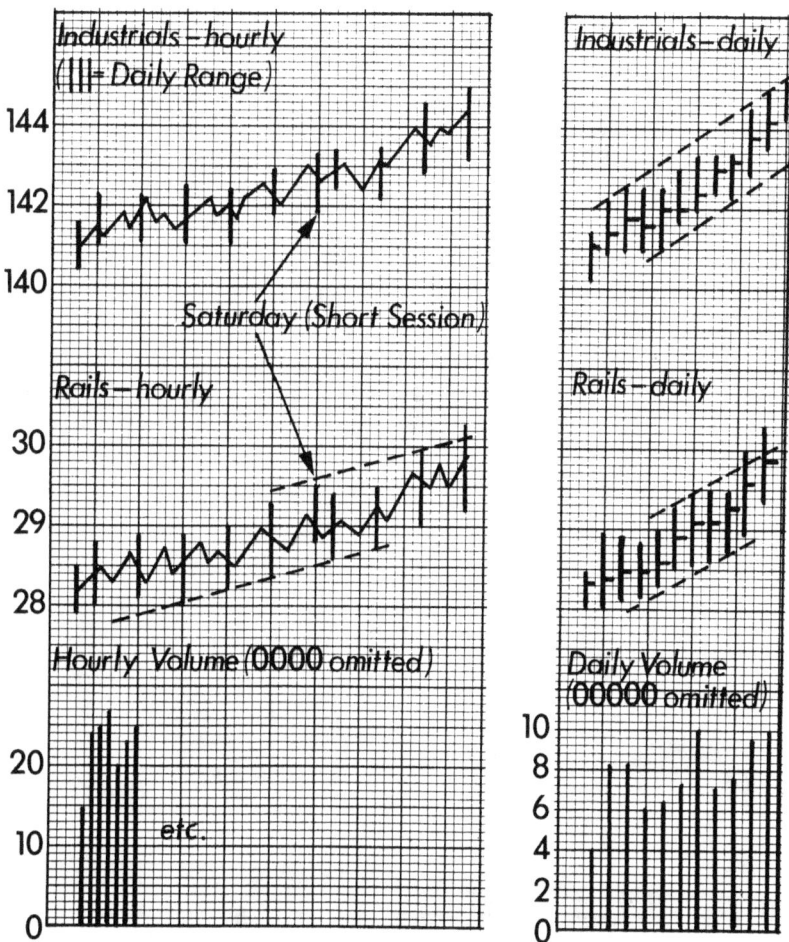

Figure 87

For individual stocks and commodities, the same general recommendations apply except that the chart paper should be subdivided by fourths instead of fifths.[1]

The weekly range should be charted on forms of the largest size charts available in order to cover a long period, one for an entire cycle. The monthly range, especially of the averages and groups, is important for observing complete cycles.

Figures 53 and 54 in Chapter VI demonstrate the value of the daily range in order to establish beforehand the extent and pattern of the weekly range. In like manner, the weekly range assists in establishing the extent and pattern of the monthly range. The monthly range assists in establishing the extent of cycles. Likewise, the monthly range facilitates observances of monthly time periods and ratio of waves.

In Figure 87, the vertical allowance for the Industrials is one point per quarter inch. The Rails and Utilities are allowed one point per half inch. The weekly range may be reduced to two points per quarter inch for the Industrials and one point per quarter inch for the Rails and Utilities. The monthly range may be reduced still further.

On the actual chart paper the cross ruled lines are pale green in color, and it will be noted that the chart patterns, which are drawn in black ink, are accentuated against the pale green background, which is highly advantageous in reading waves.

ENDNOTES

[1] For prices expressed in eighths and quarters rather than decimals.

CHAPTER XIX

INVESTMENT TIMING

Timing is one of the chief elements in the universe. We separate the times of the year into seasons: spring, summer, fall and winter. We recognize the daylight as the time of activity and the night time for relaxation and rest.

In the matter of investment, timing is the most essential element. *What* to buy is important, but *when* to buy is more important. Investment markets themselves progressively foretell their own future. Waves indicate the next movement of the market by their patterns, whose beginnings and endings are susceptible to definite and conclusive analysis.

Nature's Law embraces the most important of all elements, *timing*. Nature's Law is not a system or method of playing the market but a phenomenon which appears to mark the progress of all human activities. Its application to forecasting is revolutionary.

If one had invested $1,000 in long-term Government bonds in January 1932 and sold in June 1939, a total profit of $5000 (including interest and appreciation) would have resulted in the 89-month period. In January 1932, the yield on market value of Governments was 4%. In June 1939, it was only 2%. As for the stock market, an investment of $1,000 in July 1932 would have been increased by March 1937 to approximately $5,000 without taking dividends into account. This statement is based on the per cent change in the popular averages.

The importance of accurate forecasting has resulted in an immense increase in the use of statistics. A comparison of files of newspapers of fifty years ago with those of today will be a revelation in this respect. Millions are being spent to find a satisfactory forecasting device, but the search will be fruitless without recognition of the fact that the habit of the market is to *anticipate*, not to follow.

CHAPTER XX

SELECTION OF TRADING MEDIA

Chapter XIX demonstrated that the factor of first importance in stock trading is timing, that is, when to buy and sell. The factor of next importance is what stocks to trade. To guide you in selecting securities (either stocks or bonds) in which trading is contemplated, you should keep uppermost in mind all of the following fundamentals.

Fluctuations and Income

Fluctuations in market value of any security are much greater than its income yield, therefore the paramount factor is the preservation and appreciation of principal as a result of price fluctuations.

Bull Market Tops

In bull markets, each group of the 55 Standard Statistics list shows tops made at different times, like a fan. Bull markets are those which develop five Primary waves during a period of about two years.[1] During such a period, the several groups tend to move rather uniformly, being propelled by the powerful force of the cycle.

Bear Markets

Usually the duration of a bear market is longer than the previous bull market.[2] During the severe and relatively short duration of the decline from 1929 to 1932, the very best stocks and bonds, as well as the lower grades of both, had to be liquidated regardless of their real value. Many traders gained the erroneous impression that the bottoms of all bear markets should repeat that performance.[3] Research indicates many years will elapse before such a drastic decline may be expected.

The final bottoms of bear markets are conspicuous by bottoms of nearly all groups being made simultaneously. This is just the reverse of tops in bull markets. During bear markets, powerful leadership is less pronounced, and this is especially true during rallies. During bear swings, the market as a whole and the several groups become more sensitive to current events and extraneous factors.

Previous Experience in Trading

Many traders acquire prejudices against certain stocks because of previous unfortunate experiences. To pursue such a course, the trader would eventually find no group free from objection.

Inactive Stocks

A stock that is frequently or occasionally inactive should be avoided for trading, the reason being that waves are not registered. Inactivity clearly indicates that the stock does not enjoy thorough distribution, or else it has reached the fully-developed stage.

Inside Tips

Usually inside tips from well-intentioned friends refer to inactive and low priced stocks. It is preferable to confine one's trading to stocks that are always active.

The Age of Stocks

The life of a stock usually has three stages. The first is the youthful or experimental stage, during which such stocks should be avoided as they have not been properly seasoned. The second is the creative stage. Stocks that fall within this category have reached healthy development, thus making them a desirable medium for trading, provided they are thoroughly seasoned. The third or grown-up stage represents the period of fullest development. Dividends may be uniformly reliable and fluctuations narrow. For these reasons, the certificates become lodged in portfolios and therefore the stock is less attractive for trading purposes.

In summary, when the pattern of a reliable average is favorable, follow these recommendations:

1) Select the groups which perform in harmony with the average.

2) Then select the stocks that move in sympathy with these groups.

3) Always choose stocks that are constantly active, medium priced and seasoned leaders.

4) Diversify funds, i.e., employ more or less an equal number of dollars in from five to ten stocks, not more than one stock of a group (for example: General Motors, United Aircraft, U.S. Rubber, U.S. Steel, New York Central, and Consolidated Edison).

ENDNOTES

¹ A bull market is any advance that contains the necessary five waves. Defining the term "bull market" and "bear market" by duration or percentage price change is arbitrary.

² I think this is an unintentional misstatement. Bear markets are almost always shorter than bull markets. Over the long run, they tend to run about 61.8% of the time required for bull markets (see Chapter 4 of *Elliott Wave Principle*).

³ The same expectation is prevalent today (1980). With the crashes of 1969-1970 and 1973-1974 behind us, most are currently looking for an "instant replay" at the next four-year cycle low. Few can envision the possibility of a less "oversold" bottom despite the fact that the wave position suggests that, as Elliott puts it, "many years will elapse before such a drastic decline may be expected." [Note: This Endnote is intact as written for the original 1980 edition of this book, which was titled *The Major Works of R.N. Elliott.*— Ed.]

CHAPTER XXI

PYRAMIDIC SYMBOLS
AND HOW THEY ARE DISCOVERED

By permission of the Landone Foundation, I quote three paragraphs from pages 134 and 135 of Mr. Landone's book, *Prophecies of Melchi-Zedik*:

> The total distance around the base of the Pyramid is 36,524.22 Pyramid inches. This is exactly 100 times 365.2422, the number of days in our solar year.
>
> The height of the designed Pyramid is 5,813.02 inches.
>
> These mystic wise men formulated systems of measures of quantity, time, weight and length, and squares and cubes of the lengths. Since all of these are based on the length of the side of the square, and since that length was derived from the circle whose circumference was equal to the days of the solar year, and since the time of revolution of earth around the sun is eternal, these mystics created the only system of measurement forever exact and eternally the same.[1]

Having ascertained the circumference of the Great Pyramid Gizeh at its base, the investigators cast about for some known fact that would correspond. In this instance, it was the number of days in a year, down to the last fraction. In other words, two facts are associated, and thus establish the purpose of the symbol from which forecasts may be made.

I discovered rhythm in human activities and later learned that it is symbolized in the Great Pyramid. Egyptologists failed to recognize this symbol because they were not aware of rhythm in nature and human activities. This symbolism is described in Chapters I and II, and demonstrated in Chapters VIII through XIV.

My contribution to pyramidic symbolism follows, in the order named:

1) Discovery of patterns, degrees and numbers of waves.

2) Association of the Fibonacci number series, Hambidge's discoveries in its application to art and botany, and Pythagoras and his cryptic diagram.

3) Diagrams of the Great Pyramid from all angles.

4) Correlation of the Fibonacci ratio and the elevation of the pyramid — 5,813 inches (which is composed by the three basic numbers of the Fibonacci Summation Series: 5, 8 and 13) — to the base of the pyramid.

5) Application of the Summation Series to human activities in many fields.

Ratio Ruler

Draughtsmen use an instrument called a "proportional divider." The fulcrum is movable in order that any ratio may be obtained. These instruments are expensive and now practically unobtainable. I have therefore devised a handy substitute for ascertaining, without mathematical calculations, when the ratio between any two movements, in either amplitude or time, is 61.8%. I will send one on receipt of 25 cents in check, money order, coin or postage stamps.

R. N. Elliott

No. 63 Wall Street

New York (5), N. Y.

ENDNOTES

[1] For more on this subject, read Peter Thompkins' *Secrets of the Great Pyramid* (Harper & Row, 1971).

CHAPTER XXII

THE LAW OF MOTION

Dictionary definitions of the word "cycle" are several: "a period of time," "an entire turn or circle," "a spiral leaf structure," "a series that repeats itself." Attention has been mainly directed to cyclical rhythms in the stock market where they are very pronounced. Every movement, from wheels to planets, is cyclical. All cycles have subdivisions or degrees which facilitate the measurement of their progress.

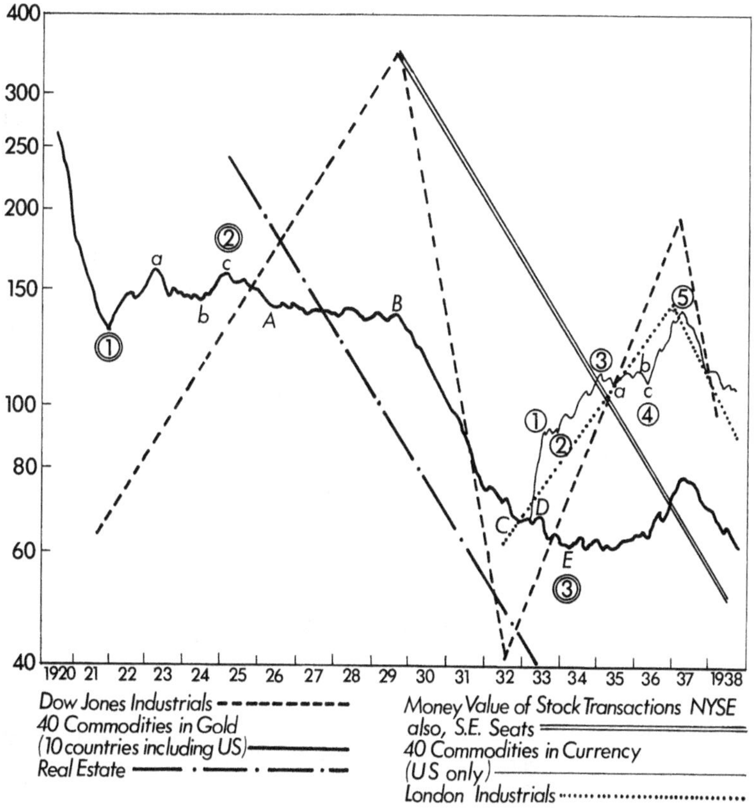

Figure 88

Planets travel in orbits and at speeds peculiar to each. The Earth revolves on its own axis and once in every twenty-four hours divides night from day. It encircles the sun once a year and thus provides the four seasons. The mechanism of planetariums may be turned backward or forward to show the relative positions and movements of planets and their satellites at any time, past, present or future.

Some elements never change their patterns. For example, water constantly observes complete cycles. The sun's rays on the ocean's surface cause water to evaporate. Air currents move the vapor until it encounters cooler atmosphere over hills and mountains, which in turn condenses the vapor. Gravity draws the water back to earth, where it again joins the sea.

Nations experience political, cultural and economic cycles, both great and small. Patterns of human life are observed in mass movements such as migration to and from cities, average age, birth rate, etc.

Figure 88 demonstrates that one human activity cannot be depended upon to forecast another. Therefore, the pattern of each factor must be analyzed by its own waves and not by extraneous factors. During the period from 1939 to April 1942, the lag in the stock market compared to that of business produced much discussion but no explanation. The answer is that eight years of inflation during the 'Twenties created a thirteen-year triangle to 1942.

The graph of temperature shown in Figure 89 is important. Temperature is not associated with human activities; nevertheless cyclical waves, over a period of one hundred ten years, formed a perfect pattern of five waves upward.

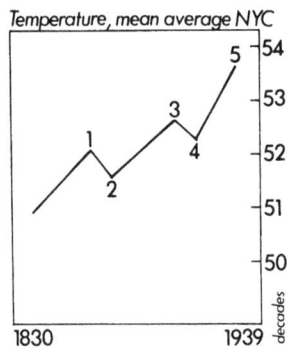

Periodicities between peaks and valleys of many items, such as epidemics, production of lynx pelts, tent caterpillars, salmon runs, etc. are fairly common. In human activities, cycles are not all uniformly spaced. They follow wave patterns in accordance with the Fibonacci Summation Series.

Dynamic symmetry is a law of nature and therefore the basis of all forms of activity.

Figure 89

Since the discovery that the earth is round, the cycle has been the subject of much research. There are three classes of cycles. First are uniform periodicities between peaks and between nadirs, such as day and night, seasons of the year, tides, epidemics, weather, swarms of insects, etc. (I recommend an article by Donald G. Cooley entitled "Cycles Predict the Future" in *Mechanix Illustrated*, February, 1944). Second are periodical fluctuations caused, in some instances, by astronomical aspects. Third are patterns, time and ratio, in accordance with a summation series disclosed by the mathematician Fibonacci.

A pamphlet entitled "The Relation of Phyllotaxis to Mechanical Laws" by Professor A.H. Church of Oxford is very interesting. Phyllotaxis is the leaf arrangement of plants. Mr. Jay Hambidge spent many years researching records, and is the author of a book entitled *Practical Applications of Dynamic Symmetry*. One chapter is entitled "The Law of Phyllotaxis." A copy of pages 27 and 28 thereof is repeated in Chapter II of this treatise.

Dr. William F. Petersen, Professor of Pathology at the University of Illinois, is the author of a very important and interesting book entitled *The Patient and the Weather*. Therein are graphed the progress of disease. The patterns are precisely the same as any other activity, including the stock market.

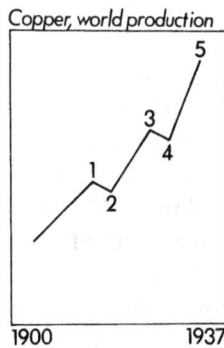

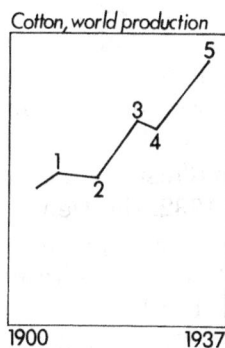

Figure 90   Figure 91

CHAPTER XXIII

THE GREAT DEPRESSION

This common expression is a misnomer insofar as the stock market is concerned. The decline of stocks from 1929 to 1932 was a correction of the previous advance, as shown in Figures 68 and 82. The dictionary defines "depression" as "below the general surface." The Grand Canyon of Colorado is a "depression" because it is far "below the general surface" for many miles on either side. From the top of the Rockies to the Pacific Ocean is a "correction," so to speak, not a "depression," notwithstanding the fact that the Pacific Coast is much lower than the bottom of the Colorado Canyon. There is no such thing as a "depression" in the stock market. If there were, it would be correct to say that from the Rockies to the Pacific is a "depression." There are numerous reasons for this erroneous expression.

The general public, which has no interest in stocks, may have enjoyed and become accustomed to continuous employment in the period from 1921 to 1929. Naturally, they assumed it to be a normal condition. When the 1929-1932 decline occurred, many people found it difficult to make both ends meet. Naturally, it seemed to them to be a "depression."

During the advance in the stock market from 1921 to 1929, traders in stocks were told that we were in a "New Era," "never would decline," "just keep on going," etc. Many common practices were "awful but lawful."

Many politicians are responsible for the erroneous use of the word "depression." During the early part of the 1929-1932 decline in stocks, when Mr. Hoover was President, some said that prosperity was "just around the corner." During the presidential campaign in 1932, the Democrats blamed the Republicans and Mr. Hoover for the "depression." The results of elections in 1932, 1936 and 1940 demonstrated that most voters believed the New Dealers. The Republicans blamed the New Dealers for the decline from 1937 to 1942. The falsity of this political claptrap, whether sponsored by Democrats or Republicans, is demonstrated graphically in Chapters X and XI.

The stock market never has a "depression;" it only corrects a previous advance. A cycle is action and reaction.

Many services and financial commentators in newspapers persist in discussing current events as causes of advances and declines. They have available the daily news and market behavior. It is therefore a simple matter to fit one to the other. When news is absent and the market fluctuates, they say its behavior is "technical."[1] This feature is discussed in Chapter XVII.

Every now and then, some important event occurs. If London declines and New York advances, or vice versa, the commentators are befuddled. Mr. Bernard Baruch recently said that prosperity will be with us for several years *"regardless of what is done or not done."* Think that over.

In the "dark ages," the world was supposed to be flat. We persist in perpetuating similar delusions.

ENDNOTES

[1] Sound familiar? Decades later, this practice is as prevalent as ever.

CHAPTER XXIV

EMOTIONAL CYCLES OF INDIVIDUALS

Cycles of mass psychology in human activities are demonstrated by graphs on other pages. A scientist now discloses his studies in the emotional cycles of individuals. In the November 1945 issue of the *Red Book* appears an article written by Mr. Myron Stearns in which he reports the results of studies, over a period of seventeen years, made by Dr. Rexford B. Hersey, scientist. The McCall Publishing Corporation has given me permission to quote from the article. I have underlined certain numbers and refer to them in the last paragraph.

Dr. Hersey is a Rhodes scholar, a graduate of the University of West Virginia and the University of Berlin.... Dr. Hersey wrote a book on his findings called "Workers' Emotionalism in Shop and Home," which was published by the University of Pennsylvania in 1932. Far-sighted officials of the Pennsylvania Railroad have supported Hersey's work.... Dr. Hersey was invited to go to Germany. He found that workers there react the same as Americans.

The periodic rise and fall of human emotions are vouched for by Dr. Hersey, who has been observing and studying them for more than seventeen years. His researches indicate that with all of us, high spirits and low spirits follow each other with a regularity almost as dependable as the tides. He found that all the checks he made on each man, over a period of weeks, fell into a fairly regular pattern. Dr. Hersey's chart showed that about every *5th* week he became more critical.

You take it for granted that a run of bad luck, in time, gets you down unless you exert strong will power. That good news, on the other hand, raises you to the top of the world. Now science says you are wrong. If you are full of energy and enthusiasm, good news will lift you higher still. Or if you are plugging dolefully through "Blue Monday," good news may help temporarily, but that is about all.

Human emotions ordinarily rise and fall at regular intervals of from *33 to 36* days. The ups and downs of these factors resemble stock market charts.

The blood cholesterol seems to have a cycle of about *56* days.... The thyroid output, which determines the total emotional cycle, usually makes a round trip from low to high and back in from *4 to 5* weeks.... In hyperthyroid cases, cycles may be as short as *3* weeks.

There seems to be no difference in cycle length between men and women.

The Fibonacci Summation Series includes the numbers 3, 5, 34 and 55. Time cycles are not always exact. Therefore when a period is given as "33 to 36," the basic period is 34, more or less. The basic period of 55 includes "56."

When members of your family, friends, employees, employers, customers, etc. annoy you, I recommend a review of this chapter. Other people have their cycles the same as you do. Do not allow your cycle to tangle with another.

PYTHAGORAS

CHAPTER XXV

PYTHAGORAS

Pythagoras, a great man, lived in the fifth century B.C. and made an impression on history that is seldom approached. The reader is urged to review a report on his activities in the *Encyclopedia Britannica*. He was a persistent investigator of the discoveries of others and visited Egypt, which is often mentioned as "The Cradle of Civilization."

Pythagoras is prominently known for his studies in mathematics. Insofar as I have seen, the most important of his discoveries has been overlooked. He drew a triangle and placed thereunder the cryptic title "The Secret of the Universe." This feature is described extensively in Chapter II.

In 1945, Mr. John H. Manas, Ph.D., President of the Pythagorean Society, wrote a book entitled *Life's Riddle Solved*, in which he disclosed a picture of Pythagoras, and I have permission from Mr. Manly P. Hall, head of The Philosophical Society of Los Angeles, California, to reproduce it (see opposite page).

There are many symbols in this picture, but we will focus our attention on two items, the pyramid[1] which Pythagoras holds in his right hand and the three squares in the lower right hand corner of the picture.

The pyramid represents the Great Pyramid of Gizeh, presumably built about 1000 B.C., although some students argue that it is much older. This Pyramid is classed as one of the "Seven Wonders of the World." The precision of measurement and placing in position of the immense marble stones employed are remarkable. However, this feature is insignificant when compared to the knowledge symbolized. It may be that a paragraph in the Bible (Isaiah 19:19) refers to it. It reads, "In that day shall there be an altar to the Lord in the midst of the land of Egypt, and a pillar at the border thereof to the Lord."

In Chapter II are graphed different views of this pyramid. For convenient reference, the view of one side is repeated in Figure 92.

The base of one side is 9,131 inches. The base of the four sides measures 36,524.22 inches. This symbolizes the number of days in our solar year, 365¼ days. Our calendar year is 365 days, but every fourth year an extra day must be added (February 29th). This is "leap year." The total days in four years is 1,461.

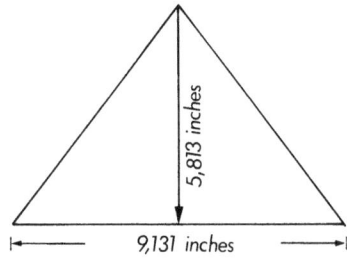

Figure 92

The elevation from base to top is 5,813 inches. The base of one side is 9,131 inches. The ratio of the elevation to the base is 63.6%. The pyramid has five surfaces and eight lines. 5 plus 8 equals 13. Note the elevation, 5,813 inches — 5, 8 and 13. 5 is 62.5% of 8. 8 is 61.5% of 13. Note the application of this ratio in Figure 71.

In human activities, an advancing movement is composed of five waves, three up and two intervening corrections. A cycle is composed of five waves up and three waves down, total eight. This is true of all degrees, Minor, Intermediate and Major. See Chapter IV.

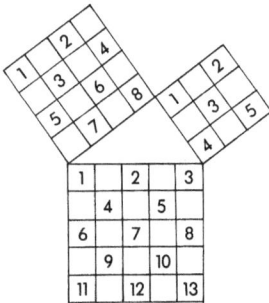

Figure 93

The diagram shown in the lower right hand of the Pythagoras picture is reproduced as Figure 93. I have numbered the squares which are shaded in the picture. The upper right square has five shaded squares. The upper left square has eight shaded squares. The lower square has thirteen shaded squares. These numbers correspond to the number of inches elevation of the Pyramid.

The same three squares are shown in Figure 94. The smaller squares are now numbered in a different manner, that is:

— 1, 2 and 3, where the square of 3 equals 9,

— 1, 2, 3 and 4, where the square of 4 equals 16, and

— 1, 2, 3, 4 and 5, where the square of 5 equals 25.

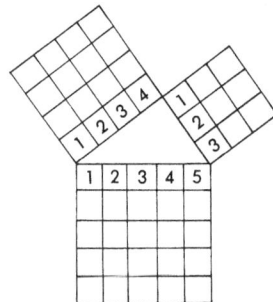

Figure 94

The theorem is that the square of the hypotenuse of a right triangle is equal to the sum of the squares of the other two sides. The discovery of this solution is the best known of Pythagoras' works.

Now return to the Fibonacci Series, 1 to 144. These numbers form the "Secret of the Universe" to which Pythagoras referred. The best example in botany is the sunflower, described by Mr. Jay Hambidge in Chapter II. In bodies of humans and animals, the numbers 3 and 5 apply. There are many other symbols in the picture of Pythagoras,[2] which is an idealistic conception.

ENDNOTES

[1] Subscriber Drew Ross points out that Pythagoras is actually holding a tetrahedron, not a pyramid. He adds, "Elliott's error is understandable because Pythagoras's hand obscures the triangular base." Pythagoras saw the tetrahedron as an elementary symbol of the three-dimensional world. "Nonetheless," adds Ross, "the triangle still leads one to the importance of the Great Pyramid, and Elliott was correct to note the incorporation of phi, which Tompkins [later] confirmed."

[2] Elliott trimmed the picture to a 5" x 8" Golden Rectangle in his reproduction.

CHAPTER XXVI

MISCELLANEOUS[1]

Volume of Waves

In an advance, the volume of wave 5 does not exceed the volume of wave 3; occasionally it is less. So long as volume increases, another advance is due, until a new high registers without an increase in volume. See Figure 95. Note also that the volume of wave 2 is less than the volume of wave 1. It is a favorable indication.[2]

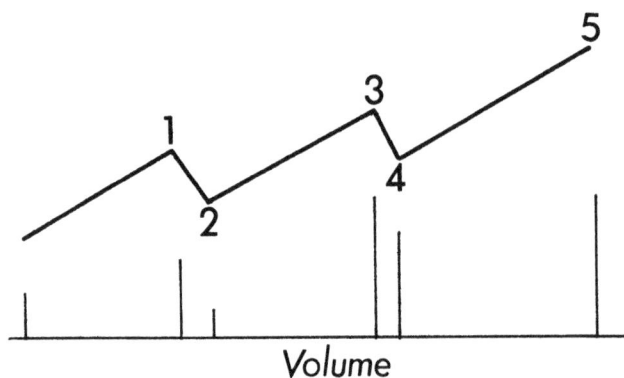

Figure 95

Circles

The word "cycle" means circle. Occasionally this feature appears in graphs of stocks. The circle in Figure 96 is divided into four segments, A, B, C and D. When a graph is rounding downward, as in segment C, and the downward pattern has been completed insofar as the number of waves is concerned, it may be expected that at the bottom, one or more series of "three-wave movements" may develop and then be followed by an accelerated advance as per segment D. The entire picture down and up will then resemble segments C and D combined, or in other words, the lower half of the circle.

The flood of strikes around the end of 1945 is simply the swing of the pendulum from left to right, 1 to 2 then to 3, as in Figure 96. Before labor was organized (previous to 1906), many, if not most employers, were autocratic, ruthless and heartless to employees, competitors and the public. The behavior of some strikers today is not worse than the behavior of management in early days. Every nation, human activity and individual has its own cycle — some long, others short, depending on the class and extent of each.

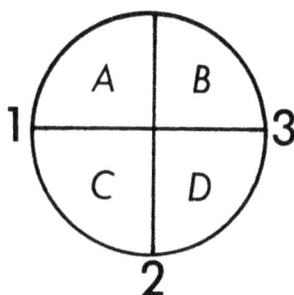

Figure 96

The "A-B Base"

The A-B base[3], shown in Figure 53, Chapter VI, is occasionally composed of double threes or even triple threes, as described in Chapter V. This is especially true when a rounding bottom is made, as discussed in the first paragraph under "Circles," above.

ENDNOTES

[1] This chapter originally contained several paragraphs that fit directly into earlier sections of the book. Apparently Elliott thought of some additional points after the bulk of the manuscript was completed and typed. I have moved these paragraphs to the appropriate areas in the previous text.

[2] That is, indicative that wave 2 is indeed in progress and that wave 3 will follow.

[3] The "A-B base" seems fine as a description for the first two waves of an A-B-C irregular correction. Elliott's reference to Figure 53 seems at first to indicate that that is what he meant. However, in the discussion of the 1942-1946 bull market that follows, he uses the A-B base concept as an *additional* wave phenomenon that can occur between the end of a corrective wave and the beginning of an impulse wave. The addition of this idea is unnecessary since a construction with that look has been, in our experience, merely part of the previous corrective wave or the next impulse wave. Apparent occurrences of an "A-B base" always have another explanation, one more consistent with the Wave Principle.

CHAPTER XXVII

THE 1942-1945 BULL MARKET [1]

The thirteen-year triangle in the Dow-Jones Industrial Average from 1928 to April 1942 is graphed in Figure 71. As described in Figures 31, 32, 37 and 38 in Chapter V, thrust follows a triangle.

In Figure 97, the Dow-Jones Industrial Average is graphed. Each vertical line represents the range of one month. Major wave ① is short. Major wave ③ is longer, and its Intermediate waves are indicated by small letters a, b, c, d and e. Note the inner base line at waves b and d. Major wave ④ is composed of three Intermediate waves indicated by the small letters a, b and c from July to November, 1943. Major wave ⑤ runs from November 1943 to December 10, 1945. Waves A and B consumed five months.[2] In the daily and weekly range for this period, all waves were composed of three waves each (see Figure 53).

From letter B to the number 1 is Intermediate wave 1, as it is composed of five waves of the daily range. Intermediate wave 3 is composed of five waves indicated by small letters a, b, c, d and e (extended). Extensions never appear in more than one of three impulse waves 1, 3 and 5 (see Figures 39 through 44). Intermediate wave 4 is the same as Intermediate wave 2. Intermediate wave 5 is composed of five waves of the weekly range and reached 196.59 on December 10, 1945. The parallel line was slightly exceeded. Subsequent to December 10, 1945, an irregular top[3] reached 207.49 on February 4, 1946.

The pattern of Major wave ⑤ from November 1943 to December 1945 is unusual in one respect. It hugged the base line from November 1943 to August 1945, instead of heading straight for the parallel line. The cause of this abnormality was a new crop of reckless speculators with more money than experience who favored low-priced stocks instead of seasoned issues of the type represented by the popular averages. In order to overcome this abnormality, I devised a Special Index that behaved normally, as will be seen in the lower chart of Figure 97. Note that Major wave ⑤ does not hug the base line, but instead follows a straight line from beginning to end.

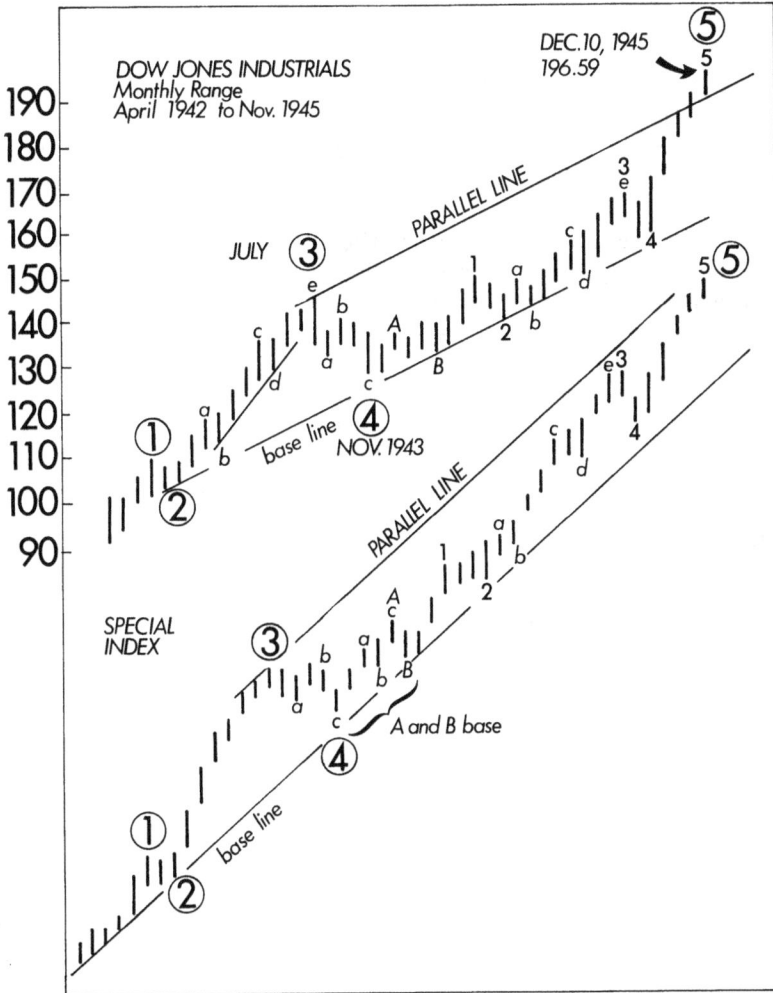

Figure 97

Note: In the upper graph in Figure 97, the Industrial Average registered its "OT" (orthodox top) at 196.59 on December 10, 1945. On going to press, an irregular top, wave B, is in process of formation. This should be followed by wave C (see Chapter VII).[4]

I expect a sub-normal bear market as illustrated in Figure 76, Chapter XII.[5]

ENDNOTES

[1] This is a great call, as the market dropped vertically a few months later.

[2] Counting A and B as waves 1 and 2 of an extended wave ⑤ would have allowed Elliott to anticipate the May 1946 peak as the orthodox top.

[3] The December peak marked the end of wave 3. The "irregular top" of February preceded a clear five-wave decline, as would have been expected. However, this top was wave B of an A-B-C irregular correction that constituted wave 4. Wave 5 then carried to the final orthodox peak at 212.50 in May 1946.

[4] Elliott would have been correctly bearish for the 1946 crash, since he was expecting the wave C decline. Since the bottom of the decline was just above 160, he probably would have "called" the bottom as well, since that bottom was at the level of the previous wave 4.

[5] Elliott was right. The correction was mild in price terms, although it lasted three years.

REVIEW AND CONCLUSION

Figure 71 depicted a thirteen-year triangle from 1928 to 1942. By reference to Chapter V, it will be noted that triangles have always appeared as wave 4 and that wave 5 exceeds the top of wave 3.

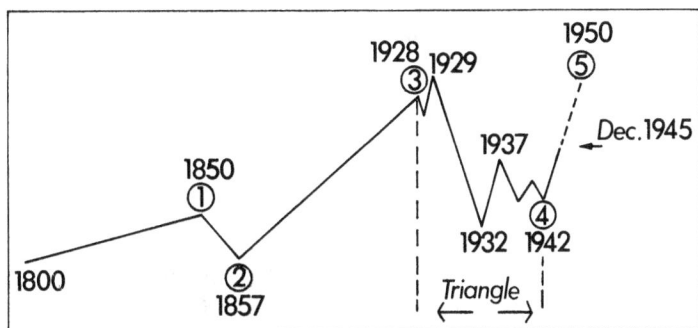

Figure 98

Figure 98 is a graph of the market from 1800 to December 1945.[1] Wave ① from 1800 to 1857 is based on business history, as stock market records are not available previous to 1857. November 1928 is the orthodox top of wave ③ from which the triangle (wave ④) started. The triangle ended, and the "thrust" (wave ⑤) started, in April 1942. A "thrust" has always exceeded the top of wave ③, which in this case is November 1928.

The movement from 1921 to November 1928 was composed of three bull markets and two intervening sub-normal bear markets. Thus far, in December 1945, one bull market has registered. It would therefore appear logical that the pattern and extent above 1942 would resemble the movement from 1921 to 1928, i.e., three bull markets and two intervening, sub-normal bear markets.

The Dow-Jones Industrial Average started in 1921 at 64 and ended in November 1928 at 299, for a 235-point advance. The thrust started April 1942 at 93. 93 plus 235 equals 328, or 29 points above November 1928, the end of wave ③.[2] The thrust may consume eight years, ending in 1950, similar to 1921-1929. The immense amount of currency in the hands of the public due to financing of the second World War would seem to confirm this indication.

There is a different sequence of procedure now as compared to 1921-1928. During 1921-1928, the first wave was a normal bull market without inflationary symptoms. The fifth wave ending in November 1928 was decidedly inflationary. Now, the *first* wave, from 1942 to 1945, disclosed inflationary characteristics. Low-priced stocks of questionable value surged ahead at the expense of the "blue chips." *The New York Sun* selected ninety-six stocks that advanced phenomenally. Every stock started at some figure below $2 per share. The highest rate of advance was 13,300%. The lowest rate of advance was 433%. The average for the group was 2,776%.

The patterns of graphs shown on previous pages furnish a historic outline of the United States. Its development is marvelous for many reasons:

— Geographic position, shape and boundaries: A square, bounded on two sides by large oceans, and on two sides by friendly neighbors.

— Latitude and climate: Semi-tropical, thus facilitating agriculture.

— Natural resources: Gold, iron, coal, oil, timber and waterways.

— Genius and individual initiative: The number and value of patents from 1850 to 1929 is marvelous. Attention is invited to Chapter XIV. Note that the graph of patent applications (Figure 81) coincides with waves of the stock market, both in time and pattern, which in turn reflects business activity and mass psychology.

— Democratic ideals: The form of government stimulates individual initiative. This does not imply that perfection has been achieved, but it does suggest that we may be on the right road.

ENDNOTES

[1] Once again, with extremely limited data, Elliott outlines correctly the entire Grand Supercycle from the late 1700s, just as he did in his essays of 1941 and 1942 (see *Selected Essays* section). His prediction of a new high above 1929 was also correct. However, in this depiction he shows a short time frame ending in 1950, which is all out of proportion to the other four waves. It seems that even a cursory examination of the chart would suggest a top much further out than 1950, and much higher than 328 on the Dow. The problem again is Elliott's 13-year triangle, since thrusts following triangles are generally swift and short. The chart that Elliott produced in his Interpretive Letter dated August 1941 and again in his Educational Bulletin of October 1942 showed a more accurate beginning date of 1776 and a more suitable projected ending date of 2012, as shown below.

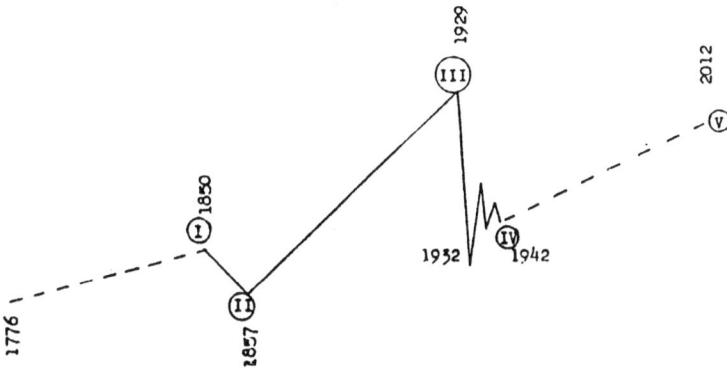

[2] This computation is based on the tenet that the thrust, or fifth wave following a horizontal triangle, is generally about as long as the widest part of the triangle.

304R.N. ELLIOTT'S MASTERWORKS

REFERENCES[1]

—Pythagoras (Greek philosopher, 500 B. C.). See *Encyclopedia Britannica*.

—Fibonacci (Italian mathematician of the thirteenth century. Better known as Leonardo of Pisa). His works were published by Count B. Boncompagni, 1857-1862.

—*Dynamic Symmetry* ("The Greek Vase"), by Jay Hambidge. Note appendix, pages 146-159.

—*Practical Applications of Dynamic Symmetry* ("The Law of Phyllotaxis"), by Jay Hambidge. See pages 27-29.

—*Nature's Harmonic Unity*, by Samuel Colman and C. Arthur Coan.

—*Proportional Form*, by Samuel Colman and C. Arthur Coan. See pages 34-35, 149-155.

—*Curves of Life*, by Theodore A. Cook.

— *The Human Situation*, by William Macniele Dixon. See pages 129-131.

—*Prophecies of Melchi-Zedik in The Great Pyramid*, by Brown Landone.

—*Nuggets from King Solomon's Mine*, by John Barnes Schmalz.

ENDNOTES

[1] The original page contained several minor errors of spelling and title, which have been corrected for this volume.

A FINAL FORECAST BY
"THE LATE R.N. ELLIOTT"

from
New Methods for Profit in the Stock Market
by Garfield Drew
(1948, 2nd edition, Metcalf Press, Boston, pp. 159-161)

The "Natural Rhythm" methods do, of course, afford a long-term picture, the question being the extent to which credence can be placed in their forecast. However, to repeat what has been said before, their indicated pattern in recent years has been far more correct than just chance seems to account for, and R.N. Elliott's record, for example, is carefully documented with unimpeachable outside sources. For that reason, the rising trend of stock prices definitely indicated for the coming years is at least interesting....

It is true that one could not see clearly just WHY prices should rise to any such extent, but the "why" is always much clearer in retrospect than it is in looking forward. Besides, if such situations were clearly defined, they would be evident to a great many, and that can never be the case on the eve of any important trend.

Elliott's Wave Principle

The "Wave Principle" [observes] that price fluctuations occur according to a definite pattern which has its basis in a law of Nature. It was first elucidated by the late R.N. Elliott. As a working theory, the Principle holds that all stock price trends, whether minor movements or major cycles, are composed of a fixed number of "waves" or fluctuations, which occur in an ordered sequence or rhythm, but are not of equal extent or duration. This applies to individual stocks, to groups, to commodities, and to "averages," since Elliott contended that it represents a natural law which dominates and controls price movements. Unexpected news, for example, does no more than affect the amplitude or time of any given wave....

The practical difficulty lies in the confusion which is likely to attend identification of the correct waves as they develop. Just as in the case of cycles, mathematical precision is ordinarily lacking. Likewise, however, the indicated sequences of advances and declines seem to have worked out more frequently than can be accounted for by the laws of pure chance.

Pattern of the '40s

Perhaps the "Wave Principle" can better be grasped at present by fitting the market fluctuations of recent years to the framework of the principle and making the necessary future projections. Elliott's hypothesis — and that of his collaborator (Mr. John C. Sinclair of the New York Stock Exchange house of Francis I. duPont and Co.) — was that from the bottom in 1942, stock prices began in important five-wave upward movement[1] which, in turn, represented[2] the last part of an even larger rhythmic move. The first upward wave of the series thus ran from 1942 to December, 1945, which was considered the true, or "orthodox" top, despite its having been overrun by a few points in the Industrial Average a little later.

Elliott felt that the second downward wave then indicated would be of subnormal extent, and this was assumed to have culminated in May, 1947. The next important move (third wave of the whole series) was, therefore, expected to be up, and to go substantially higher than the first wave. Development of the component minor waves as time goes along will afford closer clues. After a fourth downward wave, the fifth and final wave, should — if the hypothesis is correct — exceed even the 1928 high point (regarded as the true top of that particular period), although it is obvious that any such development must be considerably ahead in point of time.

ENDNOTES

[1] Elliott had presented this opinion in Chapter XXVII of Nature's Law, and it proved to be entirely correct.

[2] He means "will represent."

"ON R.N. ELLIOTT'S RECEIVING THE MARKET TECHNICIANS ASSOCIATION'S ANNUAL AWARD"

from a speech to the MTA's annual conference
May 18, 1996
by Robert R. Prechter, Jr.

Most stock market researchers who have won the MTA's Annual Award made their careers in the market. Ralph Nelson Elliott is an exception. He was not primarily a stock market guy. As you have heard from George Schade, Elliott was a businessman who built an international reputation. He was an expert in reorganizing troubled businesses so that they were profitable. His clients were often big companies, such as export-import houses and railroads. He was so well known and regarded that in the 1920s, the Coolidge administration chose him, out of all the available accountants, to straighten out the finances of Nicaragua, which the U.S. ran at the time. So he was at the top of his field in business.

Elliott was no intellectual piker, either. He contributed columns for two magazines (one business and one financial) and wrote four books: one on business, two on markets and one on foreign policy.

Could he write? Listen to some of his prose. Here he is describing Latin America, a region that he loved and in which he lived for half his life: "Riches and poverty, health and sickness, enlightenment and direst ignorance, virtue and vice rub shoulders continually, presenting contrasts perhaps as striking as in any other part of the world." That man could write.

Most of us in this room work for salaries or subscription fees or annual management fees. How many of us choose to be paid only if we make money for our clients? In his 50s, Elliott launched a financial consulting service for businesses in California. Do you know what he charged up front? Nothing. He said that he would accept payment only out of increased profits generated by the companies that adopted his recommendations. That's how sure he was that he could improve any business.

The stock market did not become Elliott's primary interest until he was in his 60s. Can you imagine someone coming from another field to the MTA and breaking new ground in market analysis when he was 67 years old? That was how old Elliott was when his first monograph was published. After building an international reputation as a business accountant through corporate service, magazine columns, books and a government commission, today Elliott enjoys a far larger reputation for what he did in the final decade of his life, when he meticulously developed the striking hypothesis that investment market behavior is patterned. So if you think you're past your prime, think again. Your best work may be years away.

To summarize my points, R.N. Elliott was competent, expressive, confident, curious, independent and versatile: an American Renaissance man.

It is difficult to appreciate the genius behind Elliott's discovery. Most people can spot wave patterns once they study what to look for. But what kind of person looks at price fluctuations cold and discerns the patterns in the first place? Only Benoit Mandelbrot, the father of fractal geometry, has accomplished a similar feat, and he did it with mountain ranges, seacoasts and rivers, in other words, other natural phenomena. He noticed it in market prices, too, but R.N. Elliott was way ahead of him in this regard, both in that discovery and in the breadth of his observations. Mandelbrot has become famous for recognizing that in nature, the smaller fluctuations, which he considers otherwise unpatterned, are exactly as complex as the larger ones, just on different scales. Elliott originated that same idea, and then went far further in discovering that there are patterns to the fluctuations.

After discerning the market's patterns, Elliott concluded that the stock market, as an expression of collective human action, is part of nature and has the same organizational properties. We all accept that there are specific laws governing cloud formation, earthquakes, and growth in a jungle. We also accept that the product of these laws is immensely complex and variable. Elliott said the same thing about the stock market: It is governed by laws, and yet the product of those laws is immensely complex and variable. What does this mean for market forecasting? It means that at times, we will know more than most people by understanding these laws, and we will have a few very important, even crucial, insights, but there is no way we will know everything or even most things, about the specific product of those laws. When people say, "Wall Street is a jungle," they are more correct than they know. The idea that markets have particular organizational laws that by their very operation require fluctuation and diversity is Elliott's great insight, and for it, he deserves the highest place in the pantheon of market researchers.

That's who Elliott was. Who was he not? Some people lump R.N. Elliott and W.D. Gann together because they both dealt with numbers. I see no similarity whatever between these two men. Elliott was not a numerologist like Gann. To illustrate the contrast, let's look at two aspects of Elliott's discoveries involving numbers. First, he noticed that markets move in five waves and three waves. Second, he noted that the Fibonacci ratio governs the market's patterns. Are these mystical assertions, or are they astute observations absolutely essential to the very idea of pattern formation in linear movement?

Elliott himself never speculated on why the market's form was five waves to progress and three waves to regress. He simply noted that that was what was happening. Well, does the essential form have to be five waves and three waves? Think about it, and you will realize that this is the minimum requirement for, and therefore the most efficient method of producing, both fluctuation and progress in linear movement. One wave does not allow fluctuation. The fewest subdivisions to create fluctuation is three waves. Three waves in both directions does not allow progress. To progress in one direction despite periods of regress, movements in the main trend must be at least five waves, simply to cover more ground than the three waves and still contain fluctuation. While there could be more waves than that, the most efficient form of punctuated progress is 5-3. And nature always follows the most efficient path. It is that simple and that profound.

O.K., why Fibonacci? Is this numerology, like Gann's mysterious tables and squares? No. A fractal progression of five waves and three waves produces numbers of waves that generate the Fibonacci sequence: 3 waves in the correction, 5 waves in the impulse, 8 waves in the full cycle. In the subdivisions, there are 13 waves in the correction, 21 in the impulse and 34 in the full cycle. The ratio between each of these adjacent numbers is .618. So Elliott's interest in Fibonacci mathematics was not something outside the market that he imposed upon the market in hopes of finding a magical revelation. It is the very essence of the market *if his empirical observations were correct.* Proving the arms-length relationship between Elliott's original modeling and his later interest in Fibonacci mathematics, he did not even become aware of the connection for years after his first book on the Wave Principle. The point is, there is not only detailed observation behind Elliott's work but also a meaningful and consistent rationale behind his conclusions. If some analysts approach the Wave Principle from a less than rigorous standpoint — and I regret having been guilty of that myself more than once — that is our error, not the Wave Principle's.

Today, thousands of institutional portfolio managers, traders and private investors employ the Wave Principle in their investment decision making. Ralph Elliott undoubtedly would have been gratified to see it. Even now, however, Elliott's legacy has only begun to manifest itself. His contribution to knowledge is far greater than simply a useful method of market analysis, as great as that is. Elliott's discovery pertains not only to market movements but to the dynamics of all social mood change. In my opinion, Elliott's contribution to sociology will someday be recognized as a breakthrough equivalent to those that occurred in the 1600s and 1700s in the physical sciences. Because he was both meticulous and principled, Elliott may have been the first social scientist, in the strict sense of the term. Given time and attention, the Wave Principle will ultimately save sociology from the realm of meandering speculation and place it firmly in the sphere of science. As a bonus, it affords a rare opportunity to appreciate the aesthetic beauty of the human experience in the abstract. Surely, few contributions to our knowledge have been greater.

I hope you will take a few minutes to look through the handout that I've prepared. One page shows exactly why R.N. Elliott was bullish on a grand scale in October 1942, calling for decades of rising stock prices at a time when most investors were too worried about World War II to picture such a thing, much less predict it. [Note: See pp. 200-205 of this book. — Ed.] Another section presents Elliott's simple drawing of a five-wave pattern within a parallel trend channel, which shows how the past 64 years in the Dow Jones Industrial Average (and the S&P as well) reflect that drawing. [Note: See Figure 64 on p. 248 of this book and compare it to the figures on pp. 171 and 173 of *View From the Top*. — Ed.] There's a condensed biography as well. And some of you might enjoy one of our recent studies, which I included at the end. We took a small handful of rules and guidelines of wave formation and had the computer draw out an idealized stock market on this highly simplified basis. Then we compared it to the Dow from 1932 to the present. I think you'll be interested in the result. [Note: See Figure 4-2 on p. 91 of *The Wave Principle of Human Social Behavior.* — Ed.]

On a light note, I observe that the MTA presented its first annual award in 1974, the year the Dow Jones Industrial Average fell to its lower channel line and kicked off our great bull market, and is giving this award to R.N. Elliott in the year that the Dow has finally, 22 years later, reached its upper channel line. That line dates back to 1937, the year Elliott began writing his first book, *The Wave Principle.* I can think of no better time to honor R.N. Elliott than when the largest version ever recorded of his five-wave pattern is up on the wall for all of us to see.

R.N. Elliott left no genetic descendants, although he has some intellectual ones. Not many people know that his biggest champion immediately following his death, A. Hamilton Bolton, the founder of *The Bank Credit Analyst*, was famous for his fundamental research into the relationship between bank credit trends and stock market trends. Bolton served a year as president of the Financial Analysts Federation, and in 1987 he became (posthumously) only the eighth person ever to be awarded the FAF's highest honor, the Nicholas Molodovsky Award, which is "presented periodically only to those individuals who have made outstanding contributions of such significance as to change the direction of the profession and to raise it to higher standards of accomplishment." In Frost's words, Bolton was a genius. But while bank credit statistics were Bolton's bread and butter, the piles of correspondence to Charles Collins, Frost and others show that he was captivated by the Wave Principle, and so were his subscribers. Simply for applying the Wave Principle so successfully, Bolton is perhaps the only man who also deserves the Market Technicians Association's highest award. Yet today the Market Technicians Association honors a man for an even greater achievement. It is an understatement to say that Ralph Nelson Elliott, the man who discerned the Wave Principle in the first place, deserves the MTA's award for "outstanding contribution to the field of technical analysis."

I hope those of you who have not added Elliott's observations of market behavior to your arsenal will do so. To summarize my feelings on the matter, Ralph Nelson Elliott is without the slightest doubt a most deserving recipient of this award, both for his pioneering work and his legacy.

When our annual award recipient is alive and with us, we always send him home with a round of applause. R.N. Elliott isn't here tonight, but I hope you will join me in giving him the same honor.